Privacy Past, Present, and Future

Leslie N. Gruis

Privacy Past, Present, and Future

Leslie N. Gruis

Academica Press
London~Washington

Library of Congress Cataloging-in-Publication Data

Names: Gruis, Leslie, author.
Title: Privacy : past, present, future / Leslie Gruis
Description: Washington : Academica Press, 2020. | Includes references.
Identifiers: LCCN 2020947527 | ISBN 9781680531268 (paperback)

Dedication

To my partner in mischief John, my son Ben, and
my feline muses,
the omnipresent P and the ephemeral Q

Contents

Foreword

Three things laid the groundwork for this book.

First, I grew up in Washington, DC – two blocks from the U.S. Capitol - in the 1960s, and 1970s. Even though I may not have understood how, my world was shaped by the events of the time. I remember the inauguration of John F. Kennedy, where all sorts of military armaments were paraded down the street as a show of force to the Soviets, who were surely watching. I remember the assassination of President Kennedy, and seeing his body lie in state in the Capitol building. I remember the riots after the assassination of Martin Luther King, Jr. My mom, a Congressional staffer, whisked my little sister and me away to stay with relatives in the suburbs, while my father, an attorney, stayed in DC to make sure those arrested were accorded their civil rights. I remember realizing when I was about ten that living where we did, we would be the first to be incinerated when the Soviet nukes came. Like any little kid, I tried to make sense of these incongruencies – the Soviet threat, American civil disobedience, and democracy. I was raised a patriot, and am still one today. I would live that patriotism for 30 years working as a mathematician for the National Security Agency.

Second, in 1989 the Berlin Wall fell. The bipolar Cold War world had been certain in its uncertainty. That suddenly crumbled, leaving us with a unipolar world, spinning tentatively around a single axis of power. It was as if we were watching the aftermath of a supernova, waiting to see how the remaining bodies of world politics would stabilize. At that point, the American psyche could not comprehend a threat posed by terrorists like that which would occur on September 11, 2001. The world changed.

Third, a project from the Cold War, the Department of Defense's ARPANET, would emerge in the 1990s, as the internet. In 1999, I read Lawrence Lessig's book *Code and Other Laws of Cyberspace*. He talked about how West Coast code (i.e. computer code from Silicon Valley, etc.)

was challenging East Coast code (federal legislation). He talked about how the virtual realm of cyberspace challenged traditional values and norms associated with the physical world.

Lessig's book got my juices flowing on the topic of cyberspace and what kind of order would emerge from it. It also made me wonder about the future of privacy. You hold in your hands the product of these musings.

I would like to thank my husband, John Kolm, my partner in mischief, adventure, and parenthood. I could not have asked for a better life partner. He encouraged me throughout the writing of this book. A professional writer himself, John spent countless hours teaching me his craft. He taught me to tell a better story, and helped me brainstorm new ideas. He commented on and edited my writing. He provided apt criticism, with the patience and guidance of a sympathetic master toward an aspiring apprentice. When I found it frustrating that his writing seemed so effortless and polished, John reassured me that he had honed this skill through decades of practice. He was right. I am not there yet, but writing has gotten easier over the last three years.

I would like to thank my son, Ben Cashman, for his patient support throughout the writing of this book. An aspiring writer, historian, and teacher himself, Ben graduated from Sarah Lawrence College at the tail end of this project. Ben reminded me about the formal rules of writing, many of which I had long forgotten. His persistent reminders helped me make sense of Picasso's quip to learn the rules like a pro so you can break them like an artist. Ben was also a valuable source of information about European history. Every time I painted myself into a corner, Ben was there to help me understand the history of Western Europe, usually England, which shaped the period I was writing about in this book. His knowledge of different periods of European history was invaluable to me. I only hope my efforts here help inspire his future success.

I would like to thank Paul du Quenoy of Academica Press. At the end of a talk I gave at the Cosmos Club in Washington, DC, he offered to be my publisher. I said yes. If I have learned anything in this life, it is to embrace good fortune when it comes. I will be eternally thankful for Paul's belief in me, and hope that this book does not disappoint.

I would like to thank Sean Kanuck, for whom I worked at the National Intelligence Council (NIC). As the National Intelligence Officer for Cyber, Sean believed I had something important to say about the future of privacy in a cyberized world. I remember the day he told me I should just go and write the book, that I was perfectly capable. His words gave me the final vote of confidence I needed to jump into an unknown future of attempted authorship. Here we are.

I would like to thank Todd Rosenthal, who patiently read chapter after chapter of my book, and offered comments.

I would like to thank all my friends, who have steadfastly stood by me while I reinvented myself as an author. I am blessed to have many friends – Anne-Marie, Becky, Susan, and others - who have always been there for me. Their belief in my abilities has given me the courage to chase rainbows.

Chapter 1
Introduction

The two greatest demands a free people places on its government are easily stated. Firstly, keep us safe. Secondly, leave us alone. At first blush, this appears to be an oxymoron. How can we cede sufficient authority to the government to guarantee our national security, while still preserving our private lives? In fact, this has been the great experiment of the United States of America.

This conflict of needs has been with us since the beginning. Our constitution says that the government must collect private information about its citizens to fairly apportion representation and taxes. The Declaration of Independence assures us that we have the inalienable right to be left in peace to enjoy life, liberty, and the pursuit of happiness.

This book is about how these two great promises can be resolved, how we got where we are today, and where we may go in the future. The ideas are immediately relevant to everyone who wants both liberty and protection, and to everyone who wants the same things for their children.

As a privacy specialist with 30 years' experience at the National Security Agency, I've heard all the jokes and fears about the government spying on its citizens. But in fact, the real threat today comes from a different and perhaps unexpected direction. It is the commercial world that is spying on you for the most part, using cyberspace to collect your most intimate personal details in giant nets as though you were one small fish in a never-ending harvest. The reason is simple, and it has nothing to do with morality or with your rights as a citizen. Countless billions of dollars are at stake.

What can we do? Is the intrusion of privacy into our private lives unstoppable? Do we just have to accept the mining of our health and financial data and the tracking of our children as the inevitable consequence of progress? And does it really matter? Is the very notion of privacy outdated, an idea that seems anachronistic to our children, an aging trope that's destined for the scrap-heap along with dancing the Charleston and fighting by Marquis of Queensbury rules?

Let's start the journey, and see what we can find out.

The Story of Alice

Alice is thirteen, going on 35.

You are her parent, and Alice is going out with friends tonight. She's all dressed up and looking like an adult. She Facetimes her plans and movements for the evening, Instagrams her friends about her romantic hopes, and Snapchats a picture of herself looking like a fashion model. And of course, she's talking on her smartphone, a device that allows her to be tracked within twenty yards anytime it's on.

Concerned about all this information going out into the ether, you and your spouse interrupt Alice's frantic preparations – she sighs and puts her hairbrush down – and you both ask her if sending her details and movements over all these hackable and mineable apps is a wise idea.

"Dad, Mom!" Alice rolls her eyes. "Are you serious? Everybody does it! It's the modern era! We're all on Instagram and Snapchat and our phones, and everyone know everything now. There are no secrets anymore. Privacy is for old people."

She shrugs at your colossal stupidity – lovingly, but pityingly – and heads out the front door towards a car full of friends. "Be back by eleven!" you yell after her.

Now that Alice is gone, the two of you start to worry. There are so many risks for kids these days. What if Alice is doing drugs, or if she's sexually active, or is using birth control? You don't really know. Searching Alice's room is creepy and mistrusting. But her safety, even her life, could be at stake. And after all, didn't she just tell you that your concerns about personal information are outdated and privacy is a thing of the past?

A thorough search of her room reveals nothing of concern. You're relieved. The two of you sit up in bed, awaiting Alice's return. A few minutes after eleven, you hear the front door slam. Before you can get up to say good night, your teenage daughter appears at your bedroom door, looking like an avenging goddess and obviously fuming.

"Mom! Dad! You've been snooping in my room!"

"Well, we …," you start to say.

"You've been snooping! How could you!"

"Look, we just …."

"Everything's been moved! You pawed into everything! Did you think I wouldn't notice? What's wrong with you?"

"Look," you finally manage to say. "Sweetheart, we are responsible for you. We love you and we want you to be safe. And you did say tonight that you didn't care about privacy, after all."

"What! Not like that! I didn't mean like that! Did you really think I want you snooping into … into all my personal stuff? There could have been anything in there! How could you! You don't trust me! You've never trusted me!"

Exit Alice, in tears.

"I'll go after her," your spouse says. Your spouse jumps out of bed, starts for the door, then turns around, grins sheepishly at you and speaks.

"People are strange, aren't they?"

Outline of the Book

Alice doesn't realize it, but privacy has a long history in the United States. In Part One, we'll discuss how ideas about individual rights evolved over the centuries, setting the framework for American privacy law and norms today. In Part Two, we'll see how specific events in the twentieth century shaped the modern American privacy ethos. These include legislation like Privacy Act, the evolution of modern corporations and government regulation, and the technologies that culminated in the information revolution. We'll also see that these activities surged and waned with the times, shaped by war, politics, and social movements. In Part Three, we'll explore how these lessons of history can inform our thinking about the importance of privacy and how to preserve it.

How We Got Here

While the word "privacy" doesn't appear in our founding documents, our first clues appear in the Bill of Rights incorporated into our Constitution. Wary of creating too powerful a federal government, our founding fathers carefully enumerated the individual rights to be preserved. The rights they described in the First, Second, Third, Fourth, Fifth, Eighth and Ninth Amendments have in modern times come to be associated with a right to privacy.[1]

The Federalist Papers provide marvelous insights into the debate that went on about designing a federal government that was just-strong-enough. The authors devote considerable space to the apportionment of representation and taxes. The Federalists believed that the survival of the fledgling government hinged on reliable sources of revenue and settling the representation issue correctly. In other words, the national security of the nation was dependent on representation and taxation that worked.

Of course, these ideas about individual rights and privacy had originally been brought to the New World by the colonists themselves. Many of them were seeking religious freedom from monarchical Anglicanism in England. Our early colonial governments were modeled on English precedents regarding governance and the law. And even after we revolted and started to create our own version of government, a lot of the concepts about fairness and appropriate treatment under the law derived from the Old World. This is why you can trace a lot of the concepts in our Constitution and our laws back to English law.

So, when we go back to jolly old England, we are struck by a few things. First, the Magna Carta was a very early form of an English constitution with a bill of rights contained therein. Second, when Henry VIII declared himself the supreme English authority over all things temporal and spiritual, he effectively began a convergence of temporal and ecclesiastical law into a single English law. The law the colonists later inherited reflected both temporal precedents and Christian values from church law. Third, libel and licensing law evolved quickly in the time of Elizabeth I, thanks to the printing press and England's entrenched power struggle against the Catholic Church. Originators of printed works which sympathized with Vatican views could find themselves charged with not just libel, but seditious libel or treason.

---

[1] Another oft-cited privacy amendment, the Fourteenth, was not adopted until 1868.

U.S. Privacy in the Twentieth Century

Privacy emerged as a legal concept in in the United States in 1890, when two lawyers wrote an article about the right to privacy for the *Harvard Law Review*. These two attorneys - Samuel Warren and (later Supreme Court Justice) Louis Brandeis - finally put a label on a concept which had existed without moniker in the American psyche since the nation's origins. The evolution of privacy from there on out was shaped by technology; war, politics and social movements; the law; and corporations and regulators.

a. Technology

First, the use of modern technologies began to raise a lot of questions about individual rights. Photography, telegraphy and telephony started to challenge traditional interpretations about where one's private domain ended and the public (interest) domain began. A 1928 Supreme Court case, *Olmsted v. U.S.*, found it constitutional to wiretap an alleged criminal's telephone from the curb. Supreme Court Justice Brandeis wrote a famous dissent. This decision would not be overturned until 1967 in *Katz v. U.S.*

Computer technologies that had been developed to help win World War II entered the civilian sector in the 1950s. A great concern began to rise in Congress about government collection, retention, aggregation, and dissemination of private information about U.S. citizens. It would take until 1974 before the Privacy Act was successfully passed.

The emergence of personal computers in the 1980s, and the internet in the 1990s, began to enable everyone to collect, retain, aggregate, and disseminate private information about individuals. Privacy concerns about medical records were addressed in the Health Insurance Portability and Accountability Act (HIPAA) in 1996. Concerns about the vulnerability of children online lead to the 1998 passage of the Children's Online Privacy Protection Act (COPPA).

b. War, Politics, and Social Movements

Governments exercise extraordinary powers during crises. In democracies, the tacit understanding is that defense of the nation trumps individual rights in a time of imminent threat. After the crisis subsides, the balance between the two needs to be restored. For example, U.S. entry into World War I in 1917 enabled passage of the 1918 Sedition Act, which effectively curtailed free speech against the government. The conclusion of the war lead to its repeal in 1920.

But there was another national security threat in the United States before, during and after World War I – communism. In America, the 1917 Russian Revolution reawakened anti-communist fears born in the previous century and galvanized Bolshevik sympathizers. The first U.S. Red Scare – an American fear of spreading communism and anarchy - occurred during 1919-1920. Believing that immigrants brought communist thinking with them from abroad, the government enacted immigration quotas to keep such undesirables out, and accelerated efforts to deport the ones that had somehow gotten in. Internal security trumped the immigrants' individual rights.

Internal security concerns about communism would once again trump individual rights after World War II during the Second Red Scare. Espionage trials of Soviet spies overlooked defendants' civil rights in favor of guilty verdicts, confirming popular fears that Communists were operating among us. New U.S. laws allowed the government to track Communists within the country and deport them. Immigration quotas once again were enacted to keep Communists out. During their hunt for Communists, the House Un-American Activities Committee called Hollywood witnesses, many of who ended up blacklisted after taking the Fifth Amendment to avoid self-incrimination. From the Senate, Eugene McCarthy chased Communists in the State Department, the Army, and across the government.

America reacted to the anti-Communist excesses of 1950s, by restoring and even extending individual rights in the 1960s. Communist claims from past decades that the U.S. majority (white, land-owning, Christian men) oppressed disenfranchised minorities (the working class) now found resonance and response with the Civil Rights Movement in America. This was the time when every citizen demanded the same rights everyone else had, regardless of race, gender, religion, and national origin. While many leaders advocated non-violence, this movement was not always peaceful. Any assembly of individuals – protesting segregation, integration, the Vietnam War, etc. - could become violent under the right circumstances. There were riots in many U.S. cities. A U.S. president and three other public figures were assassinated. But by end of the 1970s, we had settled back into quieter times when the citizenry felt the balance between individual rights and national security had been restored.

c. The Law

Legal response to privacy issues can be slow. This is particularly true as technological capabilities nibble at the edges of privacy in innovative ways, taking only one little bite each time. It's as if decades later, the law wakes up and says "Wait a minute! You ate the whole thing!" But as the citizenry comes to understand more about the technology and the possible threats it poses, social norms change. Constituents' evolving views are reflected by their elected representatives in legislative activities, and voilà, the law adapts to the technology. Judicial decisions help along the way.

Seventy years after Warren and Brandeis wrote their privacy article in 1890, the legal scholar William Prosser constrained civil privacy law into a neat framework of four torts[2]:

1. Intrusion upon the plaintiff's seclusion or solitude, or into his private affairs.
2. Public disclosure of embarrassing private facts about the plaintiff.
3. Publicity which places the plaintiff in a false light in the public eye.
4. Appropriation, for the defendant's advantage, of the plaintiff's name or likeness.[3]

Prosser developed his torts on privacy after an exhaustive study of state laws and judicial (state and federal) decisions related to privacy. These state laws and judicial decisions drove modern privacy law.

---

[2] A tort is a legal term referring to a non-criminal injury or wrong committed against a person in the absence of a formal contract. It can be committed with force or without force, intentionally or unintentionally. The injury is committed against the rights of the person, or to her real or personal property.

[3] William L. Prosser, "Privacy," 48 Cal. L. Rev. 383 (1960), accessed 5/29/18 at http s: //scholarship.law.berkeley.edu/cgi/viewcontent.cgi?ar ticle=3157&context=califor nia lawreview

The civil law associated with privacy torts is distinct from the constitutional law regarding privacy. Constitutional court cases revolve around the privacy rights enshrined in different amendments to our constitution. These protect individuals from *government* (federal, state, local) violation of their privacy. Tort law provides a *civil* law remedy for an individual whose privacy has been violated by any other entity (an individual, a corporation, a not-for-profit institution, or a government). We'll dig into this more in chapter six.

d. Corporations and Regulators

As corporations and utilities grew in the early twentieth century, the government stepped in with legislation and regulation. The Federal Trade Commission was created in 1914 to prevent unfair competition and the Federal Communications Commission was created in 1934 to regulate the telephone, the telegraph, and radio. Public entities began to use governance, compliance and risk management to ensure that their institutions were run by stated rules and in accordance with the law at an acceptable level of risk. Such corporate strategies were used to hedge against economic uncertainty, government regulation, judicial action, and anything else which might impinge on the bottom line.

Computers, cyberspace, and algorithms present many new opportunities and risks for corporations. They can now aggregate information in unprecedented ways to gain insight into potential markets. The new risks – cyber attacks, information breaches, and innovations in privacy regulation – are being woven into the corporate fabric of traditional risk management. And others have adopted this into generic information security frameworks to manage the risks associated with computer systems and the (private) information they contain.

Looking Forward: U.S. Privacy in the 21st Century

The greatest danger to our privacy today is the world's insatiable appetite for information. Cyberspace continues to be a Wild West for private information, allowing it to leak or be leaked, to propagate far afield from its origins. In the United States, we have constitutional amendments and federal laws which enshrine our private rights against violation by our government. There is no generic privacy law (yet) to protect U.S. citizens from for-profit entities, who continue to find creative ways to monetize our private information through scraping and collecting, sharing and selling, analyzing and synthesizing. Many of these U.S. companies pursue lucrative markets in non-democratic nations, refining their products to help foreign governments abridge civil rights of their people.

But there is hope. Privacy rights must be preserved, the lessons from history can inform the way forward, and every U.S. citizen must take responsibility.

First, we must reaffirm our commitment to privacy in America. Cicero said that the individual had the right to be secure in person and property. If we are still talking about this over 2,000 years later, this idea which we now denote as privacy must be worth preserving.

Second, many of the lessons from history can instruct our way forward. History tells us that the law does evolve. It may take decades, but concerted efforts can result in legal change. Risk management has evolved to include managing the risk of computer systems and the information they contain. With a little nudge, third party financial auditing practices could be extended to require privacy auditing of all data repositories containing U.S. person information.

Third, taking individual responsibility for privacy is a 21st century expression of patriotism. Taming cyberspace enough to reclaim our right to privacy is not going to be accomplished by "somebody else." Private citizens must work with government and the commercial world to insist on preserving privacy for our future, and the future of democracy.

PART I
The Origins of Privacy in England and the United States

Introduction

The United States was founded in reaction to what colonists felt were oppressive rules under a monarchy. The US Constitution legitimizes the government as a power given by the people, spelling out their expectations succinctly:

We the People *of the United States, in Order to form a more perfect Union, establish Justice, insure domestic Tranquility, provide for a common defence, promote the general Welfare, and secure the Blessings of Liberty to ourselves and our Posterity, do ordain and establish this Constitution for the United States of America.*

"We the People" says it all. This is a popular sovereignty, not a monarchy. The people are the true rulers, and the system they establish with this instrument ensure them control over the power wielded by the government.

Liberty and defense are front and center here. These are fundamental expectations the citizenry has for those they elect to represent them. Justice is important, because the people expect to be treated fairly and have their disputes justly adjudicated. Domestic tranquility and general welfare are also part of the deal. By collectively empowering the government, the people expect to be free, safe, treated fairly, and enjoy tranquility and general welfare. These are all fundamental beliefs bred into each and every American from birth.

This spirit is rooted in the Western tradition. In the 17th century, John Locke, and others espoused the idea of a social contract between the people and their government, describing the people's expectations of and obligations to the government under which they put themselves for protection. We take that for granted because it is the norm to us as Americans, but it is not the norm in all nations, with Russia and China being among the most notable exceptions.

So go back and re-read the U.S. Constitution. Therein, you'll find that the entire body of the Constitution is concerned with the constitution, responsibilities and limitations of the legislative, executive, and judiciary branches of government.

But our founding fathers felt the Constitution fell short on protecting individual rights, and ended up incorporating the Bill of Rights as amendments to the Constitution. As we shall see, this is where we will find the taproot of privacy in America.

In order to understand what motivated this, Chapter two will provide a brief study of English constitutional history up through the time of King George III, to whom our Declaration of Independence was addressed. Chapter three will pick up the story in America, starting with the fledgling colonies in Virginia and Massachusetts, and concluding with the ratified U.S. Constitution and incorporated Bill of Rights. In both chapters, we will be on the lookout for the predecessors of the individual rights which underlie our claims to privacy today.

Chapter 2
The Origins of Privacy in English Constitutional History

The foundation of English constitutionalism is not conveniently encapsulated in one seminal document. Its roots meander through interrelated events, documents, laws, court cases, and ancient practices. While the Magna Carta is often cited as the first written English constitutional document, many of the topics it attempted to address had actually been issues for hundreds of years. Important concepts emerging during this period include the definition of a freeholder or free man, the land and private property rights of freeholders, the structure of an English government, and the evolution of the law and its different jurisdictions (local, national, and the church).

Before the Norman Conquest: Law, Religion, Tradition, Justice, and Tariffs

The earliest English laws were written down about 600 CE during the time of King Ethelbert of Kent, the first Christian Anglo-Saxon king. A close alliance between law and the Christian religion is evident in these earliest English laws. Only 190 years earlier, the Roman Empire had withdrawn from the British Isles and began to be replaced by invading Angles, Saxons and Jutes. Christianity therefore came to England two ways - directly from the Romans, and indirectly with the later European invaders - and had an important influence over the legal conventions that developed in England. For example, the Roman Catholic Church favored the writing of wills as a method for receiving testamentary gifts.[4]

---

[4] Frederic William Maitland, The Constitutional History of England: A Course of Lectures Delivered. Cambridge: Cambridge University Press, 1908. Reprinted by The Lawbook Exchange, Clark, NJ, 2013, p. 5.

Before the Norman Conquest in 1066 England had different legal conventions based on the cultural traditions of the native and immigrant populations. Each king relied on the advice and consent of his wise counselors to legislate.[5] Chrimes described the king's duties during this period as "defending the people, upholding the law, and doing justice."[6] The king's laws focused on national issues, like keeping peace in the kingdom and reminding men they had an obligation to help keep the peace. These laws displaced traditional "blood feud" justice with a judicial system of tariffs to be paid by the criminal to the plaintiff and/or king. Much of the king's law in this period was devoted to describing these tariffs.[7]

The Norman Conquest: Feudalism, Individual Rights, Taxes, and Governance

As the new king, William the Conqueror claimed all English land as his own royal demesne (land held for a lord's use). He granted large estates to Norman lords and the church with feudal tenures (obligations) attached. The lords and church could grant lands to others with tenures attached. This introduction of feudalism would have a tremendous impact on individual rights, so hang tough while we digress very briefly into a discussion of tenure.

There were six kinds of tenure that the tenant could owe the king or his lord: (1) frankalmoign, (2) knight service, (3) grand serjeanty, (4) petty serjeanty, (5) free socage, and (6) villeinage. Frankalmoign was spiritual service to the lord or king by religious bodies and persons. Knight service involved providing military service, doing homage to, and swearing fealty to the king. Additional royal entitlements (incidents) associated with knight service included: freely providing (financial) aid to the king, having the heir to a knight service estate pay an inheritance relief to the king, the right of the king to keep the heir of his tenant out of the land for a year, the right of the lord to serve as a ward to and arrange marriages for minor heirs, a convention for the tenant to ask the lord's

---

[5] Maitland, 6.

[6] S.B. Chrimes, English Constitutional History. London: Oxford University Press, 1958, Second Edition, p. 73.

[7] Maitland, 4.

permission before replacing himself with another tenant, and finally, escheat or the reversion of land back to the lord or king if the tenant commits a serious crime or dies heirless. Grand serjeanty involved not military service but some special service to the king, with similar incidents. Petty serjeanty involved providing the king with warlike devices, like a sword. Free socage tenure required the tenant to pay rent with agricultural goods or money and provide several days of plowing to the lord. Villeinage described a status and tenure. People in villeinage were not free, that is, the only rights they had against their lord as Englishmen was not to be maimed or killed. As a tenure, those in villeinage held land, but their right to the land was not protected by the king.[8]

Now we can talk about individual rights under English feudal order. A *freeholder* (*lierum tenamentum*) was a person who was afforded the right to protection by the king's court when it came to his land and his possessions.[9] All individuals except those in villeinage were considered freeholders. William had severed the jurisdictions of the church (ecclesiastical) and the kingdom (temporal) so that the king's laws governed the disposition of the freehold (land) while the church's laws governed the disposition of other property (i.e. personal property). Thus, a freeholder's land could only be inherited, whereas his remaining personal property could only be willed. By this method, the king maintained control over his royal demesne and ensured a continuing income stream from freeholder payments of inheritance relief (tax).[10] The king could cite his ancient right of tallage, that is, levying land tax from his tenants for using his land. An organized system of royal taxation would emerge in the 12th century to support collection of scutage (1159), a tax paid in lieu of military service, and the Saladin tithe (1188), an early (first?) personal property tax. The tithe was levied with the consent of the

---

[8] Maitland, 25-38.

[9] Chrimes (pp. 74-75) notes that the rights of freemen (men who were free, but not necessarily freeholders in the feudal sense) were described in the ancient Germanic customs on which Anglo-Saxon law came to be based, and argues that feudal times "never destroyed the concept of the rights and duties of the freeman, the notion of the law-worthy or lawful man, fit for the responsibilities and duties of what we should call citizenship, able and willing to co-operate in the manifold and ever-growing tasks of good government."

[10] Maitland, 9, 35, 37.

king's national council to fund a crusade. Property value was assessed by neighbors, establishing precedent for taxation with representation.[11]

Well before the Norman invasion, England had been subdivided into shires (districts), each with its own shire moot – presided over by an earl and bishop - which served as a court of justice and governmental assembly. It had been an ancient practice for local freemen to participate in local government. After the Norman conquest, the shire moot became the county court, the and all freeholders were expected to participate in it. Further confusing the matter, feudal tenure also entitled each lord to have his own court for and composed of his tenants.[12]

A council of administrators – barons and clergy – made up the king's council (*curia Regis*). These individuals were called upon to exercise the regular duties of running a kingdom, to include giving advice to the king, serving as the Exchequer to mind the treasury, and a court of law for the king. These administrators exercised the king's authority by traveling out to individual counties to collect taxes and to hear court cases.[13]

Thus, the judicial system was very muddled indeed at this point in time. There were the local courts made up of local freeholders, the lord's courts, the king's court, and the king's council visiting courts mentioned above. We will have to wait until after the Magna Carta for the justice system becomes regularized.[14]

The Great Charter and the Law, Taxes and Treason

We are now ready to discuss the Magna Carta. (Bad) King John was forced to sign the Magna Carta in 1215 by clergy and barons who were tired of the king "playing ducks and drakes with the feudal custom and with certain parts of the other law of the land."[15] To address the continuing struggle between Church and King, the document guaranteed that "the English Church shall be free and shall have its rights entire and

---

[11] Maitland, 13.
[12] Maitland, 12, 13, 38, 39-41.
[13] Maitland, 63.
[14] Maitland, 106.
[15] Chrimes, 96.

its liberties inviolate."[16] To address the liberties granted to all freemen, specific rights were called out (e.g. for barons, guardians of the land, widows, and the clergy) concerning property, taxation, inheritance, and legal rights like due process[17] and habeas corpus.[18] To address past wrongs, the document cited the right to appeal for the restoration of any "lands, castles, liberties, or rights" of which the individual had been unlawfully deprived.[19] It also established a council of 25 barons empowered to redress – peaceably or otherwise - any wrongs caused by the king's disregard for the rights espoused in this charter.[20] This document, seminal to the Western tradition, affirmed that the ruler was not above the law. It was a first attempt to write down a constitution which held the king accountable.[21]

There were two jurisdictions for the law in England, ecclesiastical and temporal. The church's jurisdiction was covered by ecclesiastical law. Recall that wills were among the ecclesiastical laws that affected the individual Englishman. The Roman Catholic Church has also begun

---

[16] Carl Stephenson and Frederick George Marcham, ed. Sources of English Constitutional History: A Selection of Documents from A.D. 600 to the Present. New York: Harper and Row, 1937, p. 115.

[17] According to Black's Law Dictionary, a (modern) definition of due process of law in each particular case means such an exercise of the powers of the government as the settled maxims of law permit and sanction, and under such safeguards for the protection of individual rights as those maxims prescribe for the class of cases to which the one in question belongs.

[18] Literally, *you have the bo*dy. According to Black's Law Dictionary, habeas corpus is the name for a variety of writs having for their object to bring a party before a court or a judge. A writ is a letter issued by a court of justice in the name of the king/president/state with an official seal addressed to an officer of the law or an individual whose action the court seeks to command at the beginning or during a suit or other proceeding requiring performance of a specific act or giving authority and commission to have it done.

[19] Stephenson, 123.

[20] Stephenson, 125.

[21] In fact, these ideas had their roots in the Greek and Roman republics of the ancient world. Over a thousand years earlier, Pliny the Younger had observed *Non est princeps super leges, sed leges supra principem,* that is, Nor is the prince above the laws; rather, the laws are above the prince. Thus we can trace the origins of the US Constitution back to classical times, which is what we were learned in school. This tradition is the foundation of constitutional government and legal freedoms.

defining its own canon law in the previous century prescribing a code of behavior for all of Europe.

Temporal law was the law of the kingdom, and included statute law, ordinances, and common law. Statute (statutory) law was the law affirmed by the legislature. It might have been suggested by the king, but the legislature had to agree with it. The 1225 version of the Magna Carta became the first English statute law. This was distinct from an ordinance, a "law" mandated by the king but not agreed to by the legislature. Finally, common law was non-statutory law common to the entire kingdom.[22] This was largely determined by judicial decisions (case law) which in turn were greatly influenced by tradition.[23] The book *The Laws of England* had already normalized local customs and conventions into a book of English common law in the previous century.[24] The important point here is that by the end of the 13th century, English law and legal procedure had matured sufficiently to induce king and parliament to leave "private law and civil procedure, criminal law and criminal procedure, pretty much to themselves."[25]

In the original version of the Magna Carta, taxes were not to be raised without the advice of the landed tenants of the kingdom, that is, the agreement of the lords (bishops, abbots, earls, and greater barons) and the non-lordly tenants (e.g. who also owed tenure directly to the king).[26] This provision was removed from all subsequent versions of the document and therefore was not part of the first English statute law. In 1297, the Confirmation of the Charters would contain a provision (referred to as *De Tallagio no Concedendo,* or of not allowing tallage) specifying that no

---

[22] Maitland, 22.

[23] Black's Law Dictionary defines common law today as: "the body of those principles and rules of action, relating to the government and security of persons and property, which derive their authority solely from usages and customs of immemorial antiquity, or from judgements and decrees of the courts recognizing, affirming, and enforcing such usages and customs.

[24] Maitland, 18.

[25] Maitland, 19-21.

[26] The term *tenants in chief* has been avoided since its meaning is ambiguous in history. It can mean all individuals who owed tenure directly to the king, or non-lordly tenants to the king.

new taxes could be levied "except by the common assent of the whole kingdom and for the common benefit of the same kingdom."[27]

The Parliament summoned by Edward I (1272-1307) in 1295 would be the model for all future parliaments."[28] The king issued parliamentary summons to his earls and barons, and to England's archbishop, bishops, abbots and priors. He also commanded each sheriff (the king's county agent) to summon two elected knights from the county, two elected citizens from each city, and two elected burghers from each borough, all of whom should be empowered to act on behalf of their constituencies. These three estates – clergy, lords, and commoners - became the foundation of the House of Lords and the House of Commons. Parliament could approve the king's requests and parliamentary acts as statute law of the kingdom. The old feudal court gave way to a representative assembly of the three estates.[29]

The king's permanent council grew out of the *curia Regis* of Norman times. This came to be known as the *Concilium Regis*, and becomes distinct from the judicial body. From this kernel grew an increasingly sophisticated centralized government. The king was empowered to make ordinances – not statutes – through this council.[30]

In order to understand the evolution of the judiciary, we have to explore the relationship of law and peace. According to Maitland, "The idea of law is from the first very closely connected with the idea of peace – he who breaks the peace, puts himself outside the law, he is outlaw. But besides the general peace which exists at all times and in all places, … every man has own special peace and if you break that you injure him."[31] By the end of the 12th century, criminal acts came to be recognized as disturbances to the king's peace. At that time, the king's court acquired jurisdiction over all criminal cases (now felonies), surely motivated by the fact that felonies were a cause for escheat. Many of the legal disputes involving land came to be adjudicated in the king's court as well.[32] In the

[27] Stephenson, 164-165.
[28] Maitland, 74.
[29] Maitland, 74-75.
[30] Maitland, 91.
[31] Maitland, 108.
[32] Maitland, 109.

13th century, many civil cases (torts) were addressed by writs of trespass, requiring the guilty defendant to pay damages to the plaintiff and a fine to the king for disturbing his peace.[33] More about trespass later.

The worst crime – or disturbance of the king's peace - was high treason and was punished with death. The 1352 Statute of Treasons clearly defined what was considered treason. This included imagining or plotting the death of the king, making war against the king, or supporting the king's enemies. In 1549, the Riot Act extended the definition of treason to riotous groups of twelve or more persons assembled to kill or imprison any member of the king's council.[34] An additional provision required them to disperse upon proclamation.[35] While the 1549 Act was abolished, variations on the definition of treasonable offenses continued. By and large, the 1352 Statute was accepted down the ages as the "normal measure of treason."[36]

By the end of Edward I's reign, the county court's judicial role had waned, but its significance as a governing body had grown since it was now supplying elected representatives to the national parliament.[37] Freehold issues were heard in the king's court not the lord's court (although villeinage cases remained in the lord's court), and the king's court had become three courts – the King's Bench, the Court of Common Pleas, and the Exchequer - each with its own chief (a chief justice in the first two cases, and a baron in third). This effectively separated the judicial system from the regular governmental function, and made the chiefs nonpolitical (but still agents of the king). The King's Bench was the court that traveled around with the king, the Court of Common Pleas was the court for cases between subjects, and the Exchequer heard cases related to (and collected and disbursed) royal funds. Royal justices also continued to travel out to local jurisdictions to hear pleas and perform other judicial duties for the king. Trial by jury (a practice imported with the Normans)

---

[33] Maitland, 113-114.
[34] Maitland, 226.
[35] William Blackstone, Commentaries on the Laws of England, Book 4, Chapter 11, accessed 8/17/17 at http://lonang.com/library/reference/blackstone-commentaries-law-england/bla-411/
[36] Maitland, 228.
[37] Maitland, 42-43.

had become the norm in civil cases, and was available as an alternative to trial by battle to those accused of criminal acts.[38]

Constitutionalism in the Sixteenth Century: Royal Supremacy and Free Speech Repression

Everything did not go smoothly in England just because the Magna Carta had been signed in the 13th century and reaffirmed by many subsequent kings. During the 16th century, many of the ideas embodied in the Magna Carta were effectively eroded, setting the stage for unrest and revolution in the 17th century. Henry VIII -- maneuvering to aggrandize his power and authority - took the necessary steps to ensure separation and supremacy of the Church of England over Rome. Up until this time, the Holy See had been the legal authority on ecclesiastical appeals (for example, on divorces among other things). With the 1533 Act in Restraint of Appeals, Henry ensured that Parliament declared any appeal to the Pope in Rome illegal, centralizing the right of temporal and ecclesiastical (legal) appeal within England. The following year, Parliament recognized Henry VIII as head of the Church of England with the Act of Supremacy. With this act, Henry VIII became supreme ruler of all political and spiritual affairs. He further legitimized his role by the divine right of kings, claiming his power had been granted by God and that he was above the law and accountable only to God. In 1534, Henry VIII's First Act of Succession specifically stated that anyone that spoke out "orally, in writing, print, deed, or act" against him, his new wife (Anne Boleyn), and any heirs, would be punished for high treason.[39]

Intolerance for other people's opinions continued under Queen Elizabeth I. The Treasons Act of 1571 specified that anyone who "by writing, printing, preaching, speech, express words, or saying maliciously, advisedly, and directly publish, set forth, and affirm that … our sovereign lady, Queen Elizabeth, is an heretical, schismatic, tyrant, infidel, or an usurper of the crown" should be found guilty of high treason.[40]

---

[38] Maitland, 122, 131-137.
[39] Stephenson, 304-305, 310- 311.
[40] Stephenson, 351-352.

In 1576, a parliamentary proceeding concerning Peter Wentworth highlighted the dynamic tension between sovereign and parliamentary powers. As a member of the House of Commons, Wentworth acknowledged that "the king hath no peer nor equal in his kingdom … for otherwise his might lose his authority of commanding," but went on to attack the divine right of the sovereign by saying "the king ought not to be under man, but under God and under the law, because the law maketh him a king."[41] He defended his right to such free speech, arguing that "in this house, which is termed a place of free speech, there is nothing so necessary for the preservation of the prince and state as free speech."[42] Wentworth was imprisoned, but eventually pardoned by the queen and restored to his place in the House.

Both Henry VIII and Elizabeth exercised their prerogative to ban treasonous, heretical, and otherwise offensive books, but this discussion will be deferred until after we've had a chance to talk about the impact the printing press had on the world in chapter four.

Constitutional Crisis in the Seventeenth Century: Unification, Civil War, Restoration, and Revolution

The turbulence surrounding royal prerogative, parliamentary authority, and individual rights came to a head in 17th century England. It is also the time of the founding of the colonies in the new world, as chartered by James I and Charles I. Understanding the uproar in England at this time helps us better understand what the colonists were trying to get away from when they fled the old world for the new. It also describes the context which the colonists brought to the discussion about how the new American government should be constituted and what individual rights should be guaranteed.

James I (1603-1625)

The festering unpleasantness between Anglican England and Catholic Scotland reached its climax when Elizabeth finally executed Mary, Queen of Scots in 1587, and calmed as Mary's son James became James I in 1603. James attempted to assert his authority over Parliament

---

[41] Stephenson, 369.
[42] Stephenson, 368.

and the judicial function of common law. The House of Commons pushed back in 1604 with its Apology of the Commons, asserting the rights of free election of members of the House, freedom from restraint or imprisonment of representatives during Parliamentary sessions, and freedom of speech in debating topics within the House.[43] After James cited royal prerogative to raise new taxes, the House of Commons objected to his abridgement of their right to debate the topic.[44] Continued debate on the rights of the House of Commons led eventually to the King's dissolution of Parliament in 1622.[45]

Debate about new taxes levied by the king found judicial voice in the Bates' Case of 1606. John Bates was a merchant who refused to pay additional taxes to the King. While the court affirmed that a kingdom requires continuing sources of revenue for survival,[46] it insisted that it should be used to benefit the people.[47] While the court ruled against Bates in favor of the king, the debate of royal prerogative versus parliamentary power, and specifically how revenues were raised and spent, would continue.

Charles I (1625-1649)

James' successor Charles I continued to abridge constitutional principles, leading to Parliament's 1628 Petition of Right which cited four violated rights. First, it accused Charles of having imposed new taxes without Parliamentary debate, violating the previously mentioned *Tallagio non Concedendo* of 1297. The Commons argued that the Charles could not impose historical or new taxes "without the goodwill and assent of the archbishops, bishops, earls, barons, knight, burgesses, and other the [hic]

---

[43] Stephenson, 418-424.
[44] Stephenson, 424-427.
[45] Stephenson, 429.
[46] Baron (Judge) Clark observed that: "And as it is not a kingdom without subjects and government, so he is not a king without revenues; for without them he cannot preserve his dominions in peace, he cannot maintain war, nor reward his servants according to the state and honour of a king. And the revenue of the crown is the very essential part of the crown…." [Original, 435]
[47] Chief Baron Fleming added: "The absolute power of the king is not that which is converted or executed to private use, to the benefit of any particular person, but is only that which is applied to the general benefit of the people…, as the people is the body and the king the head." [Original, 436]

freemen of the commonalty of this realm".[48] Second, Parliament argued that Charles had violated article 39 of the Magna Carta, i.e. "No freeman shall be captured or imprisoned or disseised or outlawed or exiled or in any way destroyed, now will we go against him or send against him, except by the lawful judgement of his peers or by the law of the land",[49] specifically to include due process and habeas corpus.[50] Third, Charles had permitted the forced quartering of troops in homes, "and the inhabitants against their wills have been compelled to receive the into the houses, and there to suffer them to sojourn, against the laws and customs of this realm".[51] Fourth, Charles had permitted individuals to be forced to live under martial law during peacetime, in violation of the right to be judged by the (in this case, non-martial) law of the kingdom (first outlined in the 1353 Ordinance and Statute of Praemunire of Edward III). While Parliament passed and forced Charles to accept the Petition of Right, Charles defended his actions as divine right. In 1629, the Resolutions of the Commons were passed, outlawing any religion (e.g. Catholicism & Arminianism) besides that of the Church of England, and outlawing any new taxes without parliamentary approval.[52] Charles dissolved Parliament, and no new Parliament would be convened for 11 years.

For centuries, kings had relied on hereditary revenues and other taxes to pay for the regular expenses of his government (extraordinary expenses like those associated with military campaigns had to be raised by other means). This income stream prevented parliament from exercising any power of the purse over the king[53]. As the government grew, hereditary revenues covered less and less of the king's operating expenses. Parliament's insistence on approving new taxes further shrank the king's revenue base, creating a situation where the king needed parliament to sanction new sources of revenue and/or grant appropriations. It would not be until the time of George III that these hereditary revenues were forfeited

---

[48] Stephenson, 450.
[49] Stephenson, 121.
[50] Stephenson, 451.
[51] Stephenson, 451.
[52] Stephenson, 454.
[53] Chrimes, 84, 88-89

to Parliament in exchange for the latter granting the king an annual fee (the Civil List) to run the civil government.[54]

While it was not illegal for King Charles to continue to conduct the business of the kingdom, he had no Parliament to approve financial appropriations for the realm. He relied on old and obsolete laws and customs for raising revenue. But all was not peaceful in the kingdom. A Puritan movement took hold in Scotland, which made enforcement of the will of the Church of England increasingly difficult for the king as the head of the church. As a last resort, Charles called a Parliament, but differences remained irreconcilable and this Short Parliament (as it came to be known) was dissolved within weeks. Charles found himself unable to perform his duties without a House of Commons.[55]

What came to be known as the Long Parliament began meeting later in 1640 and would in fact continue until 1660. Parliament forced the king to accept several laws righting past constitutional wrongs and curbing royal prerogative. By the Triennial Act of 1641, Parliament made it into law that Parliament must meet at least every three years, regardless of whether the king called one or not. Another act prohibited the dissolution of the present Parliament without parliamentary assent. The Tunnage (tax on imported wine) and Poundage (tax on imported and exported goods) Act of 1641 authorized for 14 months only the collection of taxes which had been levied by royal prerogative in the past. Additional laws abolished all arbitrary courts under executive control and declared that the common law courts were the courts of the land.[56]

The Nineteen Propositions of 1642 asserted Parliament's authority and demanded the king surrender of all his powers - executive, military, and ecclesiastical. Parliament asserted its right to approve members of the king's Privy Council (the modern version of the *curia regis*) and his ministers, the right to debate "the great affairs of the kingdom", the right to advise on reformation of church government and liturgy (all along Puritan lines), the right for each judge approved by Parliament to serve indefinitely *quam diu bene se gesserint* (as long as he

[54] Maitland, 435.
[55] Chrimes, 150-152.
[56] Chrimes, 152-153.

shall behave himself well), and the right to remove and discharge military forces attending the king and prohibit the raising of such forces "but according to law, in case of actual rebellion or invasion".[57] Charles rejected this and fled London.

Civil War (1642-1649) and the Inter-Regnum (1649-1660)

The ensuring civil war unified all of Great Britain – England, Scotland and Ireland – against the tyrannical power of the king. The Heads of Proposals Act of 1647 repealed the Triennial Act, and called for biennial meetings of Parliament, free speech in the House of Commons without fear of censure or exclusion or legal prosecution, and the supremacy of judicial power. Furthermore, Parliament declared control over the militia and the raising and spending of money to support it for ten years. Additional legal reforms were intended to address the grievances of the people and extended to the availability of lands, taxes, payment of the public debt, and making a provision "that none may be compelled by penalty or otherwise to answer unto questions tending to the accusing of themselves or their nearest relations in criminal causes…."[58]

The 1649 Agreement of the People affirmed that the people and places were incorporated "for a secure and present peace upon grounds of common right, freedom, and safety."[59] It called for the ending of the current Parliament, and for elections based on population with popular elections every two years.[60]

The House of Commons passed the Act Enacting a High Court of Justice in 1649 to try King Charles as "a tyrant, traitor, and murderer, and public enemy to the commonwealth"[61] who "not content with those many encroachments which his predecessors had made upon the people in their rights and freedoms, hath had a wicked design totally to subvert the ancient and fundamental laws and liberties of this nation and in their place to introduce an arbitrary and tyrannical government, and that, besides all

---

[57] Stephenson, 489-490.
[58] Stephenson, 507-511.
[59] Stephenson, 511.
[60] Stephenson, 512.
[61] Stephenson, 518.

other evil ways and means to bring this design to pass, he hath prosecuted it with fire and sword, levied and maintained a cruel war in the land against the parliament and kingdom…."[62] Charles refused to recognize the Court, still affirming the divine right of kings: "no earthly power can justly call me, who am your king, in question as a delinquent…."[63] Perhaps not, but he was found guilty nonetheless and beheaded.[64]

In the same year, Parliament abolished the monarchy and the House of Lords, created a Council of State to perform clearly specified executive functions, and established England and its lands as a commonwealth and free state, governed "by the supreme authority of this nation – the representative of the people in parliament, and by such as they shall appoint and constituted as officers and ministers under them for the good of the people…."[65]

The Commonwealth was beset by competing interests and immobilized by the lack of legacy structure. Parliament remained at odds with Oliver Cromwell in his quest to constitutionalize his power. The 1653 Instrument of Government finally established Cromwell, the Lord Protector of the Commonwealth of England, Scotland, and Ireland, as the supreme legislative authority, empowering him to declare war and control the military, but still with the assent of Parliament. It granted a regular budget for the running of government, but additional funds for the military was granted at parliamentary discretion. All laws and specifically those concerning taxes were controlled by Parliament. Cromwell was no king, and his appointment was elective not hereditary.[66] The 1657 Humble Petition and Advice amended the Instrument, reminding Cromwell that he

---

[62] Stephenson, 516.
[63] Stephenson, 517.
[64] His sentence stated that he had: "out of a wicked design to erect and uphold in himself an unlimited and tyrannical power to rule according to his will and to overthrow the rights and liberties of the people…, hath traitorously and maliciously levied war against the present parliament and people therein represented…; and that, but the said cruel and unnatural war so levied, continued, and renewed, much innocent blood of the free people of the nation hath been spilt, many families undone, the public treasure wasted, trade obstructed and miserably decayed, vast expense and damage to the nation incurred, and many parts of the land spoiled, some of them even to desolation." [Original, 518]
[65] Stephenson, 524.
[66] Stephenson, 525-529.

was under the law, that he had to preserve the rights of Parliament, spelled out the annual budget for the army and navy, and again reminded him that he could raise no new revenues without parliamentary approval. Additionally, freedom of religion was extended to all Protestant religions.[67] The ineffectual Protectorate died with Cromwell in 1658.

The Restoration (1660-1688)

In 1660 Charles II was recalled, the Stuart monarchy was restored. As Chrimes so rightly observes "From 1660 onwards, England was never again entirely to forget that the secret of a nation's strength is to have the power of the historical past behind it, not against it."[68] The memories of bad times under an absolute monarch (Charles I), under Parliamentary supremacy (1642-1649), and under dictatorship (Cromwell) would not be forgotten. Charles II was largely unsuccessful in getting Parliament to grant him appropriations, relying instead on funding from the King of France Louis XIV.[69]

Some progressive legislation was enacted under Charles II, including a curbing of royal and noble entitlements, the creation of a post office, assistance to the poor, trade reform, and freer use and enforcement of writs of habeas corpus.[70]

Less progressive legislation included re-establishment of the Church of England and its authorities, with accompanying lesser tolerance towards non-Anglicanism, and the limiting of public petitions to the King and the Parliament.[71]

Charles II was succeeded in 1685 by James II, a devout Roman Catholic who set out during his short reign to restore the political dominance of the Catholics in England. This was an unmitigated disaster and James II fled to France, setting the stage for the Glorious Revolution.

---

[67] Stephenson, 529-532.

[68] Chrimes, 158.

[69] Chrimes, 160

[70] Stephenson, 538, 546, 551, 557-558.

[71] Stephenson, 540-546, 553-557.

The Glorious Revolution and Bill of Rights (1688-1689)

In 1688, Parliament took matters into its own hands. In the Revolution Settlement, Parliament declared that James had violated the constitutional contract between himself and the people and had abdicated, leaving the throne vacant. A Convention of Parliament invited William and Mary, the Prince and Princess of Orange, to be the King and Queen of England. Parliament subsequently enacted the Bill of Rights in 1689. This enumerated all of James II's crimes, to include subverting Protestantism; violating parliamentary authority by suspending laws and their execution, levying money, raising and keeping a standing army during peacetime, and quartering soldiers in people's homes; and by "violating freedom of election of member to serve in parliament…." [72] Immediately thereafter, the bill enumerated all the things that the new king and queen would not do, which sounds a lot like the laundry list of James II's offenses. These include "freedom of speech and debates or proceedings in parliament [which] ought not to be impeached or questioned in any court or place out of parliament."[73] As the new king and queen, William and Mary swore their allegiance to this instrument and became the new royals.

English Constitutionalism in the Eighteenth Century

18th century England was relatively calm after the uproar of the previous century. This section will highlight a few English laws and judicial decisions which influenced the proximate thinking of freedom fighters in the American colonies.

a. Freedom to Assemble

The Riot Act of 1715 spelled out a way for "preventing tumults and riotous assemblies and for the more speedy and effectual punishing the rioters." It did not challenge the freedom to assemble, but rather referred specifically to assemblies of twelve or more (as in the 1549 Riot Act) which disturbed the public peace and the safety of the king and his

---

72 Stephenson, 600.

73 Stephenson, 601.

government. While this was no longer automatically considered high treason, members of such assemblies had to disperse within one hour of notification or they would be punished with death as felons.[74]

b. Freedom of the Press

In the Commons' debate on the printing of speeches of 1738, the Commons debated whether the press should be allowed to print accounts of parliamentary proceedings in the press. It was recognized that that this was a liberty of the press issue. However, members objected because the accounts were not accurate nor comprehensive, and the Commons unanimously voted it a "high indignity to and notorious breach of privilege of this house" which would be dealt with severely.[75] In 1778, similar debates in the House of Commons about misrepresentation of their proceedings resulted in the opening of the proceedings of the House to the public.[76]

In another free speech case, the Dean of St. Asaph was found guilty of publishing but the jury was unable to decide it if was libel. An appeal went to the court of the king's bench in 1784, where Chief Justice Mansfield concluded "To be free is to live under a government by law. The liberty of the press consists in printing without any previous license subject to the consequences of law.... The judges are totally independent of the ministers that may happen to be and of the king himself." The judge upheld the verdict and the court let the matter drop.[77]

c. Private Property Rights

In *Entick v. Carrington* (1765), Entick was arrested for libel under a general warrant. Entick sued Carrington (and other messengers of the Crown) for trespass, the latter having broken into Entick's house and seized his property (books and papers). The Chief Justice Lord Camden observed that "The great end for which men entered into society was to secure their property.... By the laws of England every invasion of private property, be it ever so minute, is a trespass.... Papers are the owner's

---

[74] Stephenson, 617.
[75] Stephenson, 624-627.
[76] Stephenson, 685-687.
[77] Stephenson, 713-715.

goods and chattels. They are his dearest property…." The court found in favor of Entick and awarded him damages.[78]

d. Taxation without Representation

The Stamp Act of 1765, passed under George III's reign and allowing the "granting and applying certain stamp duties and other duties in the British colonies and plantations in America towards further defraying the expenses of defending, protecting, and securing the same" was resisted by the American colonists and repealed the following year. The Declaratory Act of 1766 was passed to remind the colonies that they had been, were, and would be "subordinate unto and dependent upon the imperial crown and parliament of Great Britain."[79] Under Townshend's Revenue Act of 1767, Parliament claimed the right to levy duties against goods in the colonies.[80]

e. Balance of Power

Concerns about undue influence of the Crown in the House of Commons led William Pitt in 1783 to suggest reform of the Parliament. Fearing that such influence was "sapping the very foundation of liberty," Pitt suggested that "The house of commons which, according to the true spirit of the constitution, should be the guardian of the people's freedom, the constitutional check and control over the executive power…."[81] He argued that his fears about corruption could be allayed by enlarging the number of representatives in the Commons. His proposal lost.

Conclusion

We have now successfully traced the highlights of English constitutional history up to the end of the 18th century. We are now ready to look at what the American colonists took away from all this as the created a new country and a new constitution for their United States.

---

[78] Stephenson, 705-707.

[79] Stephenson, 659.

[80] Stephenson, 660.

[81] Stephenson, 692-693.

Chapter 3
The Origins of Privacy in US Constitutional History

The Build-Up to the Declaration of Independence

The origins of the American colonies go back to the 1606, when King James I granted a royal charter to the Virginia Company to colonize two areas of America (located in modern day Virginia and Massachusetts). The charter granted a local governing council for each colony and an overall governing Council of Virginia in England. From its founding in 1607, Jamestown survived as the first permanent English settlement in America which some argue is "where the British Empire began."[82] The New England colony did not persist.

Participatory government was sanctioned by the Virginia Company of London with the Great Charter of 1618.[83] A representational House of Burgesses was instituted to advise the governor. Meeting for the first time in 1619, this was the first instance of self-rule in America.[84] The charter was sanctioned by a king's ordinance in 1621 designating two supreme councils for Virginia. One council – still appointed by the king - assisted the governor in governing. The other council was a representative assembly to be called by the governor annually, empowered to "make, ordain, and enact such general laws and orders for the behoof of the said colony" consistent with the practices of England and subject to approval by the Virginia Company of London.[85]

---

[82] William Kelso, retrieved on 3/19/2017 at https://www.americanhistoryusa.com/topic/jamestown-virginia/

[83] Retrieved 8/3/2017 at https://www.encyclopediavirginia.org/_Instructions_to_George_Yeardley_by_the_Virginia_Company_of_London_November_18_1618A]

[84] Retrieved on 8/3/2017 at https://www.encyclopediavirginia.org/House_of_Burgesses#its1

[85] Stephenson, 501.

Sustained colonization of New England was postponed until 1620 when the Pilgrims landed in Plymouth. Since the Virginia Company had become inactive in New England shortly after its founding, the Pilgrims felt bound by no territorial charter and created their own form of government. Their Mayflower Compact spelled out the social contract (remember John Locke) between the government and the people, and the covenant among the people:

> [We] covenant and combine ourselves togeather into a civill body politick, for our better ordering and preservation and furtherance of the ends aforesaid; and by virtue hearof to enacte, constitute, and frame shuch just and equall laws, ordinance, acts, constitutions, and offices, from time to time, as shall be thought most meete and convenient for the generall good of the Colonie, unto which we promise all due submission and obedience.[86]

Like all Englishmen, the Pilgrims had lived through tumultuous times involving kings exercising divine rights, battles for monarchical succession and religious persecution. It is therefore not surprising that their Mayflower Compact focused on the legitimacy of government. For the Pilgrims, the people empowered the government and consented to abide by the rules it established.

The Massachusetts Body of Liberties in 1641 was a pivotal document for individual liberties in America. Four centuries earlier in England, the Magna Carta had promised that the king would operate under the law and that all individuals would be treated using the regular procedures of the law before being deprived of life, liberty, or property. This is what we would call *due process* today. The Massachusetts document promised not only due process, but also freedom of speech, trial by jury, the right to bail, and the right to written notice of court proceedings, and freedom from cruel and unusual punishment. [87] This document was another ancestor of the U.S. Bill of Rights.

---

[86] Richard B. Morris, Basic Documents in American History. New York: D. Van Nostrand Company, 1965, p. 8.

[87] Accessed on 8/11/17 at http://www.nolo.com/legal-encyclopedia/content/maliberties-doc.html

Religious toleration was a big deal in the New World. Maryland had been chartered to the English Lord Baltimore (a Catholic) by Charles I in 1632 as a colony in which Catholicism was tolerated.[88] Lord Baltimore, with the advice and consent of his General Assembly, would subsequently enact the Maryland Toleration Act of 1649, spelling out religious toleration of all believers in Jesus Christ.[89]

In 1663, Charles II granted a charter for Rhode Island and the Providence Plantations which explicitly granted religious toleration for all inhabitants.[90] The colony had been founded in 1636 by the radical Puritan Roger Williams whose views on the complete separation of church and state had made him *persona non grata* in Massachusetts.[91]

England had considerable self-interest in the founding and success of the American colonies. First, it aggrandized its kingdom, and opened up new sources for trade and revenue. The raw and processed materials of the New World could be sent to the Old World in exchange for English products. Since the colonies still belonged to England, the king was obligated to protect them from attack (e.g. the French and the Indians). In exchange, as in old feudal times, these "tenants" owed the king services and revenue. Second, the mission of enlightened Englishmen included the need to civilize uncivilized societies and bring Christianity to them. Both of these reasons are mentioned in Charles II's 1681 Charter to William Penn which noted that Penn had a "commendable desire to enlarge our English empire and promote such useful commodities as may be of benefit to us and our dominions, and also to reduce the savage natives by gentle and just manners to the love of civil society and Christian religion…."[92] A third reason (which went unmentioned) was that it was easier to keep the king's peace at home if English dissenters – religious, political, and otherwise – were abroad.

---

88 Accessed 8/4/17 at http://avalon.law.yale.edu/17th_century/ma01.asp]

89 Accessed 8/4/17 at http://avalon.law.yale.edu/18th_century/maryland_toleration.asp]

90 Accessed 8/4/17 at http://avalon.law.yale.edu/17th_century/ri04.asp]

91 Accessed 8/4/17 at https://www.loc.gov/item/today-in-history/february-05/

92 Stephenson, 590.

The Declaration of Independence

Having described the origins of these United States, we now skip forward to the big event of 1776, the Declaration of Independence (see appendix B). Therein, the colonists enumerated the offenses of King George III in much the same way that Parliament had enumerated James II's offenses in the English Bill of Rights in 1689. Among his offenses, King George had obstructed the legislative process (e.g. passage of laws, royal assent to laws), subverted representation in government, dissolved representative houses, obstructed the judicial process (e.g. making judges dependent on himself), kept standing armies in times of peace without the people's assent, quartered armies in private homes, levied taxes without the people's assent, denied due process of the law (e.g. depriving people of trial by jury, bringing people back to England to answer for trumpedup charges), incited insurrection, and so on. The best bit, exactly like the charges against James II, was "He has abdicated Government hereby declaring us out of his Protection and waging War against us."[93]

We still don't see any mention of the right of privacy, but we do see "certain unalienable Rights… [which include] Life, Liberty and the pursuit of Happiness."[94] The Declaration says that these rights are to be secured by government as empowered by the consent of the governed. And "whenever any form of Government becomes destructive of these ends, it is the Right of the People to alter or abolish it, and to institute a new Government, laying its foundation on such principles and organizing its powers in such form, as to them shall seem most likely to effect their Safety and Happiness."[95]

On the Way to the U.S. Constitution of 1788 and 1791

It took a long time to get from the Declaration of Independence in 1776 to a ratified U.S. Constitution in 1788. It took another three years after that before the Bill of Rights were incorporated into the Constitution as the first ten amendments. We've already talked about how privacy is

---

[93] Morris, 28-30.
[94] Morris, 27
[95] Morris, 27.

embedded in these amendments. To tie it all together, we are going to talk about the debates that occurred along the way to these ratifications.

The first formal structure of government for the collective colonies was described in the Articles of Confederation which were finally ratified in 1781. This was our first constitution. There were some familiar features of the Articles, like the discussion about the purpose of the confederation to ensure "their common defense, the security of their liberties, and their mutual and general welfare."[96] However, the national government was weak because the states retained most of their powers. Its legislature had one chamber and each state had one vote which encouraged the states to act on individual rather than collective interests. New laws had to be ratified by nine out of 13 states which was nearly impossible. All 13 states had to agree to any amendments to the Articles, which was impossible given the rivalry between the states. The central government needed revenue to support itself and repay Revolutionary War debts, but was too weak to force the states to provide it. What truly alarmed our forefathers was Shay's Rebellion, a tax inspired rebellion in 1786 and 1787 by Massachusetts farmers which was repressed by the state militia because the national government was powerless to do so.[97]

The Constitutional Convention which met in Philadelphia in 1787 completed its work in a matter of months. In place of the Articles of Confederation arose a new U.S. Constitution. In order to inform public opinion concerning ratification by the states, our forefathers John Jay, James Madison, and Alexander Hamilton ghostwrote a series of articles which today we refer to as the Federalist Papers. There was no "continuity editor" for these articles, so differing points of view among the writers did emerge. Nonetheless, the Federalist Papers give us tremendous insight into the debate and thinking of the times, so we will digress briefly into them.

---

[96] Morris, 32.

[97] Accessed 8/17/17 at https://constitutioncenter.org/blog/10-reasons-why-americas first-constitution-failed

Federalist Paper Perspectives

Jay, Madison, and Hamilton were educated men who used lessons from history to move forward

They looked at the city states of ancient Greece. These states had been geographically compact, whereas the new United States was spreading across an entire continent. This prompted the question about how a national government could be effective across great distances. Madison answered that "the natural limit of a democracy is that distance from the central point which will just permit the most remote citizens to assemble as often as their public functions demand, and will include no greater number than can join in those functions; so the natural limit of a republic is that distance from the center which will barely allow the representatives to meet as often as may be necessary for the administration of public affairs."[98]

The vastness of America was also an advantage. Jay granted that America had the advantages of an island nation like Great Britain, "one connected, fertile, wide-spreading country … [with] a succession of navigable waters [which] forms a chain around its borders, as if to bind it together" which lent itself to trade and defense.[99] Unified, America would be able to focus on mutual interests among states and provide a formidable force against its enemies, just as the unification of England and Scotland (in 1707) spawned a stronger nation against its enemies.[100] Separated, America would be weak and forfeit "even the privilege of being neutral."[101]

The authors defined "democracy" and "republic" and explained why a republic suited the United States better

In Federalist 14, Madison said in "a democracy, the people meet and exercise the government in person; in a republic, they assemble and

---

[98] Alexander Hamilton, James Madison, and John Jay, The Federalist, Cambridge, MA: The Belknap Press of Harvard University Press, 1974, 4th printing, edited by Benjamin Fletcher Wright, Federalist 14 (Madison), p. 150.
[99] Federalist 2 (Jay), 93-94.
[100] Federalist 5 (Jay), 105.
[101] Federalist 11 (Hamilton), 139.

administer it by their representatives and agents. A democracy, consequently, will be confined to a small spot. A republic may be extended over a large region."[102]

Madison argued that more populous and territorially larger nations were better governed by republican rather than democratic government, and that carefully titrating the number of votes required for concurrence (e.g. in legislative bills) could check bias and dishonorable motivations. The representative government had to be large enough to be a voice for local constituencies, but not so large that it lost sight of national objectives.[103]

The authors were men of the Enlightenment

The authors of the Federalist papers understood the idea of the social contract between the people and the government. Jay argued that "Nothing is more certain than the indispensable necessity of government, and it is equally undeniable, that whenever and however it is instituted, the people must cede to it some of their natural rights, in order to vest it with requisite powers."[104] They granted that each citizen enjoyed "the same national rights, privileges, and protection."[105] Above all, the people wanted safety, and they looked to the government to provide "security for the preservation of peace and tranquility, as well as against dangers from foreign arms and influence, as from dangers of the like kind arising from domestic causes."[106]

The separation of powers had been an idea which originated with the French philosopher Montesquieu during the Enlightenment, and the Federalist authors cited its importance in the formation of the new national government.[107] In Federalist 47, Madison cited the absence of separate but

---

[102] Federalist 14 (Madison), 150.
[103] Federalist 10 (Madison), 133-135.
[104] Federalist 2 (Jay), 93.
[105] Federalist 2 (Jay), 94.
[106] Federalist 2 (Jay), 96.
[107] Madison quoting Montesquieu: "'When the legislative and executive powers are united in the same person or body,' says he, 'there can be no liberty, because apprehensions may arise lest the same monarch or senate should enact tyrannical laws to execute them in a tyrannical manner.' Again: 'Were the power of judging joined

equal legislative, judiciary, and executive departments as a failing of the English system.[108]

The authors were also practical men

They realized that a peaceful utopian republic was not possible. Trade was always vital to a nation's survival, and commercial competition (leading to warlike conflict) among proximate states was to be expected. Ancient Greece had been populated by nations of soldiers to address this, but the united states of America were populated by industrious people driven by commercial and agricultural interests, not warriors. This was why we had to have the discussion about standing armies - even in times of peace - in order to protect our interests. This meant ceding some legislative power to the executive. Hamilton's immortal words describe this:

> Safety from external danger is the most powerful director of national conduct. Even the ardent love of liberty will after a time, give way to its dictates. The violent destruction of life and property incident to war, the continual effort and alarm attendant on a state of continual danger, will compel nations the most attached to liberty to resort for repose and security to institutions which have a tendency to destroy their civil and political rights. To be more safe, they at length become willing to run the risk of being less free.[109]

The authors were also realistic about the human nature

They knew that different people were driven by different interests and would disagree, but somehow the representative system of government would have to accommodate such factionalism. They knew further that the "most common and durable source of factions has been the various and unequal distribution of property."[110] Man's ability to reason was fallible, and certainly no man should be allowed to judge himself

---

with the legislative, the life and liberty of the subject would be exposed to arbitrary control, for the judge would then be the legislator. Were it joined to the executive power, the judge might behave with all the violence of an oppressor.'" (47 Madison, 338)

[108] Federalist 47 (Madison), 337.

[109] Federalist 8 (Hamilton), 120.

[110] Federalist 10 (Madison), 131.

because of the potential for his biases to compromise his integrity. So a most delicate issue arose. "The apportionment of taxes on the various descriptions of property is an act which seems to require the most exact impartiality; yet these is, perhaps, no legislative act in which greater opportunity and temptation are given to a predominant party to trample on the rules of justice."[111] Nonetheless, "The interest of the man must be connected with the constitutional rights of the place."[112] As Madison famously said:

> If men were angels, no government would be necessary. If angels were to govern men, neither external nor internal controls on government would be necessary. In framing a government which is to be administered by men over men, the great difficulty lies in this; you much first enable the government to control the governed; in the next pace oblige it to control itself. A dependence on the people is, no doubt, the primary control on the government; but experience has taught mankind the necessity of auxiliary precautions.[113]

These auxiliary precautions were checks and balances.

The authors acknowledged that taxes were a hot button issue but revenue for the nation was essential

Taxes had been one of the reasons why the Articles of Confederation had failed, and the founding fathers were determined to get this right. Alexander Hamilton was the champion writer on revenue and taxes in the Federalist papers, which is probably why he became the first Secretary of the Treasury of the United States. He understood that without revenue, a nation "must resign its independence, and sink into the degraded condition of a province."[114] We have seen that in jolly old England where the king had to raise revenue to run his government through direct (land and buildings) and indirect (consumable goods) taxes.[115]

---

[111] Federalist 10 (Madison), 132.
[112] Federalist 51 (Madison), 356.
[113] Federalist 51 (Madison), 356.
[114] Federalist 12 (Hamilton), 146
[115] Note the inkling of religious condemnation of pleasure in Hamilton's comment that: "It is a single advantage of taxes on articles of consumption, that they contain in their own nature a security against excess." (21 Hamilton, 190)

Hamilton had read Adam Smith's *The Wealth of Nations* and had therefore realized that the wealth of the United States depended on many things, including "situation, soil, climate, the nature of the productions, the nature of the government, the genius of the citizens, the degree of information they possess, the state of commerce, of arts, of industry…."[116] Because of this, Hamilton concluded that "there can be no common measure of national wealth, and, of course, no general or stationary rule by which the ability of a state to pay taxes can be determined."[117]

The new U.S. Constitution called for the House of Representatives to hold the purse strings of the new federal government. Madison observed that "This power over the purse may, in fact, be regarded as the most complete and effectual weapon with which any constitution can arm the immediate representatives of the people, for obtaining a redress of every grievance, and for carrying into effect every just and salutary measure."[118] This was similar to the House of Commons' power to introduce all revenue and appropriation bills in England.

The authors emphasized the importance of a strong national government

The weakness of the national government had been a key reason why the Articles of Confederation had failed, so Hamilton brazenly articulated the authorities of national government: commerce, finance, negotiation, and war (national security) – that is, keeping the public peace and defending the nation from all internal and external threats.[119] Madison argued that national government was empowered to make national (not state and local) laws; to add states to the union; to improve roads, communication and canals; and to provide national security to every state which had a frontier which needed to be protected.[120]

The need for defense was paramount in everyone's mind. Since the national government was entrusted with the safety of the nation by its constituents, it should have "all the powers requisite to complete execution

---

[116] Federalist 21 (Hamilton), 189.
[117] Federalist 21 (Hamilton), 189.
[118] Federalist 58 (Madison), 391.
[119] Federalist 17 (Hamilton, 167 and Federalist 23 (Hamilton), 199.
[120] Federalist 14 (Madison), 152-153.

of its trust."[121] That included the authority to fund, raise, train, equip and direct its military.

Hamilton argued that state governments should be responsible for criminal and civil justice as "guardian and life and property." He reasoned that the local peace had been best kept by local law enforcement from feudal times. Noting that in a feudal system the local nobles were often abusers of the common people as well as enemies of the king, he warned that "The separate governments in a confederacy may aptly be compared with the feudal baronies…."[122]

The authors recognized that the proposed form of government was a novelty

According to Madison, the American revolution had "no parallels in the annals of human society," and only "the experiment of an extended republic" could preserve our "private rights and public happiness."[123]

The authors had something to prove and believed that union would get them there

Europe was seen as having named herself "Mistress of the World, and to consider the rest of mankind as created for her benefit. Men admired as profound philosophers have, in direct terms, attributed to her inhabitant a physical superiority and have gravely asserted that all animals, and with them the human species, degenerated in America – that even dogs cease to bark after having breathed awhile in our atmosphere. Facts have too long supported these arrogant pretensions of the Europeans. It belongs to us to vindicate the honor of the human race, and to teach that assuming brother, moderation. Union will enable us to do it."[124]

The authors disagreed on whether a bill of rights was necessary

Alexander Hamilton argued that the Constitution was a bill of rights, containing provisions like habeas corpus and the prohibition of expost-facto laws. Many of the state constitutions – which had provided

---

[121] Federalist 23 (Hamilton), 200-201.
[122] Federalist 17 (Hamilton), 169-170.
[123] Federalist 14 (Madison), 154.
[124] Federalist 11 (Hamilton), 141-142.

inspiration for the U.S. Constitution - had not contained bills of rights. In fact, Hamilton saw a bill of rights as dangerous because it specified exceptions to power *never formally given* to the national government.[125]

Historically, Hamilton argued that bills of rights were agreements between kings and their subjects, or "abridgements of prerogative in favor of privilege, reservations of rights not surrendered to the prince." In England, that had included such documents as the Magna Carta, the Petition of Right, the Declaration of Right, and Bill of Rights. But in these united states, the people surrendered nothing and retained everything, as was stated in the Preamble: "We the People of the United States, ... do ordain and establish this Constitution for the United States of America."[126]

At the end of the day, Hamilton would lose the argument, and individual rights would be incorporated as amendments to the Constitution.

The Seeds of Privacy

The U.S. Bill of Rights holds the first seeds of "privacy" in its protection of private liberties of the citizenry. In our modern era, case law and legal scholars most frequently make privacy arguments based on the First, Third, Fourth, Fifth, Ninth, and Fourteenth (which actually was not ratified until 1868) Amendments[127] For the reader's convenience, these amendments have been reproduced in appendix 3A. We will briefly look at the historical context of these amendments here, and postpone further discussion of their relationship to privacy to later.

The First Amendment

The First Amendment states:

> *Congress shall make no law respecting an establishment of religion, or prohibiting the free exercise thereof; of abridging the freedom of speech, or the press; or the right of the people peaceably to assemble, and to petition the Government for a redress of grievances.*

Let us take each of these five freedoms in turn.

---

[125] Federalist 84 (Hamilton), 532-533, 535.

[126] Federalist 84 (Hamilton), 534.

[127] Helen Nissenbaum, Privacy in Context: Technology, Policy, and the Integrity of Social Life. Stanford, CA: Stanford University Press, 2010, p. 92.

Religious freedom prohibits the establishment of a state religion like the Church of England, as well as the free exercise of any religion by any individual. We need not belabor the historical persecution of Catholics (and for that matter, all non-Anglicans) in England with which the colonists were familiar. Religious freedom was a founding value in the colonies. Why, even Catholics were tolerated in Maryland as early as 1649![128]

Freedom of speech in the First Amendment was intended to apply to all Americans.[129] In England, Henry VIII had granted this freedom *to Parliament only*, while his daughter Elizabeth I subsequently curbed it in the House of Commons.[130] Recall that the parliamentary right to freedom of speech finally appeared in the English Bill of Rights in 1689.

Freedom of the press was a uniquely colonial ideal, a reaction to English licensing rules to preview and approve all publications before public release. Remember in the 18th century, the only kind of freedom of the press issue the English House of Commons debated concerned printing accounts of parliamentary proceedings.

Henry VIII had required the licensing of all publications, and Elizabeth I required prior review before release. Early colonial governments in America tried to implement similar restrictions.

In 1735, the seditious libel case of *John Peter Zenger vs. US* would set the path for a free press in America. Zenger was an immigrant who had printed articles from wealthy lawyers criticizing the royal government. When asked for his sources, he refused to reveal them. Zenger was acquitted after his lawyer mounted the successful defense that the articles contained the truth.[131]

At the same time, Thomas Paine was writing *Common Sense*, a prime example of the kind of free speech that thrived in America and stuck

---

128 Roman Catholics would not be emancipated in Great Britain until 1829. [Source, 678]

129 Yes, our forefathers were thinking of white men like themselves. Subsequent amendments about the rights and freedoms of all Americans today have translated the First Amendment in time so it applies to all Americans.

130 Chrimes, 135.

131 Linda R. Monk, The Words We Live By: Your Annotated Guide to the Constitution. New York: Stonesong Press, 2015, p. 150.

in the craw of her English overlords.[132] As Supreme Court Justice Hugo Black would say nearly 200 years later, "the press was to serve the governed, not the governors."[133]

In English law, non-peaceful assembly that upset order in the kingdom (rioting) was subject to the full force of the law and its punishments. Treason – which included just imagining the killing of the king - and rioting had been tied together for centuries in England.

The right to petition goes back to the Magna Carta, which empowered a subset of barons to hear and personally redress or petition the King to redress wrongs. The 1628 Petition of Right included the right to know the charges whereby someone was imprisoned (habeas corpus), which was reiterated in the Habeas Corpus Act of 1669. The 1689 English Bill of Rights again affirmed "that it is the right of the subjects to petition the king, and all commitments and persecutions for such petitioning are illegal".[134] The Declaration of Independence had specifically faulted King George for not hearing petitions from his colonists.[135]

The Third Amendment

The Third Amendment states: "No Solider shall, in time of peace be quartered in any house, without the consent of the Owner, nor in time of war, but in a manner to be prescribed by law."[136] Yes, Parliament had faulted Charles I for this in 1628 under the Petition of Right, and James II

---

[132] England would see a significant decision regarding freedom of the press during George IV's reign in the case of The King v. Burdett in 1820. Sir Francis Burdett was found guilty of writing and publishing seditious libel. Appealed to the king's court bench, the higher court upheld the finding. What is particularly illustrative is Judge Best's restatement of his opinion: "My opinion is that every man ought to be permitted to instruct his fellow subjects; that every man may fearlessly advance any new doctrines, provided that he does so with proper respect to the religion and government of the country; that he may point out errors in the measures of public men; but he must not impute criminal conduct to them. The liberty of the press cannot be carried to this extent without violating another equally sacred right; namely the right of character. This right can only be attacked in a court of justice, where the party attacked has a fair opportunity of defending himself. Where vituperation begins the liberty of the press ends." (Stephenson, 718-720)

[133] *NY Times v US, 1971.*

[134] Stephenson, 601.

[135] Monk, 153.

[136] Morris, 63.

for this in the Bill of Rights of 1689. And yet Parliament went on to pass the First Quartering Act in 1765, requiring the colonies to pay for or provide room and board to British soldiers in America. The colonists objected to this, arguing it was a tax for services they never wanted. The Second Quartering Act of 1774 authorized the housing of British troops in private homes.[137] And that's how we got the Third Amendment.

The Fourth Amendment

The Fourth Amendment will become our favorite as "*The right of the people to be secure in their persons, houses, papers, and effects, against unreasonable searches and seizures, shall not be violated….*"[138]

This amendment is succinct but complicated. There are several ideas at work here. First, there is the idea of land as property, but also personal property. Remember there had been a devoted history of English laws about land, but less so regarding personal property, which historically had been governed by ecclesiastical law. Second, what arises here is a discussion about what is public (e.g. king's lands tenured to a tenant) and what is private (e.g. my papers). Third, there are concepts of peace and safety. The feudal (and later social) contract specifies that the people essentially exchange freedom for safety. The king's peace needs to be kept – by the king and by his people - because the king is obliged to keep his people safe. Of course, this service isn't free, and so the people will have to pay in some way as the beneficiaries of such governance.

These ideas are all wrapped up in the associated Fourth Amendment epithet "a man's home is his castle." We have Attorney General of England, Sir Edward Coke, to thank for this. While reporting on an English common law case in 1604, he penned the popular words:

> The house of every one is to him as his castle and fortress, as well as for his defence against injury and violence as for his repose.[139]

---

[137] Monk, 158-159.

[138] Morris, 63.

[139] Sir Edward Coke. The Selected Writings and Speeches of Sir Edward Coke, ed. Steve Sheppard. Indianapolis: Liberty Fund, 2003, v. 1. Accessed on 6/27/17 at http://oll.libertyfund.org/titles/coke-selected-writings-of-sir-edward-coke-vol-i-5#lf0462-01_head_075

James Otis' "Against Writs of Assistance" speech of 1761 is an early example arguing for individual rights and the sanctity of the home in the colonies. Defending a group of merchants in the Superior Court of Massachusetts who were tired of having their premises wantonly searched, Otis argued that such general writs required little/no justification, and granted excessively wide powers to a broad range of government officials who were free to abuse their powers and become petty tyrants. He saw these writs at "the worst instrument of arbitrary power, the most destructive of English liberty and the fundamental principles of law...."[140]

Otis argued that while such general warrants had been used in the past, the current law called for the use of special warrants that authorized search of a specific location based on evidence sworn (official) by a complainant. Such writs violated "one of the most essential branches of English liberty ... the freedom of one's house.... [where a] man's house is his castle...."[141]

John Adams – who attended the trial – paraphrased the later part of Otis' defense concerning individual rights (the original version having been lost). Otis argued that every man is an "independent sovereign" with "inherent, inalienable, and indefeasible" rights, and that these rights were embodied in the English constitution and went back to Anglo-Saxon law and the Magna Carta.

Otis further "asserted that the security of these rights to life, liberty, and property had been the object of all those struggles against arbitrary power, temporal and spiritual, civil and political, military and ecclesiastical, in every age. He asserted that our ancestors, as British subjects, and we their descendants, as British subjects, were entitled to all those rights by the British constitution...."[142]

The Fifth Amendment

In the American vernacular, the phrase "I'll take the Fifth" means the right to not have to bear witness against oneself during a criminal trial. In 1770, John Adams had written about the importance of concealing one's

---

[140] James Otis, "Against Writs of Assistance," 1761, accessed 5/28/18 at http://www.constitution.org/bor/otis_against_writs.htm [139]Otis.

[141] Otis.

[142] Otis.

thoughts and opinions. He saw it as a right, and as an intelligent thing to do so enemies cannot use such knowledge against you. Adams also observed that there are things you tell your discreet friends but not your indiscreet individuals who make exploit the knowledge to your "loss, disgrace, or mortification." Finally, he conceded that there were times that a man had a duty to "make known his sentiments and intentions boldly and publicly." He also conceded that there was no hard and fast rule about what can and cannot be lawfully concealed.[143]

But there is considerably more in the Fifth Amendment:

> *No person shall be held to answer for a capital, or otherwise infamous crime, unless on a presentment of indictment of a Grand Jury, except in cases arising in the land or naval forces, or in the Militia, when in actual service in time of War or public danger; nor shall any person be subject for the same offense to be twice put in jeopardy of life or limb; nor shall be compelled in any criminal case to be a witness against himself, nor be deprived of life, liberty, or property, without due process of law; nor shall private property be taken for public use, without just compensation.*

We think of the individual rights described in the Fifth Amendment as due process under the law. As we have seen, many of these grow out of the English legal tradition. Trial by jury came to America as a legacy of the Norman invasion. The seizure of private property without just compensation had been an issue in the Magna Carta.

The Ninth Amendment

This amendment was clearly inspired by Alexander Hamilton's concern that a bill of rights enumerated exceptions to the power of the state, implicitly affirming all others. The Ninth Amendment states:

> *The enumeration in the Constitution, of certain rights, shall not be construed to deny or disparage others retained by the people.*

---

[143] John Adams, Diary, 1770 Aug. 20. Monday. Accessed 5/28/18 at https://www.masshist.org/digitaladams/archive/doc?id=D15&bc=%2Fdigitaladams%2Farchive%2Fbrowse%2Fdiaries_by_date.php

The Fourteenth Amendment

The Fourteen Amendment was not adopted until after the Civil War in 1868. It was intended to resolve the ambiguity about the status of former slaves who would now be recognized as citizens with equal protection under the law. The 14th Amendment extended the individual rights described in the U.S. Constitution to all citizens within all states, effectively extending the full legal force of individual rights to state governments.[144]

Conclusion

So what is privacy? Is it a "a claim, a right, an interest, a value, a preference, or merely a state of existence?"[145] We have already seen it is not a right affirmed in the U.S. Bill of Rights, but lawyers still based privacy arguments on amendments incorporated into the Constitution. Chapter five will delve into how judicial interpretation of privacy has evolved over time. But first, we need to talk about how technology challenged and shaped privacy in America during the 19th and 20th centuries.

Appendix 3A

Amendments typically associated with Privacy

1st Amendment

Congress shall make no law respecting an establishment of religion, or prohibiting the free exercise thereof; of abridging the freedom of speech, or the press; or the right of the people peaceably to assemble, and to petition the Government for a redress of grievances.

3rd Amendment

No Soldier shall, in time of peace be quartered in any house, without the consent of the Owner, nor in time of war, but in a manner to be prescribed by law.

4th Amendment

The right of the people to be secure in their persons, houses, papers, and effects, against unreasonable searches and

---

[144] Monk, 218.
[145] Nissenbaum, 2.

seizures, shall not be violated, and no Warrants shall issue, but upon probably cause, supported by Oath or affirmation, and particularly describing the place to be searched, and the persons or things to be seized.

5th Amendment

No person shall be held to answer for a capital, or otherwise infamous crime, unless on a presentment of indictment of a Grand Jury, except in cases arising in the land or naval forces, or in the Militia, when in actual service in time of War or public danger; nor shall any person be subject for the same offense to be twice put in jeopardy of life or limb; nor shall be compelled in any criminal case to be a witness against himself, nor be deprived of life, liberty, or property, without due process of law; nor shall private property be taken for public use, without just compensation.

9th Amendment

The enumeration in the Constitution, of certain rights, shall not be construed to deny or disparage others retained by the people.

14th Amendment [adopted in 1868]

Section 1. All persons born or naturalized in the United States, and subject to the jurisdiction thereof, are citizens of the United States and of the State wherein they reside. No State shall make or enforce any law which shall abridge the privileges or immunities of citizens of the United States; nor shall any State deprive any person of life, liberty, or property, without due process of law; nor deny to any person within its jurisdiction the equal protection of the laws.

Section 2. Representatives shall be apportioned among the several States according to the respective numbers, counting the whole number of persons in each State, excluding Indians not taxed. But when the right to vote at any election for the choice of electors for President and Vice President of the United States, Representatives in Congress, the Executive and Judicial officers of a State, or the members of the Legislature thereof, is denied to any of the male inhabitants of such State, being twenty-one years of age, and citizens of the United States, or any way abridged, except for participation in rebellion, or any other crime, the basis of representation therein shall be reduced in the proportion which the number of such male citizens shall be to the whole number of male citizens twentyone years of age in such State.

Section 3. No person shall be a Senator or Representative in Congress, or elector of President and Vice President, or hold any office, civil or military, under the United States, or under any State, who, having previously taken an oath, as a member of Congress, or as an officer of the United States, or as a member of any State legislature, or as an executive or judicial officer of any States, to support the Constitution of the United States, shall have engaged in insurrection or rebellion against the same, or given aid and comfort to the enemies thereof. But Congress may by a vote of two-thirds of each House, remove such disability.

Section 4. The validity of the public debt of the United States, authorized by law, including debts incurred for payment of pensions and bounties for services in suppressing insurrection or rebellion, shall not be questioned. But neither the United States nor any state shall assume or pay any debt or obligation incurred in aid of insurrection or rebellion against the United States, or any claim for the loss or emancipation of any slave; but all such debts, obligations, and claims shall be held illegal and void.

Section 5. The Congress shall have the power to enforce, by appropriate legislation, the provisions of this article.

Chapter 4
What Hath God Wrought, and Other Perils of Technology

What's past is prologue.
Shakespeare

In this chapter, we're going to talk about four technologies – the printing press, the telegraph, the telephone, and the – that revolutionized how people could communicate. It is an important part of our story, because it explains how communications evolved from more basic methods to the free flow of information across communications infrastructure which we take for granted today. Along with these revolutions, the idea of privacy emerged and evolved, which is something we will talk more about in chapter five.

The Printing Press

The mechanical printing press was invented around 1440 on the European continent and spawned a revolution. Up until this time, books and other written documents had been laboriously copied by hand, and reading was a skill mastered by few. The easier reproduction and availability of written communications through moveable type would contribute to the cataclysmic cultural change associated with the Renaissance, the Reformation, the Enlightenment and the Scientific Revolution. Historians vociferously debate the relationship of the printing press to these movements and we will not be going down that rabbit hole! However, we will briefly look at what these movements were about, and then consider the synergies between them and the printing press.

Introduction

Much of Western knowledge had been lost, misplaced, or scattered across Christian and Moslem lands by 1440. Preservation of this knowledge was thwarted by both man and the environment. Wars and the fall of empires led to abandonment and burning of libraries and to the exodus of scholars able to read and understand these texts. Environmental effects eroded the quality of the media (e.g. papyrus roll, vellum, parchment codex) on which the knowledge was recorded. Inadvertent errors were introduced by scribes when they made new copies of a text, and pictures or diagrams were left out because there was no easy way to make copies. Original texts were translated into new languages, and errors in translation were introduced. The great library at Alexandria, founded by the Greeks around 295 BCE and inadvertently burned by the Romans during a war in 48 BCE, had contained many ancient texts in Greek, Egyptian, and other languages. Its daughter library in the nearby Serapeum temple had been intentionally destroyed around 491 CE to in an effort to eradicate paganism as Christianity took hold in the Roman Empire.[146]

After the fall of the Roman Empire in the 5th century CE, the church was the only safe home for books. Monasteries contained both libraries and scriptoria, the place where monks made copies of books by hand. They produced luxurious copies of manuscripts and books using elaborate scripts and illuminated illustrations. Byzantine monasteries typically contained books in Greek whereas Western monasteries contained books in Latin.[147] Many Greek classics migrated and were preserved in the Muslim world. Education, learning, and books were largely controlled by the church.

Greek classics would be recovered in the West later, having found their way to the Arab world.

The rise of European universities in the 12th century coincided with renewed interest in Greek classics. The universities needed less expensive copies of these books for their students, and stationers (*stationarii*) associated with the universities came into being. Fortuitously, many Greek classics had migrated to and been preserved in the Muslim world. Western stationers were able to provide students with Latin

---

[146] https://www.britannica.com/topic/Library-of-Alexandria

[147] https://www.britannica.com/topic/publishing#ref28609, retrieved 2/25/18.

translations of Arabic language versions of Greek classics recovered from the Muslim world.[148]

A Little Background on the Renaissance

The Renaissance began around 1400 and lasted until around 1650.[149] The early Renaissance reinvigorated learning, renewing interest in Classical studies and values. It emerged initially in Italy with the humanist movement and spread to northern Europe. Humanists were secular scholars who focused on human dignity and accomplishments. They intended on making philosophical and religious world views consistent and compatible (!). One source tells us: "The effect of humanism was to help men break free from the mental strictures imposed by religious orthodoxy, to inspire free inquiry and criticism, and to inspire a new confidence in the possibilities of human thought and creations."[150] The humanist movement benefited greatly from the flight of scholars with classical books and manuscripts from Constantinople after it fell to the Turks in 1453.[151]

A Little Background on the Reformation

The Reformation was a revolution in the Western Christian church in the 16th century. Historians attribute its origins to a reaction against an increasingly powerful and corrupt Catholic Church in Western Europe. Its beginnings date to Martin Luther's posting of his 95 Theses in 1517 in Wittenberg, Germany. Luther believed that the church had perverted the ideas of redemption and grace. He condemned the system of indulgences (particularly their commercialization), acts which sinning Catholics could perform to minimize their time in Purgatory. He viewed Scripture as authoritative, and believed that justification (God's movement of an individual from a state of sin to a state of grace) was achieved through faith, not works, calling into question gospel doctrine that the exceptional

[148] https://www.britannica.com/topic/Library-of-Alexandria, retrieved 1/1/18.
[149] https://www.britannica.com/place/Italy/The-age-of-Charles-V#ref318656, retrieved 1/1/18.
[150] https://www.britannica.com/event/Renaissance, retrieved 1/1/18.
[151] https://www.britannica.com/event/Renaissance, retrieved 1/1/18.

good deeds of saints had earned them grace. Luther also rejected transubstantiation, the Catholic belief that the bread and wine of the Eucharist actually became the body and blood of Christ. Yes, Luther was on a collision course with the Catholic Church.[152]

A second advocate of reformation was John Calvin, a French Protestant who fled France for Switzerland. He agreed with Luther's views on justification, believed that Holy Communion represented a *spiritual* sharing of the body and blood of Christ, and emphasized predestination. In Geneva, he experimented with a representational community, leading Geneva to come to be known as the Protestant Rome.[153]

Protestantism spread across northern and eastern Europe, and jumped the English Channel, while Italy, France, and Spain remained Catholic strongholds. As we already know, in England Henry VIII repudiated papal authority (still bitter about that annulment issue) and created and headed the new Anglican Church. This allowed the English church to prepare the liturgy in English and as well as a Book of Common Prayer. John Knox, greatly influenced by John Calvin, established Protestantism in Scotland which would ease the unification of England and Scotland under James I.[154] But we are getting ahead of ourselves.

A Little Background on the Scientific Revolution

The Scientific Revolution was the revolution in the sciences of the 15th, 16th and 17th centuries in which classical views of science were displaced by more modern views. Science was now seen as distinct from philosophy and technology with utilitarian goals. Common sense was replaced with abstract reasoning, and the "scientific method" was used to substantiate or refute hypotheses within a theoretical framework. The natural world was modeled more as a machine than a living organism, and these scientists emphasized *how* rather than *why* as the Aristotelians had.[155]

---

[152] https://www.britannica.com/event/Reformation, retrieved 1/1/18.

[153] https://www.britannica.com/event/Reformation, retrieved 1/1/18.

[154] https://www.britannica.com/event/Reformation, retrieved 1/1/18.

[155] https://www.britannica.com/science/scientific-revolution, retrieved 1/1/18.

The Printing Press and the Renaissance

We all know that Johannes Gutenberg established the first European printing press in Mainz (then in the Holy Roman Empire) around 1440. The press spread to German and Swiss-German towns (Strasbourg, Cologne, Augsburg, Nuremberg, and Basel) in the 1460's and over the Alps to Italy.[156] The first English printing press was established by William Caxton in 1476 who had learned printing in Cologne.[157] The availability of paper from Italy was a necessary condition for the proliferation of the printing press in Europe.[158] The earliest record of an English paper mill dates to 1495.[159]

The printing press made ancient texts readily available to scholars, who ended up comparing different versions of the same classics. Comparison between ancient Greek versions and later Latin versions revealed corruption in translation. Scholars "purified" texts back to their original meaning. During this period, Erasmus became famous for purifying St. Jerome's Latin version of the Bible or the Vulgate produced in the 4th century CE. There was a sense in this time that the purification of texts helped restore their original messages as revelations God had given to man.[160]

And a subtle social change took place. Individual achievement and the accompanying fame took over from the anonymity of the scribe. Things like copywriting written works or patenting inventions became important. Intellectual property started to have a place in the world.[161] Artisans could now be recognized as inventors, the secretiveness of the guild was being challenged by individuals with initiative, and ingenuity could be recognized with fame and fortune.[162]

---

156 Eisenstein, Elizabeth L. The Printing Press as an Agent of Change: Communicati ons and Cultural Transformations in Early-Modern Europe. Cambridge, UK: Cambridge University Press, 2009, 14th printing, 272

157 http://www.bbc.co.uk/history/historic_figures/caxton_william.shtml, retrieved 1/ 1/18.

158 Eisenstein, 217.

159 http://baph.org.uk/ukpaperhistory.html, retrieved 1/1/18.

160 Eisenstein, 191.

161 Eisenstein, 229.

162 Eisenstein, 240.

Writers like Montaigne began to write in a personalized style which captured the power of the pulpit in an individual message to a reader. This individualistic style connected the reader to the author in a way that connected individuals with common interests and concerns indirectly.[163]

The availability of books meant an increase in the number of people who were self-educated. No longer did one have to apprentice at a guild to acquire the skills of a trade nor attend university to have access to books. This opened up the authorship market to non-academic writers who were disdainful towards academics. They wrote self-help and self-improvement works which the increasingly literate population snatched up. A sense of independence and self-reliance rose up in populations.[164]

Which brings us to an interesting point. In the past, guilds had secretively passed down the skills and recipes of their professions through oral tradition and on-the-job training. These practices all appeared to be very mysterious. So, when this 'underworld of learning' all of a sudden became visible in printed form, it was hard for the reader to distinguish between legitimate sources (like apothecaries) and charlatans (like alchemists). Potential authors became fearful of censorship, largely driven by Catholic Church beliefs that some printed work violated God's word.[165]

This all became part of what I'll call the sorting out period. The Renaissance recovered ancient texts and used them to come up with authoritative versions in Latin (for the academics) and in the "vulgar" vernacular language of the region for the non-Latin readers. The wider availability of these texts made it possible for scholars and non-scholars to look at printed copies of diverse classics at once and begin to recognize inconsistencies across sources. This helped set the stage for the Scientific Revolution, in which classical texts would be challenged and – based on scientific discoveries in more modern times – discarded.[166]

---

[163] Eisenstein, 230-231.
[164] Eisenstein, 244.
[165] Eisenstein, 273.
[166] Eisenstein, 502.

The Printing Press and the Reformation

Which brings us to the Reformation. The printing press made it possible to disseminate Luther's 95 Theses across Europe. It created a tidal wave of influence which even the Pope could not control. In modern parlance, Luther went viral. It was the first movement that used the power of the press "for overt propaganda and agitation against an established institution."[167] The printed caricature was born. Eisenstein argues that the printing press "probably contributed more to destroying Christian concord and inflaming religious warfare than any of the so-called arts of war ever did…."[168]

From the time of Luther on, the German people felt God had blessed them with Gutenberg's printing press, intending to emancipate them "from bondage to Rome and brought the light of true religion to a God-fearing people."[169] Protestant leaders came to see the printing press as "a providential device which ended forever a priestly monopoly of learning, overcame ignorance and superstition, pushed back the evil forces commanded by Italian popes, and, in general, brought Western Europe out of the dark ages."[170]

The power of the press was also leveraged by Henry VIII. Eisenstein argues that "No episode … shattered the unity of the Church as decisively or permanently as did the contested divorce case of a sixteenthcentury English king." [171] In support of the king's actions, Thomas Cromwell used the printing press to mount the first government propaganda campaign against the Catholic Church. He did this as skillfully as Lutherans, using propagandists and publications in the vernacular.

In response to the Protestant challenges to Catholic doctrine and practices, the Catholic Church convened the Council of Trent during three periods from 1545 to 1563. The Council refuted Luther's justification and anti-transubstantiation doctrines, reiterating Catholic belief in

---

[167] Eisenstein, 304.
[168] Eisenstein, 319.
[168]Eisenstein 305.
[169] Eisenstein 305.
[170] Eisenstein, 305.
[171] Eisenstein, 312.

transubstantiation. The Council also declared that the Latin Vulgate was the authoritative source for doctrinal proof and rejected any other Bibles. Italian and French printers who had been making money on vernacular Bibles relocated to Protestant nations, and a huge black-market book trade sprang up.[172]

It was not only differences in beliefs or the corruption of the Church that fueled a split in Christianity. It was the fact that all those scholars looking to original sources to produce authoritative versions of the Bible were discovering inconsistencies. As Eisenstein tells us, "Given the believe that true eloquence was a token of divine inspiration, Biblical scholars faced a painful predicament: either they had to conceal all the discrepancies and lapses they uncovered, or else they cast doubt on the divine authorship of the scriptures."[173]

Which brings us to another significant difference between the Catholic and Protestant faiths.

Eisenstein tells us that Catholics defended use of Latin because of tradition, "but also because it was esoteric and kept mysteries veiled from the profane. The power of the press could be used to improve clerical education but had to be controlled by clerical censors to foster lay obedience."[174] Alternatively, the Protestant doctrine empowered the individual to practice his faith himself. The salvation promised through Bible reading in vernacular language spurred literacy rates.[175]

In 1538, Henry VIII of England authorized the first English version of the Bible, known as the Great Bible, which enjoyed some popularity. The English language Geneva Bible, first published in Geneva in 1557 and in England in 1576, was published by English Presbyterians living abroad during Queen Mary's (Catholic) reign and became popular among Puritans. King James I authorized a new version of the English Bible in 1604, leading to publication of the King James Bible in 1611.[176] The Anglican Book of Common Prayer was first authorized for use in

---

172 https://www.britannica.com/event/Council-of-Trent, retrieved 1/2/18.
173 Eisenstein, 323.
174 Eisenstein, 344.
175 Eisenstein, 333.
176 https://www.britannica.com/topic/King-James-Version, accessed 1/2/18.

1549 and revised several times thereafter.[177] During the Tudor dynasty, the Englishing of law books was justified on patriotic grounds. During the Stuart dynasty, John Lileburne argued that laws should be in English so anyone could read them, and English laws began to be printed in the 1480's.[178] Not just in England but across Europe, the printing press drove language standardization, formalizing the vernacular and unifying a people around their mother tongue.[179]

The rise of printing and Protestantism induced an awakening of the individual spirit in Europe. Printers and their associates (e.g. artisans, academics, preachers) became the new capitalist bourgeoisie, nibbling away at the antiquated authority of the feudal aristocracy and the church.[180] Printer's workshops – salons of artisans, printers, academics, aspiring authors, and others – became centers of patriotism and democratic thought which vexed the Counter-Reformation.[181] As Eisenstein tells us: "the printer not only helped to shape a competing hedonistic and utilitarian ethic; he also made possible a fuller orchestration of all the old anti-clerical themes."[182] It also necessitated an expanded government bureaucracy to regulate this new industry.[183]

Printing centers migrated from Catholic nations in southern Europe to Protestant nations further north. Geneva, the European center of Calvinism, began to function as a Protestant Rome after French Protestant refugees immigrating there in the 1550's caused explosive growth in the number of printers in that city.[184] When the Calvinists won in Holland, Dutch printing entered its golden age, first in Leiden with the Elseviers and later in Amsterdam. It was the Elsevier press that would published Catholic philosophers like Galileo and Descartes who were prohibited from publishing in their native lands.[185] Across the Channel, King James

---

177 https://www.britannica.com/topic/Book-of-Common-Prayer, accessed 1/2/18.
178 Eisenstein, 104, 362.
179 Eisenstein, 117-118.
180 Eisenstein, 388.
181 Eisenstein, 389.
182 Eisenstein, 394.
183 Eisenstein, 395-396.
184 Eisenstein, 402, 410.
185 Eisenstein, 409.

I allowed the publication of the work of Paolo Sarpi,[186] an Italian theologian and statesman who disagreed with papal absolutism and believed in separation of church and state.[187]

The Catholic Church began publishing an Index of Forbidden Books (Index Librorum Prohibitorum) in 1559 which it would continue to update.[188] Publishers discovered that appearance of their publications on such banned book lists enhanced the reputations of authors and spurred sales, leading booksellers to understand the power of such passive publicity.[189]

In Protestant regions, learning from books became a part of everyday life. Parents, not priests, became responsible for the spiritualization of the household. As a result, Eisenstein says, "Puritan tradesmen who had learned to talk to God in the presence of their apprentices, wives, and children were already on their way to selfgovernment."[190] It bred self-esteem, self-mastery, and self-worth.[191] Book learning invaded the privacy of the family home and became part of family life.[192] Children could now receive formal instruction from primers and other textbooks instead of living the life of an apprentice or page.[193] In Scotland, wealthy households could be fined for not having a copy of the Bible and the psalter in the vernacular.[194] The English Puritan preacher John Foxe published his *Book of Martyrs* in England in 1559 which became very popular in English Puritan households.[195] In Catholic regions, learning to read was not similarly incentivized among the general population.

Interestingly enough, a rising concern about Satanic forces arose during the Reformation and printing revolution. Religious unrest often

---

186 Eisenstein, 412.
187 https://www.britannica.com/biography/Paolo-Sarpi, retrieved 1/3/18.
188 https://www.britannica.com/topic/public-opinion#ref397875, accessed 1/3/18.
189 Eisenstein, 406, 639.
190 Eisenstein, 425.
191 Eisenstein, 427.
192 Eisenstein, 133.
193 Eisenstein, 432.
194 Eisenstein, 415.
195 https://www.britannica.com/biography/John-Foxe, accessed 1/3/18.

bred accusations that the opposing camp was working for the Devil. The book learning advocated by Protestants - which undermined Catholic orthodoxy - was painted as the devil's work by the Catholics.[196] The first edition *Malleus Maelficarum*, a demonology encyclopedia, was published in 1486 and, according to Eisenstein, fueled Satan preoccupation. Indeed, all good bible-reading Protestants would have understood minister John Wesley's words "Giving up witchcraft is in effect giving up the Bible" as a reference to Exodus xxii, 18, "Thou shalt not suffer a witch to live."[197] Every story needs its villain.

The Printing Press and the Scientific Revolution

OK, we finally have all the background we need to talk about the Scientific Revolution (whew!). Prior to this time, the classicists were reveling in the new availability of original sources and translations facilitated by the printing press. People were able to compare different sources as well as different versions of books for the first time. An effort to descramble and correct knowledge began, much as Erasmus had tried to correct St. Jerome's Vulgate. The experimentalists realized that classical texts were inconsistent with what they saw in the real world. This gave rise to new theories, some of which would challenge Catholic beliefs (trouble ahead). It would take time, but the classical sources would be discarded, and a new science would "couple empiricism and rationalism and ... develop theoretical frameworks for ordering collected facts."[198] This work could be printing and distributed with books, and corrections could be made in future editions through *feedback* for the first time.[199] The idea of man's knowledge continuing to expand would challenge fundamental Christian beliefs in the infinitude and unfathomability of God's mysteries.[200]

This happened in many scientific fields, but the top three usually mentioned include astronomy, physics, and anatomy. The major players in astronomy were Nicolaus Copernicus (1473-1543, Prussia/Poland),

---

[196] Eisenstein, 438.
[197] Eisenstein, 439.
[198] Eisenstein, 477, 511.
[199] Eisenstein, 479.
[200] Eisenstein, 518.

Tycho Brahe (1546- 1601, Denmark), Galileo Galilei (1564-1642, Italy), and Johannes Kepler (1571-1630, Germany). The major players in physics were René Descartes (1596-1630, France) and Isaac Newton (1642-1727, England), while the major players in anatomy most frequently mentioned are Andreas Vesalius (1514-1578, Belgium) and William Harvey (1578-1657, England). Their work would supplant the astronomy of the Egyptian astronomer Ptolemy (100-160 CE), the physics of Greek philosopher Aristotle (384 – 322 BCE), and the anatomy of the Greek physician Galen (129-216 CE). We will focus on the astronomy story.

Ptolemy's *Almagest* was lost to the West until the 12th century, when it was recovered from the Moslem world in Arabic. Very few copies were available before the printing press.[201] Copernicus had three copies of this and many other classical sources, and was able to study and compare them side by side. He saw discrepancies in the data and the theory, and came up with his alternative heliocentric theory.[202] Brahe taught himself astronomy and mathematics from books, and as a young man also observed that things were misplaced in the sky according to existing texts.[203] New astronomical data – desperately needed – had to be collected over a long period of time to be most useful. The publication of mathematical and astronomical tables freed up scientists from tedious calculations so they could spend more time designing experiments, making observations, coming up with new theories, and getting their words into print. Copernicus' studies motivated Brahe to collect new astronomical data which Kepler would use.[204] Copernicus' book *De Revolutionibus* was published in 1543 in Nuremberg shortly before his death. It was re-published in Amsterdam in 1616 shortly after the latest Catholic Church Index condemned it.[205] Kepler by that time was working on a publication to clarify Copernicus' work, and then part of Kepler's work was banned.[206] Kepler's astronomical model turned Copernicus' heliocentric view into a dynamic universe where the sun pushed the

---

201 Eisenstein, 463-464.
202 Eisenstein, 603, 629.
203 Eisenstein, 597.
204 Eisenstein, 585.
205 Eisenstein, 480.
206 Eisenstein, 639.

planets around in non-circular orbits, setting the stage for Newton in the 17th century.[207]

Understanding of celestial phenomena was important to Christianity, especially when it came to figuring out when Easter should be. Easter falls approximately on the first Sunday after the first full moon on or after the Spring Equinox.[208] The phases of the moon are not aligned with the Equinox. Nor did the Julian calendar (replaced by the Gregorian calendar in 1582) align with the solar year, causing more confusion.[209] This meant that the Christian church always had work for astronomers.[210]

Many scholars and scientists were reticent to publish their works.[211] Some authors - like Copernicus - realized that their writings at least *appeared* to challenge the beliefs of the Catholic Church. That could get a book banned and/or an author condemned for black magic and/or heresy. Some authors may have also feared that their work would be stolen. Evolving legal concepts would address intellectual property concerns, and over time real science would become common knowledge and understood as distinct from magic.[212] The Royal Society of London was founded in 1660 and clarified the bounds of science by beginning to publish it Philosophical Transactions five years later.[213]

A Special Case: Galileo

The Reformation raced across Europe as the printing press spread knowledge to a broader reading community. Protestantism eroded the power of the Catholic Church, which desperately tried to hold on to the preeminent role it had had during the Middle Ages. But a sense of individualism and naturalism had started to take hold, and it would prove

---

[207] https://www.britannica.com/biography/Johannes-Kepler, accessed 1/3/18.

[208] http://aa.usno.navy.mil/faq/docs/easter.php, retrieved 1/3/18. Passover falls on the first full moon after the spring equinox.

[209] https://www.britannica.com/science/Julian-calendar, retrieved 1/3/18.

[210] Eisenstein, 612.

[211] Eisenstein, 453.

[212] Eisenstein, 620-621.

[213] https://royalsociety.org/about-us/history/, accessed 1/3/18. Not that they were completely above the Christian uproar. Eisenstein quips that the Royal Society and the Anglican Church were aligned anti-Papists (page 668).

impossible for the Catholic Church to put the genie back in the bottle. No story better illustrates this conundrum than that of Galileo.

In the spring of 1609, Galileo Galilei began making observations using a newfangled thing called a telescope. His book *The Sideral Messenger* – published in 1610 by a Catholic press – described his astronomical discoveries and made him famous.[214] In 1613, Galileo wrote letter to a student about inconsistencies between Copernican theory and the Bible, which garnered negative attention from Rome. The Catholic Church believed that the Bible had been passed down to man as the word of God, and scientific discovers that contradicted the Bible were heresy. Galileo expanded on his original thoughts in *A Letter to Grand Duchess Christina of Tuscany* in 1615. There were several key thoughts in this letter. First, he suggested that scientific evidence appeared to contradict passages in the Bible only because the Bible had been historically interpreted incorrectly. Galileo affirms that "the holy Bible can never speak untruth – whenever its true meaning is understood."[215] Second, he believed that the clerics condemning him did so out of spite and (mathematical) ignorance, not having studied Copernicus' or Galileo's work and not having provided any cogent counter arguments to the heliocentric theory. Third, Galileo reiterated the words of an eminent ecclesiastic (Cardinal Baronius): "That the intention of the Holy Ghost is to teach us how one goes to heaven, not how heaven goes."[216] Even though this had been uttered by one of their own, the Catholic Church took exception to the idea that their authority did not extend to the physical as well as spiritual world. The promulgation of Copernican views in vernacular language was arrested by the Vatican's decree of the Congregation of the Index (banned book list) in 1616. Copernicus' book was withdrawn until it could be "corrected," and it became risky for Catholic presses to publish such work.[217] Galileo effectively got the message to sit down and shut up.[218]

---

[214] Eisenstein, 652.

[215] https://sourcebooks.fordham.edu/mod/galileo-tuscany.asp, accessed 1/6/18.

[216] https://sourcebooks.fordham.edu/mod/galileo-tuscany.asp, accessed 1/6/18.

[217] Eisenstein, 653.

[218] https://www.britannica.com/biography/Galileo-Galilei, accessed 1/6/18.

In 1624, Galileo asked and received permission from the Pope to write a book about his understanding of the universe. The Pope warned him to only treat Copernicanism as hypothetical, which was the spirit in which Copernicus' work had been "corrected." Galileo completed his work *Dialogue Concerning the Two Chief World Systems, Ptolemaic and Copernican* around 1630 and it was published in Florence in 1632. Galileo was summoned before the Inquisition in 1633 and accused of not treating the Copernican model as hypothetical. Galileo admitted he had gotten carried away. He was found guilty, suspected of heresy, and condemned to life imprisonment (in comfortable surroundings), where he remained until his death in 1642.[219] His last work, *Dialogues Concerning Two New Sciences*, were smuggled out of Italy and published in the Netherlands in 1638.[220]

Summary on the Effects of the Printing Press

Francis Bacon[221] acknowledged the revolutionary effect of the printing press in 1620. He stated that this invention (along with gunpowder and the compass) "changed the appearance and state of the whole world."[222] He also understood that such inventions gave rise to ambition. The ambition bred by the printing press made Christian populations uncomfortable. The sinful greed and pride of printers and authors violated the Christian virtues of charity and humility. But printed books helped people. Therefore, Bacon argued that it was noble to put personal ambition aside and "to endeavor to renew and enlarge the power and empire of mankind … over the universe."[223] A modern historian puts it this way: "By

---

[219] https://www.britannica.com/biography/Galileo-Galilei, accessed 1/6/18.
[220] Eisenstein, 637.
[221] Sir Francis Bacon (1561-1626) was a famous English philosopher, lawyer, eloquent Parlimentarian, and senior advisor to King James I. He set out to develop a new plan for all of the sciences which was intended to make man once again the master over Nature since his fall from grace at the time of Adam. He was an early empiricist (e.g. discovery through observation) and believer in inductive reasoning. He was also much admired by Thomas Jefferson.
[222] From Francis Bacon's Novum Organum, 29, originally published in England in 1620, http://www.gutenberg.org/files/45988/45988-h/45988-h.htm, accessed 1/6/18.
[223] Ibid.

a marvelous alchemy, print transmuted self-seeking activities into a public good."[224]

The Protestants abandoned Catholicism, not their faith in an almighty Christian God. They disagreed with the Vatican claim that all scientific discoveries were heresy unless they were consistent with the Catholic interpretation of the Bible. Many believed that God empowered man with the ability to make discoveries about God's mysteries. As Bacon reasoned: "… let mankind regain their rights over nature, assigned to them by the gift of God, and obtain that power, whose exercise will be governed by right reason and true religion."[225] The printing press helped end the Vatican's stranglehold over scientific discovery.

Protestantism emphasized the importance of reading in Protestant nations. The spread of reading to a more general population created new markets for vernacular Bibles, devotional literature, primers, and self-help books.[226] The notoriety of banned books brought increased sales in Protestant markets.[227] Literacy empowered people – individually and collectively – to act against the tyranny of Rome, fueling political consciousness, activism, and nationalism.[228]

Galileo did end up influencing the Scientific Revolution positively. Because of the printing press, his condemned *Dialogue* could be republished in Protestant lands and made widely available. His *Discourses* were published and there as a foundation for Newton and his classical physics. And luckily, Newton would come along later, in the right country at the right time, after the Glorious Revolution had brought freedom of the press permanently to England.[229]

In order to trace the impact of the printing press all the way up to the time of the American Revolution, one must make mention of the Enlightenment movement of the 17th and 18th centuries. As successors to the minds of the Scientific Revolution, Enlightenment thinkers believed

---

224 Eisenstein, 558.
225 From Francis Bacon's Novum Organum, 29, originally published in England in 1620, http://www.gutenberg.org/files/45988/45988-h/45988-h.htm, accessed 1/6/18.
226 Eisenstein, 78.
227 Eisenstein, 676.
228 Eisenstein, 422.
229 Eisenstein, 677-678, 682.

that reason could and should be used to make sense of the universe and improve their lives. John Locke believed the human mind was a blank slate (*tabula rasa*) at birth, and that the individual character was shaped by individual experience. Original sin had nothing to do with it. Thomas Hobbes believed that humankind was driven by survival and pleasure seeking. He saw the state not as some representation of Heaven on Earth, but a pragmatic solution for preserving individual rights and personal interests. This idea of a social contract was interesting as philosophy, but left something to be desired in practice. John Locke, Jeremy Bentham, Montesquieu, Voltaire, Jean-Jacques Rousseau, Denis Diderot, Condorcet, Thomas Jefferson and Thomas Paine criticized the authoritarian nature of the governments they saw in Great Britain, France and the American colonies. Enlightenment spokesperson saw the need for the preservation of natural rights within a framework of democracy. And it's thinking like that brought great reform in England and revolution in America and France.[230]

The Telegraph

The story of the telegraph is a typical story of new inventions. There were fits and starts, advances and setbacks, and many cooks over many decades contributing to the broth. In fact, a similar evolution of the telegraph occurred in both the U.S. and United Kingdom around the same time.[231] But this book is not about the history of the telegraph, so we'll pick up our story in the United States in the mid-19th century.

"What Hath God Wrought?" were the first words signaled across the 40 mile Washington-to-Baltimore telegraph line by its inventor Samuel F. B. Morse on 24 May 1844. With this auspicious biblical quotation, the modern era of communication was born in America. While Morse had been previously dismissed as a charlatan, he had won over a majority of congressmen to secure government funding for this demonstration. Unfortunately, it was taken as just that, a demonstration which garnered no government interest. People just couldn't understand

---

[230] https://www.britannica.com/event/Enlightenment-European-history, retrieved 2 / 25/18.

[231] Tom Standage, The Victorian Internet: The Remarkable Story of the Telegraph and the Nineteenth Century's On-line Pioneers. New York: Walker and Company, 1998.

its potential usefulness, and Morse turned to private sources for funding. In 1845, the fledgling Magnetic Telegraph Company was created and began to build telegraph lines from New York to Philadelphia, Boston, Buffalo, and further west. The technology took off, and by 1850 there were over 12,000 miles of telegraph line in America operated by 20 different companies. The telegraph was adopted by the banking and general business community as a vital way of transmitting and receiving information across great distances faster than ever before. In 1861, the transcontinental telegraph was completed, bringing an end to the short-lived Pony Express.[232] Time compressed further for the business world in 1867 when the first stock "tickers" began telegraphically transmitting stock prices to investors (with a paper tape at the receive end they could read) from the exchange on Wall Street as they fluctuated.[233]

It would take several attempts between 1857 and 1865 before the first reliable trans-Atlantic cable linked the United States to Great Britain. The fourth attempt in 1858 provided a cable that worked for less than a month, leading to accusations, investigations, and disenchantment. By 1865, the science had become better understood and a reliable cable between the U.S. and Europe became available and began to turn a profit.[234]

Criminals exploited the technology, doing things like placing bets on winning horses after the race but before the bookies had received the information by conventional means.[235] The law and regulatory environment raced to prohibit criminal advantage provided by telegraphy, and the scofflaws found new loopholes to exploit. The game between the law and the citizen over telegraphic communications was afoot.

An important part of Morse's success involved the code he developed to transmit telegraphic information. Morse code was made up of short signals (corresponding to a "dot" of one unit) and long signals (corresponding to a "dash" of three units). He designed his code so that the more often a letter occurred in English, the less signal was sent. So, for

---

[232] Standage, 53, 58-59.
[233] Standage, 175.
[234] Standage, 80, 84-89.
[235] Standage, 107.

example, the most frequent letter E was represented by a single dot (one unit). This was an early example of efficient usage of the available communications channel, something that we'll see became increasingly important in the 20th century.

There were two reasons that other codes besides Morse came to be used for telegraphy. First, as in Morse code, codes were designed to use the available telegraph channel efficiently. Since telegraph companies charged more for longer messages (e.g. charging by the letter or word), it was cheaper for consumers to send shorter messages. So, banks and businesses came up with codes to describe transactions (like buy 100 bales of cotton or send $100) with fewer characters to reduce the per telegram cost. These banks and businesses were sending lots of telegrams each business day, so the savings for them would have been enormous!

The second reason people used codes was to communicate secretly. It was common in Victorian times for young lovers to communicate by placing secret codes in newspaper classified ads, and they adapted these methods to the telegraph. After all, telegrams were handled by many strangers (including the person that accepted it from you at the telegraph office, the transmitter, the receiver, and the person that delivered it) and therefore there was no guarantee that your message would remain private. Banks and the businesses also wanted their private business information to remain private, so it made good sense to use secret codes in their telegraph communications. And of course, the criminal element also desired to transmit information secretly to communicate with their accomplices and evade the law.[236]

Telegraph technology proliferated in Europe as well, leading to interconnections between companies in different countries.[237] England, not being on the continent, was prohibited interconnection until the challenge of telegraphy across the English Channel could be solved. It was not until 1852 that direct cabled telegraphic communications became possible between London and Paris. This lead to a proliferation of submarine cabling from England to Belgium, Ireland, Germany and Russia. Submarine cable was also installed from Italy to Sardinia and

[236] Standage, 109-110.

[237] Standage, 68-69.

Corsica.[238] Urban telegraph lines became congested, and hubs became bottlenecks. This was addressed in the mid-19th century by introduction of steam-powered pneumatic tube messaging networks in London, Paris, and other cities.[239]

In most countries in Europe, the telegraph was owned by the government. This had the monopolistic advantage of creating common practices across the telegraphic system, thus enabling standardization. For example, after the private telegraph companies were taken over by the British government in 1869, companies and individuals were able to register private telegraphic addresses. Companies and organizations paid for leased lines to get a direct feed from the telegraph office. Large companies with several offices began using internal private telegraphic lines to communicate directly among themselves.[240] Bilateral agreements between governments were signed to facilitate telegraphic services across frontiers. Eventually it became such a nightmare that an international meeting was called in Paris in 1865 which resulted in the founding of the International Telegraph Union (ITU, which today stands for the International Telecommunication Union) to regulate telegraphic practices across Europe. Whereas individual countries had tried to ban the use of codes except by the government, now they were allowed under ITU rules.[241]

In America, the telegraph companies were private, and there was never any prohibition against the use of codes, so they proliferated far earlier in the U.S. than in Europe.[242]

Finally, everywhere, it was considered acceptable for governments to intercept telegrams in the name of national security.[243] It would take some time before privacy law caught up with this technological capability in the U.S.

Near real time communications across vast distances all of a sudden became possible. The telegraph was a boon to the newspapers, now

---

238 Standage, 73.
239 Standage, Chapter 6.
240 Standage, 172-173.
241 Standage, 111.
242 Standage, 111.
243 Standage, 121.

placed in a position to be able to report the most recent developments from far flung corners of the world to inquiring minds. But governments realized that the rapid acquisition of timely information could provide advantages to their enemies, particularly during wartime. The first war in which the telegraph played a role was the Crimean War (1853-1856) in which Britain, France and the Ottoman Empire fought against Russia. The telegraph was extended to the front lines, enabling an unprecedented amount of what English and French field commanders saw as central government interference.[244]

In the United States, the telegraph was first used during the Civil War by both the Union and Confederate armies. Even today, the building across the street from the White House where President Lincoln used to go read and send telegrams is still there. In 1861, the first U.S. transcontinental telegraph initiated service.

The telegraph had a profound impact on economic activities worldwide. Businessmen became addicted to the telegraph, now able to buy and sell goods quickly across telegraphic channels. The rate of business transactions was complemented by the new railroad systems which could transport goods across vast distances.[245]

The telegraph had a profound impact on the human psyche, raising hope of greater peace for the future. Some argued that the hostilities engendered by diplomatic miscommunication in the past would no longer occur in the telegraphic era. Indeed, one government could quickly communicate with another government without the time delays and diplomatic chicanery of the past. Still others believed that peace would follow because the shared human experiences made possible by the telegraph would increase empathy across mankind.[246] They were wrong.

Before our story of the telegraph draws to a close, there are a few more technological advances worth mentioning. First, Charles Wheatstone in England patented the first automatic telegraph - using pre-punched tape to transmit messages ten times faster - in 1858 which was widely adopted by 1867. Second, in 1872, Joseph B. Stearns of Boston patented a design

---

[244] Standage, 154-157.
[245] Standage, 166.
[246] Standage, 161-163.

which could simultaneously send and receive messages on the same telegraphic wire (duplex). This effectively doubled the capacity of the telegraph system for minimal cost. Third, in 1874 Thomas Alva Edison patented a telegraphic terminal which could handle two send and two receive messages as the same time (quadraplex). And finally, in France in 1874 Jean-Maurice-Émile Baudot implemented a new automatic telegraph using his Baudot terminals which essentially combined twelve transmitters into one transmission and achieved a theoretical transmission rate of 360 words per minute. Today we call this multiplexing. He also designed own code – composed of five binary digits per character – to replace Morse's code, a code which is still used today.[247] All of these advances set the stage for the technology that would oust the telegraph.

The Telephone

Alexander Graham Bell was awarded U.S. Patent No. 174,465 for the telephone on March 3, 1876, having filed his patent hours before his competitor Elisha Gray. Bell's patent was actually entitled "Improvements in Telegraphy" and described the electrical transmission of "vocal and other sounds," that is, not necessarily speech.[248] Six months later, Bell demonstrated the first successful one-way telephone call across several miles using borrowed telegraph wires.[249] In January 1877, Bell was granted U.S. Patent No. 186,767 which protected the combined transmitter-receiver device and a number of other features. The telephone was first used for news reporting the next month, and by May the first Bell telephones had been rented to a business.[250]

Popular culture had begun to talk about speech being transmitted at a distance in the 1850's, once the English Channel had been bridged by telegraph cables.[251] It's not that it was achievable yet, but it was within the realm of imagination. Some people dismissed the new telephone

[247] Standage, 190-194.

[248] John Brooks, Telephone: The First Hundred Years. New York: Harper & Row, 1976, p. 47. In fact, the word "telephone" comes from the Greek "tele -"meaning at a distance while "phon" means "sound."

[249] Brooks, 52.

[250] Brooks 53.

[251] Brooks, 36.

technology as trickery or witchcraft, while others saw it as a golden business opportunity with which to get involved.

The fledgling Bell Company spent considerable time and money defending its patent rights over their 17-year lifetimes. For example, after Western Union (now in league with Elisha Gray) created the American Speaking Telephone Company in 1877,[252] the Bell Company filed a patent infringement suit against them in 1878.[253] IN 1879, the companies came to a settlement whereby Western Union gave up all patents claims and telephone facilities in exchange for 20 percent of Bell's telephone rental revenue over the life of the Bell patents.[254] Bell was involved in over 600 patent infringement lawsuits over the next ten years, and won every one of them.[255]

Bell telephone service continued to grow, improve, and expand across the United States in spite of financial depressions in 1884, 1890, and 1893.[256] Bell accomplished this not only by defending its original patents, but also by buying up new patents and working to monopolize the telephone market. This enabled the company to keep charging customers the same or higher prices even during times of economic downturn. Bell acquired controlling interest in Western Electric from Western Union (!) in 1881, and Western Electric became the sole Bell equipment supplier in 1882.[257] Bell also encouraged the establishment of local telephone companies, licensing its product to the company in exchange for a cut of the profits. In this way, telephone service was made available in local markets, providing a public service in even rural areas while still being profitable to the Bell company.[258]

The first telephone services relied on a single wire between communicants, with a connection to ground being used to complete the circuit. This was subject to interference from telegraph traffic, as well as

---

[252] Brooks, 62.
[253] Brooks, 64.
[254] Brooks, 71.
[255] Brooks, 77.
[256] Brooks, 81.
[257] Brooks, 83-84.
[258] Brooks, 84.

electric lights and electric trolleys when they came into service.[259] Early long-distance service was hindered by such static, until the Bell innovation of using an entirely metal circuit (versus using the ground to complete the one wire circuit) was used to reduce the interference. With this problem solved, the next problem was that sound gradually grew weaker over the miles and completely faded out if the distance was great enough. This is called attenuation. The use of copper (versus galvanized iron) wire reduced this attenuation effect sufficiently to make long-distance service possible across the nearly 300 miles from New York to Boston in 1884.[260] The American Telephone and Telegraph Company (AT&T) came into being in 1885, given responsibility for creating and operating the longdistance network, and later for negotiating connection agreements with local telephone companies.[261]

The great blizzard of March 12-13, 1888 left local and long-distance telephone wires dangling and downed from New York to Boston. This incentivized Bell to move wires underground, and technological advances in dry core cabling made underground wires more effective over longer distances.[262] Throughout the 1890's, the Bell system improved it physical infrastructure, replacing single wire with two wire service which significantly reduced static and attenuation. It laid more long-distance lines, and the first central battery switchboard made the individual battery at each phone obsolete. Bell was stimulated to expand and compete, seeing a rise from 240,000 phone customers in 1892 to over 800,000 in 1899. What had been incorporated as American Bell in Massachusetts was reconstituted within AT&T in New York.[263]

As its initial patents expired, the Bell company it had to find a new way to better compete against independents. In some cases, Bell met this competition by cutting its own rates. Less respectable measures included setting up bogus companies to protect Bell interests in local markets, and using influence to force local banks not to underwrite independents.

---

259 Brooks, 85.
260 Brooks, 87-88.
261 Brooks, 90.
262 Brooks, 99.
263 Brooks, 106-107.

Another method involved secretly buying up local companies. AT&T's main clout still resided in its persistent refusal to allow independents to interconnect with the Bell network. Since AT&T owned all the longdistance service, anyone wanting long distance service was coerced into doing business with Bell.[264]

As for its human effects, the telephone shrank time and space. In financial markets, Wall Street became truly national. Stocks and bonds could be traded in near real time from coast to coast. This synergy applied to the bankers as well. For example, J.P. Morgan was able to head off the financial crisis of 1907 by supplying $25 million in credit to banks just in time.[265] In the rural environment, isolation was replaced with connectedness to neighbors and the outside world. The resulting rural morale improvement led to increased farming productivity. And eavesdropping on party lines would become a form of entertainment.[266]

In 1907, Theodore N. Vail became the new president of the struggling AT&T. Bell had 3,132,000 telephones in service while the independents had 2,987,000. Long distance service still suffered from delays and noise on the lines.[267] Whereas AT&T had cultivated an atmosphere of secrecy around itself in the past, Vail began to provide greater transparency to both stockholders and customers. Vail also held the unpopular belief that maximizing profit was not the primary driver of the company. True, profit was necessary in order to maintain and modernize the company and its infrastructure, but it was not the only driver. In order to provide the best service to the most people at the cheapest price, Vail believed that monopoly was necessary. Nor did he object to the idea of public regulation of telephone rates as a way to ameliorate pricing to the consumer in the absence of competition. Vail continued to resist interconnection with independent telephone companies.[268]

---

[264] Brooks, 112-114.

[265] Brooks, 115.

[266] Brooks, 116.

[267] Brooks, 127.

[268] Brooks, 131-132.

Vail went on to unify the telephone and telegraph systems. In 1909, AT&T purchased a controlling interest (30 percent) in Western Union. Vail became the president of Western Union and the companies began to be intermingled. The result of the converged technologies was that customers were extended credit across both companies. Telegrams could be sent by telephone, and by default, any telegram placed by telephone went to the Western Union and not a competitor. Telegraph and telephone lines provided some redundancy, and a consolidation of staff and physical facilities brought savings.[269]

Telephone service had grown up as utility instance of the big business monopolies (e.g. steel, oil, etc.) which began to be reined in after the Sherman Antitrust Act became law in 1890. U.S. appetite for trustbusting brought more hostility towards AT&T's monopoly status. By 1912, the Department of Justice began looking into an antitrust complaint filed against AT&T, and in 1913, the Interstate Commerce Commission (ICC), the regulator responsible for the telephone business since 1910, began an investigation. This would become a turning point for AT&T.[270]

Vail compromised. In what came to be known as the Kingsbury Commitment of 1913, AT&T made a number of concessions. First, it disposed of its Western Union stock so that Western Union once again became an independent company. Second, it stopped buying up independent telephone companies except with prior approval from the ICC. Third, it agreed to allow independent phone companies to provide long distance service by connecting to the Bell system.[271] The Kingsbury Commitment would be formally accepted by Congress in the Graham Act of 1921.[272]

Meanwhile, technology continued to march forward. The loading coil, which took advantage of induced current (inductance) to reduce attenuation, was first used in 1906 for long distance service between New York and Philadelphia. This technology made longer distance service possible at lower costs since thinner wires could be used with the loading

---

[269] Brooks, 134.
[270] Brooks, 135.
[271] Brooks, 136.
[272] Brooks, 160.

coil. The 1912 invention of a workable repeater, a device to amplify signals over long distances would make transcontinental telephone service possible. This technology made a considerable splash when transcontinental telephone service debuted between New York and San Francisco at the Panama-Pacific Exposition in 1915. That same year, Bell engineers demonstrated long distance (250 miles) voice transmission over a wireless channel, setting the stage for the wireless communications revolution.[273]

The telephone had become a national necessity, and whispers of government ownership of the telephone company began. After the British government had taken over the telephone system in 1912, the U.S. was the only major nation with non-federal telephone service. And people were focused on what was going on in Europe as the world ramped up towards World War I. Demand on the telephone industry soared after the U.S. enter the war. President Wilson finally took control of the telephone and telegraph companies in mid-1918, shortly before the end of the war.[274] After one year, Congress voted to return telephone (and telegraph) service to private hands. The government had been unable to provide telephone service without raising rates significantly. Bell received back its assets, showing an operations deficit of over $13M for the year. The idea of government ownership of the telephone system had been put to rest in the United States.[275]

AT&T played a tremendous role during World War I. A total of 15,000 Bell employees ultimately staffed fourteen Army Signal Corps battalions for the American Expeditionary Force. They established a new telephone network in France using Bell/Western Electric equipment. Bell engineers created the first two-way air-to-ground radio communications between pilots and the ground during 1917. They installed a high-powered radio transmitter in France to communicate with the United States since trans-Atlantic telegraph cables were rendered useless by German submarine damage.[276]

---

[273] Brooks, 138-140.

[274] Brooks, 148, 150-151, 156.

[275] Brooks, 158-159.

[276] Brooks, 157.

While work in trans-Atlantic radio telephony continued after the war, a new application appeared: broadcast radio. The first radio stations appeared in 1920, and by 1922 AT&T got into the act. Radio commercials provides a new source of revenue when interspersed with news and other information, music and other entertainment. AT&T opened additional stations, and worked assiduously to ensure competing radio stations did not have access to its telephone lines (e.g. which were necessary to link radio stations). Once again, competitors brought suits against AT&T both for patent infringement and for access to AT&T telephone lines.[277] This would be resolved in 1926 when A&T, under new leadership, got out of the radio broadcast business and agreed to provide telephone line access to broadcasting companies.[278]

In 1927, AT&T's president Walter S. Gifford stated that the telephone industry was responsible for providing "the best possible telephone service at the lowest cost consistent with financial safety." In the spirit of Theodore Vail, AT&T said it put public service was first and profits second.[279]

Bell did well during the 1920's and was able to reduce rates. Advanced in mechanical switching were made, and short-distance cable telephony was demonstrated. Bell Labs was finally officially created on 1925. By 1927, trans-Atlantic telephone service was possible between New York and London by radio. And by 1929, Bell Labs demonstrated the first color television to the public. The Depression and the Second World War would delay its commercialization.[280] The development of coaxial cable – developed at Bell Labs and first installed in New York City in 1936 – would introduce another necessary innovation for the future of television (and telephone) with its high capacity and low attenuation. In 1937, Dr. Clinton J. Davisson would be the first individual at the labs to win a Nobel Prize for his research into the wavelike behavior of the electron.[281]

---

[277] Brooks, 161-165.
[278] Brooks, 171.
[279] Brooks, 172-173.
[280] Brooks, 168, 179-180, 185.
[281] Brooks, 202-203.

AT&T had a record 15,193,000 telephone subscribers in 1930. The effect of the Depression on AT&T was felt first at its equipment manufacturer General Electric, geared to always be producing more and more devices for a growing telephone market. Declining telephone demand, and declining prices overall would lead state legislators to insist on lowest telephone service prices. Reduced revenues meant that profits would not cover the traditional dividend of $9 per share. The AT&T Board of Directors decided in favor of the dividend and laid off 20 percent of its workforce. Long distance calls had decreased from fifty million in 1930 to thirty million in 1933. This engendered loyalty among stockholders, and dissatisfaction among workers.[282]

In 1935, the Wagner Act was passed, assuring all employees of freedom to "unions of their own choosing." This would lead to the end of local company unions and the creation of a new national union for telephone workers. AT&T went along with it. The new union, initially known as the National Federation of Telephone Workers, would change its name to the Communications Workers of America after World War II and become a powerful collective bargaining force.[283]

In 1934, the Federal Communications Act marked the beginning of serious telephone regulation. The Act created the Federal Communications Commission (FCC) whose primary interest was regulating the telephone industry. The FCC initiated a complete and thorough investigation into all telephone companies which would last until 1938. AT&T complied. The final report, far less critical of AT&T than the original version, was issued shortly World War II began. While its issuance went unheralded, it did have the effect of drawing regulatory lines in the sand for the future.[284]

A hurricane on September 21, 1938 left much of the Northeastern United States without telephone service. The Bell system responded with the military discipline of the American Expeditionary Force, and all

[282] Brooks, 187-191.
[283] Brooks, 194-195.
[284] Brooks, 198-199.

outages fully resolved by the end of November. Bell had risen as a hero in public opinion.[285]

Bell Labs and Western Electric would devote the vast majority of their resources to the war effort during U.S. involvement in World War II. "Modern" telephone services now existed in foreign lands, so Bell would not be called upon to install such systems overseas this time. Nor with the government even consider taking over the telephone system this time. [286]

Bell Labs and Western Electric were now shrouded in secrecy, designing and manufacturing military equipment, most notably radar and the M-9 gun director. Radar would pay Bell handsome dividends later on since the related research into microwaves would pave the way for microwave radio relays after the war. The M-9 gun director was the predecessor of missile and antiaircraft guidance systems.[287]

Bell Labs research that had been started before the war resumed and matured after the war. The first mobile telephone service went into commercial world in 1946, linking moving vehicles to the telephone network by radio. The first New York – Washington TV transmission via coaxial cable also occurred that year. But none was so earth-shattering as the 1947 invention of the transistor, a semi-conductor amplifier that could be used for electronic switching at telephone exchanges. Transistors would replace vacuum tubes, which required too much power and generated too much heat to be used as amplifiers in such switches. The development of transistors made integrated circuits possible, leading to such innovations as modern computers, communication satellites, and cellular telephones. Three Bells Labs researchers shared the Nobel Prize for developing the transistor in 1956. That same year, Bell Labs research into undersea repeaters finally made trans-Atlantic telephony possible via undersea cable. [288]

In 1949, the Justice Department filed suit against AT&T and Western Electric arguing violation of the Sherman Antitrust Act in telephone rates and equipment pricing. This suit would drag on to 1956,

---

[285] Brooks, 199-200.
[286] Brooks, 208-210.
[287] Brooks, 211.
[288] Brooks, 203, 223-224, 247.

through a change of government administration when a consent order was reached. The consent order specified four things: that AT&T and Western Electric would not be separated, that Western Electric would not manufacture anything except equipment of the type bought by the Bell System and the Department of Defense, that Bell would only engage in common carrier communications, and that Bell would grant non-exclusive licenses and technical details to anyone on fair terms.[289]

Along the way to this agreement, AT&T had agreed to take over management of Sandia National Labs, which was now responsible for the manufacture of atomic weapons. In 1949, the Sandia Corporation was created as a subsidiary of Western Electric. This was only the beginning of AT&T and Western Electric's support to the defense of the United States in the post-war period. Both became key players in the development of guided anti-aircraft missions and the Early-Warning air-defense radar. In 1962, the Bell system surged over eight days to provide new longdistance services to support the U.S. military during the Cuban Missile Crisis. It supported much of the communications for the U.S. space exploration program. And also in 1962, Bell was able to get its first experimental communications satellite Telstar into orbit.[290] Shortly thereafter, the Communications Satellite Act was passed by Congress and the corporation Comsat was created. Initially a part-owner, AT&T was forced by the FCC to divest itself of Comsat in 1973. By that time, Comsat was carrying one-half of all international calls on its circuits and AT&T was its best customer.[291]

With regards to privacy, there was a big change during the 1950s. In 1950, three out of four residential telephones shared a party line. Anyone on the party line could listen in on anyone else making a call on the party line. By 1960, that ratio had been reduced to 27%, made possible by the line concentrator innovation. The line concentrator provided privacy at the cost of others not being able to get a dial tone.[292] Increased privacy would also give telephone abusers and stalkers greater opportunity to harass individuals with less fear of apprehension and prosecution. In

---

289 Brooks, 233, 235, 2x37, 255.

290 Brooks, 252-253, 274, 276.

291 Brooks, 276-277.

292 Brooks, 267.

1966 alone, 375,000 complaints of abusive or obscene phone calls were reported to the Bell System.[293]

Before 1968, it had been illegal to attach non-Bell equipment to Bell telephone lines. Which was not to say that there wasn't a thriving bootleg business in telephone equipment during the 1950s, and 1960s. In 1968, the FCC decided that consumer equipment could be attached to the Bell network provided that Bell have the opportunity to install protective equipment between the equipment and the line. In 1970, the FCC decided to allow independent companies to set up intercity microwave relays to lease telephone service to businesses. All of a sudden, AT&T found it was competing in the market for equipment and leased line services to businesses.

As many probably remember, 1974 marked the huge antitrust suit brought by the U.S. Government against AT&T, Western Union, Bell Labs, and all the Bell operating companies. The most specific charge was against AT&T for its attempts to prevent interconnection of competing telephone equipment and common-carrier equipment.[294] In 1982, AT&T agreed to divest itself of its local operating companies (where the government felt monopoly was still appropriate) and retain long distance, research and development and manufacturing concerns (which the government felt should be open to competition). In exchange, the government lifted the constraints imposed on AT&T by the 1956 decree. Divestiture took place on 1 January 1984.[295]

Technological innovation continued to march on. In the mid-1970s, Bell installed its first digital electronic switch in Chicago which was able (initially) to handle 350,000 calls per hour. In 1977, AT&T installed the first fiber optic cable for commercial communications in Chicago. By 1988, AT&T had laid the first fiber optic submarine cable across the Atlantic, able to handle ten times more calls than the last copper cable. In 1994, AT&T completed its acquisition of McCaw Cellular Communications Incorporated, the largest wireless service provider in the U.S., and renamed it AT&T Wireless. And in 1996, the

---

[293] Brooks, 286-287.

[294] Brooks, 312, 215.

[295] https://www.corp.att.com/history/history3.html, retrieved 25 February 2018.

Telecommunications Act became law, promoting competition between local operating companies, long distance companies, and cable companies.[296]

The Digital Age

It would be impossible to enumerate all the technology firsts that brought us to our current digital age. All the technology we have already talked about did not singlehandedly get us to the internet, the personal computer, or the smart cell phone of the digital age. The internet began life as the ARPANET, a project funded by the U.S. Department of Defense to connect 16 universities and research centers across the United States. It was conceived after the SAGE (Semi-Automatic Ground Environment) system of the 1960s, demonstrated it could track enemy aircraft and coordinate military response. Remember, it was the Cold War and we feared the Soviets would use their aircraft to launch a nuclear attack against the United States. AT&T had a big role in the SAGE system since it relied on the telecommunications backbone for intercommunication. ARPANET introduced packet switching, the switching of packets of data across complex networks, on which the internet today relies. TCP/IP (transmission control protocol/internet protocol) was first invented for ARPANET to allow one network to pass off packets to another network. It too is foundational to today's internet.[297] Internetworking began to be commercialized in the 1990s, leading to the internet we know today.[298]

The personal computer emerged in the 1970s, once large-scale integration made it possible to put a powerful multiprocessor on one semiconductor chip at a price-point individual users could afford.[299] It built on many of the successes of Bell Labs during and after World War II. The first computers were primitive and appealed only to techno-geeks, who were also tantalized at the prospect of being able to get on the ARPANET. Over time, the human-machine interfaces improved (e.g. MS Windows, browser windows), making interactions with the personal

---

[296] https://www.corp.att.com/history/milestones.html, retrieved 25 February 2018.
[297] https://www.britannica.com/topic/ARPANET, retrieved 25 February 2018.
[298] https://www.britannica.com/technology/Internet, retrieved 25 February 2018.
[299] https://www.britannica.com/technology/personal-computer, retrieved 25 Febru ary 2018.

computer and the internet more approachable to the layperson. Personal computers continued to pack more computing power into smaller devices such that the personal computer became portable.[300]

The first cellular telephone system used in the United States was AMPS (Advanced Mobile Phone System). This first generation (IG) cell phone used analog technology. It was introduced in 1983 in Chicago by AT&T and Motorola, and was a tremendous success. After one year, it had it 200,000 subscribers within the year. After five years, it had 2M users and the system was running out of capacity to support this growth rate. During the late 1980s, and early 1990s, the first digital cellular telephones became available. Known as 2G, they used the available bandwidth more efficiently and were able to support far more users. Enhancements that come after that started to make additional services and internet access available in your pocket.[301]

Summary

In this chapter, we've talked about technologies from 1440 up to the turn of the 21st century, a span of 450 years. Each had huge effects on communications and the evolution of privacy in Western civilization. Once the telegraph came along, however, the pace of innovation in communications technology accelerated at an exponential rate, bringing us up to our current digital age.

Here are a couple generic observations:

1. It takes time for a culture and society to accept and digest the innovations made possible by technology. Early adopters will embrace new technology with reckless abandon, while others will reject it with Luddite conviction.
2. It is easier to assess the impact of new technology at a distance. We're already talked about the huge effects the printing press had on the Western world. Grand cultural changes are possible, but may take generations.

---

[300] https://www.britannica.com/technology/personal-computer, retrieved 25 February 2018.

[301] https://www.britannica.com/technology/mobile-telephone, retrieved 25 February 2018.

3. Entities may respond negatively when they see new technology threaten their interests. The Catholic Church responded negatively to printing press technology by trying to control what printers produced. The tighter they clung to this model, the more quickly printers slipped through their fingers and relocated to Protestant lands. Printed books replaced hand copied ones. Western Union battled Bell Telephone/AT&T for market dominance for years, but ultimately the telephone supplanted the telegraph.
4. Entities may respond positively if they see new technology present new opportunities. The transistor, radio transmission, and fiber optic cable created new markets for new companies to provide cellular telephony, video on demand, high-speed internet, etc. It is far harder for existing entities (old dogs) to embrace innovative technology and migrate into new markets (new tricks).
5. Government response to new technology is measured. As a republic, the United States Government is responsible for representing its citizenry and acting in the public interest. The overall opinion of the citizenry must be taken into account by Congress members because they want to be reelected. But the opinion of constituents towards new technology takes time to mature. Complaints from other businesses or consumers raise awareness among legislators and regulators. Judicial decisions may generate case law precedents. If complaints or decisions always seem to go in one direction, perhaps there really is a legal or constitutional issue here worth taking on.

We now understand how technology can be an agent of change, challenging existing norms and beliefs. We are now ready to dive into how U.S. law evolved to respond to the challenges technology posed to common conceptions of privacy.

Chapter 5
How the Printing Press Shaped Free Speech Law in Great Britain

The use of the [common] law consistent principally in these three things:

i. To secure men's persons from death and violence.
ii. The dispose the property of their goods and lands.
iii. For preservation of their good names from shame and infamy.

Sir Francis Bacon, *The Use of Law* (1635)[302]

Francis Bacon's concise summary of the uses of the law make no reference to privacy. Privacy was not a subject of discussion in England before the mid-17th century, but its seeds had been spreading for centuries before. And sometime after 1640 and before the American Revolution, even the English realized that privacy was conspicuously absent from their lives.

In this chapter, we will see thoughts about privacy emerge. The printing press turbocharged language regulation in English law, building on Roman law, and sprinkled with Christian values along the way. This is the heritage that the American colonists took to the New World and inculcated into their United States.

The Mischief Wrought by the Printing Press in English Law

The printing press gave broad availability to the common man to books in the vernacular. This enabled broad dissemination of what the Vatican and European rulers saw as "dangerous ideas" like heresy and treason which could undermine their authority. One source reports that

---

302 https://archive.org/stream/elementsofcommon00baco#page/n123/mode/2up/search/prefervation, accessed 3/16/18.

there were ten lists of banned books – some royal, some ecclesiastical - in England between 1526 and 1555 before the first Vatican Index appeared in 1559. All based their censorship on heresy law.[303]

English censorship based on heresy declined after England restricted its definition to the denial of Christian fundamentals in 1558.[304] Starting in 1559, the dangerous ideas promoted in written (oral comes along for the ride) works were prosecuted in England as libel (slander), seditious libel, and treason. Such English language regulation was derived from the Roman law concerning injury (*iniuria*), with subsequent Christian influences along the way.

a. Language Regulation under Roman Law

The regulation of language under Roman law – in the *Corpus iuris civilis* - treated all written and spoken transgressions as an attack on another person, to include injury against their dignity or good name. The attack has to be with malicious intent in order for it to truly apply as an injury. This got carried over into English law by way of canon law. The injury done was causing someone infamy (*infamia*) in two senses. Someone was not only injured in the sense he became ashamed, but also in the sense that his legal rights and protections might be abridged (e.g. he might lose his freedom, or become ineligible to serve on a jury, etc.).[305]

Citing François Baudoin's analysis, Shuger notes that Roman law had two concepts involving transgressive language intended to cause injury. The first, verse libel (*malum carmen*), involved the composition or chanting of injurious verses about someone[306]. This law was also used to rein in satirical literature and may have even been applied to magical incantations. Cicero specifically cited state censorship as appropriate when satirical poets – imagining themselves as unofficial legislators - poked fun at magistrates, undermining the authority of the judicial system

---

[303] Debora Shuger, Censorship and Cultural Sensibility: The Regulation of Language in Tudor-Stuart England. Philadelphia: University of Pennsylvania Press, 2006, 56.
[304] Shuger, 65.
[305] Shuger, 78-79.
[306] Francois Baudouin, Ad Legis de Famosis Libellis et de Calumniatoribus, Commentarius. PARISIIS: Apud Andream Wechelum, 1562. Accessed 18 March at https://ia800504.us.archive.org/6/items/bub_gb_1KfLKIXMhoEC/bub_gb_1KfLKIXMhoEC.pdf

and denying the magistrate the right to defend himself in court.[307] While later classified as a civil injury, in earlier times Cicero observed that the danger posed by verse libel extended beyond the individual to the entire community and could therefore be considered sedition.[308] So much for poetic license!

A second Roman law involving transgressive language concerned calumny (*calumnia*), malicious false accusation of a crime. Someone could be accused of a crime in two ways, by signed accusation delivered directly to the appropriate government official (*libellus*), or by an anonymous accusation made publicly available (*famosus libellus*). Over time, Roman law came to view *malum carmen* and *calumnia* as two types of *libelli famosi*, the first a civil injury against someone's good name and reputation, the second a criminal accusation which could put the accused in danger of the law.[309]

Roman law prohibited the use any *famosus libellus* as evidence to investigate or prosecute an alleged crime. This prohibition extended to even to the Emperor, eliminating the tempting prospect of getting rid of one's enemies by falsely accusing them of sedition, treason, and the like. As Shuger tells us, "The Roman laws regulating language show no concern for the speaker or writer, for their freedom of expression, because the whole point of these laws was to protect the victim, the person injured by another's words."[310]

Political libel, that is, libel against public figures, was a specific form of *iniuria* that was covered under Roman law. By the medieval era, English law distinguished between libel against peers (*scandulum magnatum*, or great offenses) as opposed to (other) people holding public office. In either case, political libel was uniquely distinguished by its potential to undermine the authority of the King and disturb his peace.[311]

---

[307] Shuger, 85-86.
[308] Shuger, 82-83.
[309] Shuger, 83.
[310] Shuger, 95.
[311] Shuger, 87-88.

b. Language Regulation under English Law

Heresy and treason are the only two ideological (thought) crimes in the Western tradition. As we saw in the previous chapter, scientists pointing out inconsistencies between the observed order of the universe and Christian beliefs were branded as heretics by the Catholic Church.

England too had had heresy laws, including the harsh 1401 statute which specified that anyone who "openly or secretly shall preach, hold, teach, or impart anything, or *compose or write any book*, contrary to the catholic faith or the decisions of Holy Church" and convicted of this heretical crime should be burned at the stake.[312]

Henry VIII's 1530 Proclamation against Erroneous Books specified that "blasphemous and pestiferous English books" from other regions were intended to undermine Christianity, to incite sedition and disobedience, to cause people to turn away from law and customs to the detriment of the kingdom. Not only were these books banned, he required all books to be examined, approved, and printed by the diocese.[313] Henry established a licensing procedure for books by proclamation in 1538.[314] Elizabeth repealed the heresy laws in 1559 with her Act of Supremacy.[315] This act also narrowed the definition of heresy to the refutation of broad Christian fundamentals, setting the stage for future censorship laws to focus on libel instead of heresy.[316]

The history of English libel law could be traced back to chapter 34 (*de scandalis magnatum*) of the Westminster Act of 1275,[317] which had been refreshed several times since then.

Both Mary and Elizabeth followed Henry's lead. Mary issued a Charter to Stationers in 1557,[318] which Elizabeth affirmed two years later.

---

312 Stephenson and Marcham, 274.
313 Stephenson and Marcham, 388.
314 http://www.british-history.ac.uk/letters-papers-hen8/vol13/no2/pp353-369, acess ed 14 March 2018.
315 http://members.shaw.ca/reformation/1554heresy.htm, retrieved 13 March, 2018.
316 Shuger, 63.
317 http://self.gutenberg.org/articles/eng/Statute_of_Westminster_1275?View=embed ded, accessed 14 March 2018.
318 http://www.copyrighthistory.org/cam/pdf/uk_1557_1.pdf, accessed 14 March 2018.

With this act, Elizabeth also licensed the printing of books which had been approved only by the Queen, members of her Privy Council, university chancellors, or by ecclesiastical authorities. It prohibited the printing of books that were "heretical, seditious, or unseemly for Christian ears."[319] Under Elizabeth's rule, the Court of the Star Chamber (more about this shortly) issued a Decree Concerning Books in 1566 which reiterated the ban on importation, printing and selling of prohibited books; described the punishments associated with the commitment of such crimes; and empowered the wardens of the Company of Stationers of the City of London (chartered by the crown) to search printers' and booksellers' facilities and shipments, and seize offending books. The Chamber went further in 1585 with a Decree Concerning Printers, requiring certification of printing presses, review and approval for release of all books, and the right of the wardens to inspect printing premises and seize printing presses which had been used to break the law.[320] Such a licensing system would stay in place until 1641.

Elizabeth did focus considerable effort on the other thought crime: treason. The 1558 Act of Supremacy specifically stated that any subject(s) "shall by writing, printing, teaching, preaching, express words, deed, or act, advisedly, maliciously, and directly affirm, hold, stand with, set forth, maintain, defend the authority, pre-eminence, power, or jurisdiction, spiritual or ecclesiastical, of any foreign prince, prelate, person, statue, or potentate" – if lawfully convicted – will be punished appropriately, "culminating in punishment for high treason on the third offence."[321] The 1571 Treasons Act specifically prohibited any treasonous activities, including those in "printing, writing, ciphering, speech, words, or sayings," which imagine or devise the death of the Queen, allege that she should not be Queen, accuse her of being a "heretic, schismatic, tyrant, infidel, or an usurper," or in any other way question or undermine her authority and legitimacy.[322]

---

[319] http://www.copyrighthistory.org/cam/tools/request/showRecord?id=commentary_uk_1559, accessed 13 March 2018.
[320] Stephenson, 388-390.
[321] Stephenson and Marcham, 346.
[322] Stephenson and Marcham, 351-351.

A great deal of the literature banned in England under Elizabeth was written by English Catholics exiled to the continent.[323] Mounting political tension between Anglican England and Catholic Spain spurred English regulation of seditious, libelous, and treasonous writings about the English monarchy. The English Sedition Acts of 1580-81 specifically prohibited "seditious words and rumors uttered against the Queen's most excellent Majesty."[324] The types of seditious literature Elizabeth intended to ban included things like Cardinal Allen's 1588 *Admonition to the Nobility and People of England*, which urged nobility to rise up against the queen, outlined her horrible crimes, questioned her legitimacy, and faulted her unchasteness.[325] Had the Spanish Armada of 1588 been successful, it was intended that Allen's writing would be printed in England.[326]

But early English language regulation was not exercised by statutes and proclamations alone.[327] Ecclesiastical law, civil law, and criminal law could also exercise language regulation.[328] The precedent for ecclesiastical law had been the Constitution of the Council of Oxford in 1222 which authorized excommunication of anyone who defamed with malicious criminal accusations whether the accusation was true or false. In 1599, the Bishops' Ban signed by the Archbishop of Canterbury (John Whitgift) and the Bishop of London (Richard Bancroft) – the licensers of books – prohibited satires and epigrams, called for the destruction of some existing satirical books, and extended governmental control over plays and histories. Shuger describes the Bishops' Ban as "the single most sweeping act of censorship during the entire period from 1558 to 1641."[329] In 1606, the non-ecclesiastical Act to Restrain the Abuses of Players was passed "for the preventing and avoiding of the great Abuse of the Holy Name of

---

[323] Shuger, 15.
[324] http://www.nationalarchives.gov.uk/pathways/citizenship/citizen_subject/transcripts/rumours.htm, accessed 13 March 2018.
[325] https://quod.lib.umich.edu/e/eebo/A16774.0001.001/1:2?rgn=div1;view=fulltext, accessed 14 March 2018.
[326] http://www.newadvent.org/cathen/01727c.htm, accessed 14 March 1588.
[327] Shuger, 75.
[328] Shuger, 69.
[329] Shuger, 76.

God in Stage Plays, Interludes, May Games, Shows and such like."[330] The banning of satire and profanity in dramatic productions caused William Shakespeare and his contemporaries no end of troubles.

Depending on the nature of the offense, defamation cases were tried in the ecclesiastical, civil or criminal courts. The ecclesiastical courts could resolve a case by having the defamer ask for forgiveness, take back his words to restore the slighted person's reputation, and affirm the victim's innocence to the community. It didn't matter whether the accusation was true or false.[331] Alternatively, the common law courts could award damages, and in some cases the defamer could plead truth as a defense.[332]

We now come to criminal (scandalous) defamation cases, which were heard in the Court of the Star Chamber before 1641; after the Restoration, the term was changed to seditious libel and it was tried in common law courts as a misdemeanor. The Star Chamber was a court composed of the king's council. It was best known for dealing with political crimes like sedition. It was also used to prosecute crimes for which the common law had not yet devised any punishment, like libel. The court originated from ancient tradition and appears to have come into being in the mid-15th century (around the time of the invention of the printing press). While considered legitimate and lawful earlier on, by the time it was abolished in 1641 it was tyrannical and meted out cruel punishments.[333] Populated by justices and Privy Council members, it derived its power from royal prerogative outside the common law. The Star Chamber did not follow the due process procedures of the common law court, did not have jury trials, and was not authorized to pass the death sentence. During the 16th century, it expanded its scope to include all sorts of breaches to the peace to include slander.[334] It could award damages and force the maligner to confess, that is, issue a retraction and ask for

---

[330] https://archive.org/stream/statutesatlarge02raitgoog#page/n727/mode/2up/search/to+restrain+abuses, accessed 13 March 2018.

[331] Shuger, 110.

[332] Shuger, 71.

[333] Maitland, 261-263.

[334] https://www.britannica.com/topic/Court-of-Star-Chamber, accessed 15 March 2018.

forgiveness. We're focusing on the Star Chamber because, as Shuger tells us, it "was where the political implications of defamation law emerged most clearly, and it was here that the principles governing the regulation of language were hammered out and articulated."[335]

The 1605 case of Lewis Pickering was, according the jurist Edward Coke, the Star Chamber case which served as the precedent for all future criminal libel cases. Mr. Pickering was accused of pinning a defamatory note to the hearse of Archbishop Whitgift (yes, the same Whitgift that authored the Bishops' Ban, how about that).[336] [337] Coke's words outline the following basic principles:

1. All libel deserves severe punishment. If it is about a private person, it will incite the person, his family and society to revenge, causing disturbances to the peace. If it is about a Magistrate or another public person, it is a greater crime because it not only causes disturbances to the peace, but sullies the reputation of the government.
2. It doesn't matter whether the person libeled is dead or alive, the effect is the same.
3. Libelers can be punished in the common law court or the Star Chamber.
4. It is irrelevant whether the libel is true or not.[338]

At the very end of his piece on Pickering, Coke added: "… libeling and calumniation is an offence against the law of God." In the next section, we are going to talk about why he would say this.

c. The Christian Context of English Law

Christian values were still important, even in post-Reformation England. Ideas like loving one's neighbor, charity and forgiveness were still woven into the fabric of everyday life. These values came from the Bible.

---

[335] Shuger, 71-72.
[336] Shuger, 72.
[337] The text of Pickering's poem appears here: http://www.earlystuartlibels.net/htdocs/early_jacobean_section/B11.html, accessed 14 March 2018.
[338] http://lawlibrary.wm.edu/wythepedia/library/ReportsOfSirEdwardCoke1738Pt5.pdf, accessed 14 March 2018.

When we compare these Biblical values to some of the terms in legal use at the time, things start to make sense. The ideological (thought) crime of heresy violated the first of the Ten Commandments: "I am the Lord thy God. You shall have no other gods, nor create false idols to which you bow down and worship."[339] The tricky part of course was that heresy was in the eye of the beholder. For the Catholic Church, heresy was anything contrary to the views of the Vatican. For England after the Reformation, it was anything contrary to the views of the Church of England.

Blasphemy was a violation of the Second Commandment: "Do not take the Lord's name in vain."

Defamation violated the Eighth Commandment which said: "Do not bear false witness against your neighbor." Furthermore, defamation of one's parent(s) violated the Fourth Commandment: "Honor you father and mother." In Deuteronomy, God commanded that any man bearing false witness should be punished in the same way the accused would have been punished had he been adjudged guilty in order to drive sin away (Deuteronomy, 19:16-19). Slander and libel are two types of defamation, and therefore violate God's commandments. The bottom line here is that these are sins which must be driven away.

The respected Dominican theologian Thomas Aquinas ca. 1224-1275 talked about fraternal correction and court justice (through public denunciation) as the two ways in which to drive away sin. Fraternal correction is secret (private) admonishment to someone that he has sinned. It is appropriate when the sin is the type of private sin which hurt only the sinner and the person sinned against. Fraternal correction is an act of charity (a virtue) because its intent is to help the sinner cast out evil, which is the same as helping him obtain goodness. Court justice – which not only admonishes but punishes - is appropriate when the sin is a public sin, a sin which hurt not only the individual against whom it was directed, but other people and/or the common good. It is also appropriate for private sins like treason and heresy, because they are sins committed in private which

[339] https://www.kingjamesbibleonline.org, accessed 16 March 2018.

affect others in "body or in … soul."[340] This view about defamation being a sin persisted into the 16th and 17th century.

The penitential ethics of the medieval church embraced this idea of private admonition.[341] Private confession of sins could, with penance, lead to absolution. This played out in the acts of contrition we already talked about in the ecclesiastical and non-ecclesiastical courts of TudorStuart England.

The confessional privacy minimized the amount of injury done to an individual's name (by which we mean internal dignity and external reputation). The Bible talked about this in a story about Noah (Genesis 9:21-27). His son Ham sinned by telling his brothers Shem and Japeth that he had seen his drunk father asleep naked.[342] Shem and Japeth averted their eyes while covering Noah up, but Noah woke up and knew what Ham has done. Ham shamed his father by telling other people about Noah's nakedness. Shem and Japeth charitably tried to preserve their father's dignity by discretely correcting the situation. As a result, God cursed Ham and blessed Shem and Japeth.

Honor is about relationships. The relationship may be as equals or not, but honor is inextricably intertwined with ideas of charity and privacy. Writers like Thomas Aquinas and Edward Coke talked about the two components of honor – the inward one (dignity) and the outward one (fame or reputation). Defamation – with the malicious intent of causing dishonor - was considered both a crime and a sin, because damage to one's honor could lead to severe consequences.[343] In the case of a public figure, political legitimacy was grounded on a good reputation.[344] William Ames took this one step further where he wrote in 1639: "Every man has title to a good repute, as a commodity trusted in the bosoms of other men, till such

---

[340] Thomas Aquinas, Summa Theologica, SS Treatise on the Theological Virtues, Q[33] Of Fraternal Correction, trans. The Fathers of the English Dominican Province, 1947. http://www.sacred-texts.com/chr/aquinas/summa/sum288.htm, accessed 16 March 2018.

[341] Shuger, 135.

[342] Shuger, 153-154.

[343] Shuger, 158-159, 161.

[344] Shuger, 275.

time as he himself by his own misdemeanors shall, as it were, fetch it away hence."[345]

So how did charity and privacy exactly play out? Elizabeth had said 'that she did not make windows into men's souls.'[346] In other words, there was no way she could "see" what their true beliefs were, so their words had to be taken at face value. You had to choose your words carefully. Luckily, from Elizabeth's time through the 17th century, the English legal system did rely on *mitior sensus* (milder sense) rule. If someone said something that could be interpreted in an innocent or a defamatory sense, *mitior sensus* said to use the one most favorable to the speaker.[347]

d. Constitutionalism and English Law

In 1607, John Cowell published a law book which very nearly caused a constitutional crisis. Entitled *The Interpreter*, it was the first English example of a comprehensive common law dictionary. In 1610, the House of Commons received a complaint about this book. The complaint objected to Cowell's portrayal of the prerogative powers of the Crown in absolutist terms, which was not atypical for the times.

James I agreed with suppression of the book for two reasons. First, books licensed by state take on quasi-official status. They represent the voice of the times (*vox temporis*), describing the norms of their era, "bearing an authority with respect to England's unwritten constitution similar to the authority granted judicial decisions with respect to its unwritten legal code. Books establish precedent." A dangerous precedent that suggested that the king intended to introduce absolutism into civil law.[348] Second, James I did not want to leave any wiggle room in what the laws of the kingdom were. He wanted to prevent a constitutional crisis which he knew the Pope would try to exploit, and he to avoid constitutional crisis which his opponent the Pope could and would exploit.

---

[345] https://archive.org/stream/conscpo00ames#page/146/mode/2up/search/good+repute, accessed 15 March 2018.

[346]http://www.historic-uk.com/HistoryUK/HistoryofEngland/Queen-Elizabeth-I/, acessed 14 March 2018.

[347] Shuger, 219.

[348] Shuger, 239, 242-243.

Furthermore, he wanted to make sure his subjects continued to respect the laws of the kingdom, so they couldn't be up for grabs. Whether or not this is something the king believed or just thought he had to say, Parliament happily went along with it.[349]

By 1644, John Milton was able to neatly summarize the blending of religion and individual rights in his anonymous essay *Aeropagitica.* Subtitled "A Speech for the Liberty of Unlicensed Printing to the Parliament of England," Milton cited St. Dionysius' vision (around 240 CE) in which God told him: "Read any books whatever come to thy hands, for thou art sufficient both the judge aright, and to examine each matter."[350] This was the thrust of Milton's argument – that God had given man reason and expected him to exercise it. Man could only successfully seek God's truth by understanding both good and evil. Milton saw any licensing of books as "a tyranny over learning"[351] which abridged man's liberty.

In *On Liberty* in 1859, John Stuart Mill wrote "There is a limit to the legitimate interference of collective opinion with individual independence: and to find that limit, and to maintain it against encroachment, is on indispensable to a good condition of human affairs, as protection against political despotism."[352] The individual's right to control himself, insofar as it does not affect others, is sovereign.

Mill goes on to define liberty as:

1. Freedom of conscience, thought and feeling, "opinion and sentiment on all subjects, practical or speculative, scientific, moral, or theological," expression and publication.[353]
2. Freedom to do what we like (and live with the consequences) as long as it does not harm others.
3. Freedom for the individuals with all these liberties to unite for whatever purpose they choose, again as long as it doesn't harm others.

---

[349] Shuger, 244-245.
[350] John Milton, "Aeropagitica", in Little Masterpieces. New York: Doubleday, Page and Co., 1901, ed. Bliss Perry, p. 155.
[351] Milton, 183.
[352] John Stuart Mill, On Liberty. London: Longmans, Green, Reader and Dyer, 1880, p. 3.
[353] Mill, 7.

Conclusion

The English monarchy had a tradition of language regulation born out of Roman law. By the time of Henry VIII, Mary, and Elizabeth, the printing press had empowered individuals to run afoul of conventions about heresy and treason, requiring government intervention. Elizabeth removed heresy as a major issue by narrowing its definition, but that ended up focusing more attention on treason, libel, and seditious libel. It is interesting to note that there was no licensing act in place from 1641 to 1662 (essentially, the time between the monarchies of Charles I and James II), when a new act was enacted to prevent "the frequent abuses in printing seditious, treasonable, and unlicensed books and pamphlets, and for regulating of printing and printing-presses."[354] Once again arguing that "the well-government and regulating of printer and printing-presses is a matter of public care and of great concernment," the act set out to stop the printing and selling of "heretical, schismatical, blasphemous, seditious, and treasonable books pamphlets, and papers."[355] Such licensing of printers and printing presses, and registration of every book to be printed[356] did not go down well with the Empire's colonists in the New World. Mill's message came too late.

---

[354] Stephenson, 548.

[354]Stephenson, 548.

[355] Stephenson, 548.

[356] In 1695, the House of Commons considered reviving the Licensing Act of 1662, but was unable to reach consensus and therefore it lapsed.

Chapter 6
How Privacy
Emerged in the United States

The colonists took their English heritage – so shaped by the printing press - with them to the New World. English legal norms regarding libel (slander), sedition, treason, and heresy migrated to America. In chapter three, we noted that the colonists rebelled against England's efforts to regulate speech. The case of Peter Zenger affirmed an anti-Royalist belief in freedom of the press as a core American value. It also set American legal precedent that the truth could be used as a defense in cases of seditious libel (check). Thomas Paine took freedom of the press to new heights, fueling the flames of American independence with *Common Sense* in 1776.

Christian values also came to the New World. A new land held out promise for all Christians to practice Christianity as they wished. The Maryland Toleration Act of 1649 set a precedent for religious tolerance in America. Many colonies were founded as refuges for people practicing different kinds of Christianity – Maryland for Catholics, Pennsylvania for Quakers, and across the Virginia and Massachusetts Bay regions for Puritans. That is not to say that all Christian sects were tolerated well across all colonies, but eventually freedom of religion would be enshrined as a core American value in the original Bill of Rights.

Constitutionalism also migrated to America. Individualism – born out of the Reformation - came with the colonists, who had dreams of new lives, religious freedom and - perhaps for the first time ever - happiness. Restraints exercised by the British Empire chafed against these dreams. The colonists' revolution against the monarchy would lead to the unique brand of U.S. constitutionalism guaranteeing "life, liberty, and the pursuit of happiness."

Setting

All the ideas we've talked about - English law, Christian values, and individual rights - laid the foundation for the formal concept of privacy to emerge in the United States in the late 19th century. In *Privacy Law and Society*, [357] Allen and Rotenberg argue that population, geography, literacy, and technology all contributed to the emergence of privacy in the 1890's. First, people had been migrating from rural environments since the end of the Civil War and U.S. cities had become more crowded. Farmers and homesteaders had to adapt to less personal space in their living arrangements, but experienced greater anonymity than in rural areas. People's perceptions about privacy in the city were very different than they had been in the countryside.

Second, the era of U.S. expansion to its frontiers was coming to an end. Historian Frederick Jackson Turner wrote in 1893 that U.S. colonization across the continent was nearly complete and frontier was closing fast, causing a limitation on "independence and secluded lifestyles." [358]

Third, increased rates of literacy created a market for popular (as opposed to scholarly) journalism and vice versa. The media was available to and had a greater impact on the public than ever before.

Fourth, technology was changing the rules of the privacy game. A telegram had to be touched and/or read by numerous individuals to be successfully conveyed from the sender to the intended recipient. The development of personal cameras gave individuals the capability to take pictures much more easily than in the past. Some of these pictures would find their way into newspapers as matters of public interest, garnering unwanted publicity for their subjects. Other technologies – the telephone (and its party lines) and audio recording - and later wiretapping, radio and motion pictures - would raise all sorts of privacy issues.[359]

---

[357] Anita L. Allen and Marc Rotenberg, Privacy Law and Society. St. Paul, MN: West Academic Publishing, 2016, 3rd edition.

[358] Frederick Jackson Turner, "The Significance of the Frontier in American History 1893. Accessed 5/31/18 at http://nationalhumanitiescenter.org/pds/gilded/empire/text1/turner.pdf

[359] Allen and Rotenberg, pp. 35-38.

This author would like to add a fifth. The War between the States marked the beginning of the end of rampant paternalism in the United States. The Fourteenth Amendment, passed in 1868, guaranteed all citizens – not just white men like our forefathers - due process and equal protection under the law. In reality, the extension of equal rights to minorities and women had only begun.

In 1859, John Stuart Mill had actually talked about heavy handed government regulation of intoxicating liquors as an abuse of power, "suited only to a state of society in which the laboring classes are avowedly treated as children or savages" [and that all efforts should be made] … "to educate them for freedom and govern them as freemen…."[360] The Eighteenth Amendment – banning the "manufacture, sale, or transportation of intoxicating liquors" – was a late example of paternalism aimed at the working classes. This paternalism was largely made possible by the women of the converged temperance and suffrage movements exercising their newly recognized rights.

How Technology Helped Birth "Privacy" in the Late 19th Century

In order to drive home relevant legal and individual views in this era, we will consider a landmark 1881 case which unified disparate ideas about privacy in a single judicial proceeding. *De May v. Roberts* illustrated the breaking of many traditional laws, values, and rights, including: "a private home violated, a married couple mortified, a woman's modesty compromised, the intimate body observed, health information disclosed, and … expectations of privacy shattered."[361]

Here are the circumstances. Dr. De May was summoned on a stormy night to the home of Mr. and Mrs. Roberts because Mrs. Roberts had gone into labor. Dr. De May was tired, overworked, and feeling under the weather and brought an assistant named Mr. Scattergood to carry his things. The Roberts made no objection and Mr. Scattergood settled in the kitchen. During the labor, Mrs. Roberts was being attended by a Mrs. Parks along with Dr. Scattergood. When Mrs. Parks had to step out for a

---

[360] Mill, 60.

[361] Allen and Rotenberg, pp. 20-21.

few minutes, Dr. De May asked Mr. Scattergood to come in and hold Mrs. Roberts' hand during her labor to prevent her from falling. The baby was born and all went well. The Roberts' later learned that Mr. Scattergood was not a medical professional (they also objected because he was a young unmarried man). Believing they had been misled, they sued the physician and his assistant in De May v. Roberts (46 Mich. 160, 9 N.W. 146 (Mich. 1881).

Some people may find the circumstances of this case curious, but that is because norms have changed a lot since then. It was the norm then to give birth at home, in the presence of only a medical professional and/or other women. Today, a woman in the U.S. typically gives birth at a hospital attended by medical professionals, and the father is frequently present at the birth. In the late 19th century, women were much more modest in their attire than we are today. And women's health issues were not a matter of public discussion, especially with (unmarried) men!

But this birth took place at home. And a man's home is his castle. Dr. De May and Mr. Scattergood had been invited into the Roberts home. At some point, the Roberts mistakenly assumed that Mr. Scattergood was a medical professional. It's not clear that either the doctor or his assistant ever intended to mislead the Roberts nor understood that they had. But the norms of the time made the Roberts feel as if Mrs. Roberts had in a sense been "violated" by Mr. Scattergood by seeing her body, perhaps even her genitals during the very private act of childbirth.

The suit pivoted on the fact that Dr. De May and Mr. Scattergood had been given consent to enter the Roberts home under *false pretenses*. The courts found in favor of the Roberts in both the lower court and on appeal in the Michigan Supreme Court.

So now that we have a sense of the legal and social norms of the time, we talk about the formalization of privacy as a right. In 1890, E.L. Godkin published an article on "The Rights of the Citizen" in the popular *Scribner's Magazine*. He opened his article by observing that societies formed for mutual assistance, and its members required mutual respect.[362]

---

[362] E.L. Godkin, "The Rights of the Citizen. IV. To His Own Reputation." Scribner's Magazine, New York, 1890, v. 8, p. 58. Accessed May 15, 2018 at https://babel.hathitrust.org/cgi/pt?id=coo.31924097287480;view=1up;seq=66

That need for respect created first form of personal property - social repute – which Godkin claimed is necessary for happiness in life. Members of the society who fail to provide this help or to adhere to the group's customs open themselves up to social penalty.

Godkin went on to observe that historically the law did not take slander – a violation of a norm - as seriously because its effect was limited (e.g. geographically), and because the offended party exacted his own recompense (albeit violently). By 1890, newspapers (made possible by the printing press) magnified the effect that defamatory remarks, enabling broad public dissemination of said remarks and having greater potential to disturb the peace, thus requiring governmental intervention. By In his modern times, Godkin could write: "it is as much the duty for the state to provide security for reputation as for property, and that it is … [in] the interest of the state to do so…."[363]

Godkin also talks about newspapers as the communications medium by which the public got information about its government and its players. Democracy encourages public discussion about government and its machinations. And party politics and their parochial influences can sway public opinion, especially when it comes to the election cycle (apparently Publius knew what he was talking about in the *Federalist*). Godkin concludes: "There is nothing more important to the state than the voter should have accurate knowledge as to the character and history of the men whom he puts into important official places; and attempts of any kind to prevent his getting it, or to furnish it to him in a spurious condition, are quite fit objects of punishment as attempts to prevent his voting according to his conscience through corruption or intimidation."[364] While Godkin acknowledges that there is an economic incentive for the newspapers to report sensational information, he wishes that social mores kept it in better check.

Finally, Godkin talks about privacy as a modern concept. Privacy is a right, a boundary a man draws between his public life as a citizen and his private life as an individual. Godkin references Coke's words about a man's home being his "'castle and fortress as well for his defense against

[363] Godkin, p. 62.
[364] Godkin, p. 64.

injury and violence as for his repose.'" As we saw in the DeMay v. Roberts case, this is a concept imbued with social and legal underpinnings in America in 1890 which demonstrates respect for a man's "personality as an individual, for that kingdom of the mind, [and] that inner world of personal thought and feeling in which every man passes … time…."[365] It is, Godkin concludes, a natural right of modern man.

U.S. legal scholarship on privacy quickly followed. Samuel D. Warren and Louis Brandeis (later Supreme Court Justice) published an article in the *Harvard Law Review* entitled "The Right to Privacy," citing Godkin's call for legal remedies to the "evil of invasion of privacy by newspapers, long keenly felt."[366] Brandeis and Warren neatly synopsized the dynamic nature of the protections afforded by the law we've attempted to trace thus far:

> That the individual shall have full protection in person and in property is a principle as old as the common law; but it has been found necessary from time to time to define anew the exact nature and extent of such protection. Political, social, and economic changes entail the recognition of new rights, and the common law, in its eternal youth, grows to meet the new demands of society. Thus, in very early times, the law gave remedy only for physical interference with life and property, for trespasses *vi et armis* [with force and arms]. Then 'the right to life' served only to protect the subject from battery in its various forms; liberty meant freedom from actual restraint; and the right to property secured to the individual his lands and his cattle…. [Protection against injury also extended to reputation.] Gradually the scope of these legal rights broadened; and now the right to life had come to mean the right to enjoy life – the right to be let alone; the right to liberty secures the exercise of extensive civil privileges; and the term 'property' had grown to comprise every form of possession – intangible as well as tangible.[367]

This is reminiscent of 1635 description of the uses of law which opened the previous chapter, with one notable exception. By 1890,

---

[365] Godkin, p. 65.
[366] E.L. Godkin, 58.
[367] Samuel D. Warren and Louis Brandeis, "The Right to Privacy," Harvard Business Review, 1890, accessed 6/2/18 at http://www.jstor.org/stable/pdf/1321160.pdf?refreqid=excelsior%3A0df8ef50658f2e2204b9fb82667f3e28

Brandeis and Warren argued that the legal framework designed to protect the individual, his property and his reputation had evolved to encompass the right to be left alone, or privacy.[368] It's not a right which appears explicitly in our Bill of Rights, but a right nonetheless.

Warren and Brandeis were prompted to write this article after at least one instance of a newspaper publishing a journalist's photograph of a private individual in a private social setting without permission. There are several ways in which this fits into our overall theme of technology shaping law. First, the authors themselves noted the advances in photographic technology which now permitted pictures to be taken quickly and surreptitiously (in the past, the subject would have to sit for an extended period for a photograph to be taken). Second, the photograph was published in a newspaper, a communications method that widely disseminated information to the public by use of printing press technology. Third, the image may even have been transmitted via telegraph using an early telegraphic version of what we think about as facsimile. The specific details of the incident(s) are lost to history, so we'll just move on knowing that somehow technology was shaping the thinking of legal scholars in a significant way. Any which way, Warren and Brandeis feared that such technology might "make good the prediction that 'what is whispered in the closet shall be proclaimed from the house-tops.'"[369]

Modern U.S. Privacy Torts Emerge in 1960

The Brandeis and Warren law review article on privacy is today cited as the starting point for formalizing privacy law in the United States. Unlike Athena, privacy law did not spring into the world fully formed, but would take another 70 years to be formalized in four privacy *torts*.

A tort is a legal term referring to a non-criminal injury or wrong committed against a person in the absence of a formal contract. It can be

---

[368] In point of fact, Brandeis and Warren had borrowed this idea from jurist and law professor Thomas M. Cooley who had written that "The right to one's person may be said to be a right of complete immunity: to be let alone." See Thomas M. Cooley, Treatise on the Law of Torts or the Wrongs Which Arise Independent of Contract. Chicago: Callaghan and Co, 1879, p. 29. Accessed 6/2/18 at https://repository.law.umich.edu/books/11/ [368]Warren and Brandeis.

[369] Warren and Brandeis.

committed with force or without force, intentionally or unintentionally. The injury is committed against the rights of the person, or to her real or personal property. So, tort law covers non-criminal *iniuria* we have been talking about since the beginning of this chapter.

In 1960, Prosser finally put privacy law into a neat framework of four torts:

1. Intrusion upon the plaintiff's seclusion or solitude, or into his private affairs.
2. Public disclosure of embarrassing private facts about the plaintiff.
3. Publicity which places the plaintiff in a false light in the public eye.
4. Appropriation, for the defendant's advantage, of the plaintiff's name or likeness.[370]

Prosser developed his torts on privacy after an exhaustive study of state laws and judicial (state and federal) related to privacy. These state laws and judicial decisions actually drove modern privacy law.

In order to understand this, we will look at some of the precedent cases for each of these torts. With respect to intrusion, we've already talked about De May v. Roberts in 1881. With respect to disclosure, we consider the 1890 case of *Manola v. Stevens*, cited by Warren and Brandeis in their paper. Marion Manola was a popular performer in New York City who was surreptitiously photographed in her tights by a photographer. Manola sued, claiming that her modesty was offended (remember, mores were different then). She won, and the photographer was forever banned from displaying her photograph.[371]

Disclosure was also used to argue cases in favor of "right to be forgotten," a subject we will talk about more in the second half of this book. In the case of *Melvin v. Reid* (112 Cal. App. 285 (Cal. Ct. App. 1931), superseded by statute), Mrs. Bernard Melvin (nee Gabrielle Darley) sued the producers of "The Red Kimono," a film about her earlier life under her maiden name as a prostitute who was tried and acquitted for

---

[370] William L. Prosser, "Privacy," 48 Cal. L. Rev. 383 (1960), accessed 5/29/18 at https://scholarship.law.berkeley.edu/cgi/viewcontent.cgi?article=3157&context=californialawreview

[371] Allen and Rotenberg, 23.

murder. Rehabilitated and now a respectable member of society, Mrs. Melvin was scorned by her social circles and suffered emotional distress. Judge Marks found in favor of the plaintiff, stating: "The use of the appellant's true name in connection with the incidents of her former life in the plot and advertisements was unnecessary and indelicate and a wilful and wanton disregard of that charity which should … keep us from unnecessarily holding another up to the scorn and contempt of upright members of society."[372] Catch that Christian value there?

In the case of *Sidis v. F-R Publishing Corporation*, William James Sidis had been person of public interest since the age of 10 when he was recognized as a math prodigy. He graduated from Harvard at 16. After an emotional breakdown, Sidis was repulsed by the life he had known and assiduously worked to live in obscurity. The *New Yorker* did a follow-up "Where Are They New?" article on him years later. There was no dispute about the truthfulness of the article, but the judge opined that it was "a ruthless exposure of a once public character, who has since sought and has now been deprived of the seclusion of private life."[373] However, the judge found in favor of The New Yorker because the article was of public interest and the reporting of such information what within the mores of the times.

In the case of false light, we consider the 1905 case of *Pavesich v. New England Life Insurance Company*. Mr. Pavesich complained that his image had been used without permission to advertise New England Life Insurance, and the accompanying text falsely implied that he had purchased this insurance. The first trial in 1904 found for the insurance company. On appeal to the Georgia Supreme Court under Judge Cobb, the court found for the plaintiff.

In his judicial opinion, Cobb notes that just because a "right of privacy" hadn't previously described didn't mean it wasn't a right that didn't exist. True, earlier "privacy-like" cases had been argued on ideas related to property rights, breach of trust, et al. Cobb argues that privacy stems from the absolute rights to be safe to be free. The individual is safe

---

372 Allen and Rotenberg, 126.

373 Sidis v. F-R Pub. Corp. 113 F. 2d 806 (@d Cir. 1940), in Allen and Rotenberg, 127-128

to enjoy his life (and reputation) in whatever way he pleases as long as it doesn't infringe on the rights of others or break the law. The individual is free from restraint/imprisonment except under due process of the law. Cobb argues that the right to privacy is "derived from natural law, recognized by the principles of municipal law, and guaranteed … by the constitutions of the United States and of the State of Georgia…."[374]

An early privacy case concerning appropriation was *Robertson v. Rochester Folding Box Co.* in the New York Supreme Court in 1902. In this case, the Rochester Folding Box Company put an image of Abigail Robertson without her permission on labels and advertisements for Franklin Mills flour. Rochester furthermore labelled the picture "Flower of the Family." Robertson argued she had been humiliated and suffered mental distress and asked for an injunction against further use of her picture. Judge Parker concluded that Robertson's privacy complain was invalid, stating that his "examination of the authorities leads us to the conclusion that the so-called 'right of privacy' has not as yet found an abiding place in our jurisprudence, and, as we view it, the doctrine cannot now be incorporated without doing violence to settled principles of law by which the profession and the public have long been guided."[375] The New York legislature, less than a year later, passed a law recognizing the right to privacy.[376]

Constitutional Privacy

State laws lead the way in privacy law.[377] But we have not yet considered constitutional challenges. Cases involving constitutional challenges end up in state courts, federal courts, and the U.S. Supreme Court.

We will now walk through privacy cases related to the amendments to the U.S. Constitution. We will emphasis the First, Second, Third, Fourth, Fifth, and Fourteenth Amendments. There are a couple

[374] Pavesich v. New England Life Insurance Co. et al. 122 Ga. 190, 50 S.E. 68 (Ga. 1905). Accessed 6/2/18 at http://faculty.uml.edu/sgallagher/pavesich_v.htm

[375] Robertson v. Rochester Folding Box Co. 171 N.Y. 538 (N.Y. 1902), in Allen and Rotenberg, 41-42.

[376] Allen and Rotenberg, 42.

[377] "How U.S. State Law Quietly Leads the Way in Privacy Protection," Special Report by Privacilla, July 2002. Accessed 5/31/18 at http://www.privacilla.org /releases /Torts_Report.pdf

other amendments which talk ensure certain freedoms but are not usually the emphasis of privacy law. We will at least mention their privacy aspects here. Along the way, we will try to call out how technology is shaping outcomes over time. Spoiler alert, the Fourth and Fourteenth will jeopardize most of our time.

First Amendment

Many privacy issues have been raised in First Amendment cases. They include freedom of religion, freedom of private association (often highlighting race politics), sensitive data, anonymous speech, freedom of ideas, and freedom of association (often related to exclusion of LGBTQ persons).

a. Freedom of Religion

The classic Supreme Court case regarding freedom of religion is Reynolds v. United States (1878). Mr. Reynolds was a Mormon who took a second wife, after Congress passed a statute banning polygamy. Having acknowledged the First Amendment guarantee of religious freedom, Chief Justice Waite noted that "from the earliest history of England, polygamy has been treated as an offence against society,"[378] prosecuted first in the ecclesiastical courts, later as a violation of a statute of James I, and carried over in law to the New World. He then added:

> In the face of all this evidence, it is impossible to believe that the constitutional guaranty of religious freedom was intended to prohibit legislation in respect to this most important feature of social life. Marriage, while from its very nature a sacred obligation, is nevertheless, in most civilized nations, a civil contract, and usually regulated by law. Upon it society may be said to be built, and out of its fruits spring social relations and social obligations and duties with which government is necessarily required to deal.

Chief Justice Waite ruled in favor of the anti-polygamy law, and concluded:

> To permit ... [polygamy] would be to make the professed doctrines of religious belief superior to the law of the land, and,

[378] Reynolds v. United States, 98 U.S. 145 (1878), accessed 6/13/18 at https: //supreme.justia.com/cases/federal/us/98/145/case.html

> in effect, to permit every citizen to become a law unto himself. Government could exist only in name under such circumstances.

b. Freedom of Association

Next, we'll consider the right of association in *NAACP v. Alabama* 357 U.S. 449 (1958). Alabama accused the NAACP of having failed to file its corporate charter with the state before doing business in that state. The state filed suit and requested that among other things the NAACP provide its membership lists. The Supreme Court found that this violated its members rights to free association and privacy in one's associations as well as due process (see Fourteenth Amendment).

c. Sensitive Data

In *Ostengren v. Cuccinelli* (2010),[379] Betty Ostengren was a private citizen of Virginia concerned about the open availability of private information. She brought attention to the Commonwealth's practice of placing land records on the internet without first redacting Social Security Numbers (SSN's) by reposting the same information on her own website. Additionally, she linked the SSN's to additional public records. While Virginia argued that the SSN's should be protected under the First Amendment, the Virginia court found in favor of Ostengren, citing words from the earlier *Cox Brod. Corp. v. Cohn* (1975):

> Public records, by their very nature, are of interest to those concerned with the administration of government, and a public benefit is performed by the reporting of the true contents of the records by the media. The freedom of the press to publish that information appears to us to be of critical importance to our type of government, in which the citizenry is the final judge of the proper conduct of public business. In preserving that form of government, the First and Fourteenth Amendments command nothing less than that the States may not impose sanctions on the publication of truthful information contained in official court records open to public inspection.[380]

---

[379] Ostengren v. Cuccinelli, 2010 WL 2891576 (C.A. 4 (Va.)), in Allen and Rotenberg, 333-334.

[380] Cox Broad. Corp. v. Cohn, 420 U.S. 469 (1975), accessed 6/13/18 at https://supreme.justia.com/cases/federal/us/420/469/case.html [380]Allen and Rotenberg, 337.

d. Anonymous Speech

i. *Talley v. California* (1960)

With respect to anonymous speech, we consider the case of *Talley v. California* (1960), in which the Supreme Court struck down a California ban against distributing leaflets "that did not bear the names and addresses of the people responsible for their distribution."[381] In his opinion, Justice Black noted that even the Federalist Papers had been published anonymously, part of a wave of publications across the British Empire which defied the "obnoxious press licensing law of England."[382]

ii. *Doe I and Doe II v. Individuals, Whose True Names are Unknown* (2008)

Skipping forward to the cyber age, we consider another case regarding anonymous speech. In *Doe I and Doe II v. Individuals, Whose True Names are Unknown*. This case was lodged by two female Yale Law School students who were being harassed, threatened, and subjected to defamatory remarks by an anonymous individual (John Doe 21) on the law school admission website AutoAdmit.com. The plaintiffs petitioned the Internet Service Provider (ISP) AT&T Internet Services for information in order to reveal the identity of John Doe 21, and John Doe 21 attempted to quash this petition. The court denied the quash on the grounds that the First Amendment right to free speech (in this case, anonymous internet speech) "is not absolute and must be weighed against Doe II's need for discovery to redress alleged wrongs."[383] Furthermore, the court commented that John Doe 21 had little expectation of privacy when he was committing tortious acts which could be open to discovery under legal action.

e. Freedom of Ideas

At this point, Allen and Rotenberg note that the First Amendment "protects the mind's encounters with the sacred and the profane."[384] This

---

[381] Allen and Rotenberg, 337.

[382] Talley v. California, 362 U.S. 60 (1960), accessed 6/13/18 at https://supreme.justia.com/cases/federal/us/362/60/case.html

[383] Doe I and Doe II v. Individuals, Whose True Names are Unknown, 561 F.Supp.2d 249 (D. Ct. 2008), in Allen and Rotenberg, 357.

[384] Allen and Rotenberg, 363.

extends to things like pornography and adultery. So, in the case of *Stanley v. Georgia*, Mr. Stanley's home was lawfully searched for evidence of alleged bookmaking activities. In the course of the search, obscene material was found. Having been convicted of possession of obscene material, Mr. Stanley appealed to the Supreme Court. The Supreme Court overturned his convict on First Amendment grounds, stating:

> It is now well established that the Constitution protects the right to receive information and ideas.... Moreover, in the context of this case - a prosecution for mere possession of printed or filmed matter in the privacy of a person's own home - that right takes on an added dimension. For also fundamental is the right to be free, except in very limited circumstances, from unwanted governmental intrusions into one's privacy.[385]

f. Freedom of Association

Finally for the First Amendment, we consider the 2000 Supreme Court case of *Boy Scouts of America v. Dale*.[386] James Dale, who had achieved the prestigious rank of Eagle Scout, became an adult member of the Boy Scouts and was approved to be an assistant scoutmaster. His adult membership in the Boy Scouts was revoked after the Boy Scouts learned he was a homosexual. They learned this because the newspaper local to his university reported his role as co-president of the Lesbian/Gay Alliance. The Boy Scouts argued that homosexuality was counter to their teachings and values as a private association, and that they had a longstanding policy against putting homosexuals in leadership positions. The Supreme Court found for the Boy Scouts of America, reasoning that Dale's re-admittance would hinder the Scouts' First Amendment right to freedom of association.

Second Amendment

The right to keep and bear arms is as American as apple pie. The case law is exhaustive. What I want to call out here is the newish debate about anonymous gun ownership. Our electronic age has made it

---

[385] Stanley v. Georgia, 394 U.S. 557 (1969), accessed 6/13/18 at https://supreme.justia.com/cases/federal/us/394/557/.

[386] Boy Scouts of America v. Dale, 530 U.S. 640 (2000), accessed 6/13/18 at https://supreme.justia.com/cases/federal/us/530/640/

technically possible for there to be electronic access to gun ownership and licensing records. This has stirred a tempest in a teapot about privacy rights in regards to the Second Amendment.

Third Amendment

The famous no-quartering-of-soldiers-in-my-home amendment to the Constitution. While it may have been highly relevant historically (see chapters two and three), it doesn't seem so today. Or is it? According to Allen and Rotenberg, some legal scholars are talking about government intrusions into the home digital domain are Third Amendment issues. Could this shape cybersecurity policy in the future?[387]

Fourth Amendment

There are many Fourth Amendment cases related to privacy. We will emphasize the searching telephone communications, house and curtilage, and medical testing and records (including alcohol, drug, disease and DNA).[388] It is interesting to note that many of them cite the 1765 English case of Entick v. Carrington as discussed in chapter two.

a. Telephone Communications

This is our first really meaty topic concerning how technology shapes the law over time.

i. Olmstead v. U.S.

We consider first the famous 1928 Supreme Court case of *Olmstead v. United States*. Roy Olmstead was an alleged bootlegger. He was prosecuted based on evidence collected from wiretapping Olmstead's phone without trespass on Olmstead's property. The Supreme Court subsequently took up this issue as a Fourth (and Fifth) Amendment issue.

In his majority opinion, Chief Justice Taft stated:

> The Amendment itself shows that the search is to be of material things - the person, the house, his papers, or his effects. The description of the warrant necessary to make the proceeding

---

[387] Allen and Rotenberg, 395.

[388] Other issues concern school searches, hotel and workplace searches, traffic and identify stops, and airport searches.

> lawful is that it must specify the place to be searched and the person or *things* to be seized.

With regard, for example, to the U.S. mail, Taft argues:

> It is plainly within the words of the Amendment to say that the unlawful rifling by a government agent of a sealed letter is a search and seizure of the sender's papers or effects. The letter is a paper, an effect, and in the custody of a Government that forbids carriage except under its protection.

However, Taft continues:

> The United States takes no such care of telegraph or telephone messages as of mailed sealed letters. The Amendment does not forbid what was done here. There was no searching. There was no seizure. The evidence was secured by the use of the sense of hearing, and that only. There was no entry of the houses or offices of the defendants.

The majority opinion of the Supreme Court was that the wiretapping was legal.

But wait. The three Supreme Court justices dissented with this opinion, including our old friend Louis Brandeis. In his dissenting opinion, Brandeis quotes an earlier Supreme Court decision which said:

> Legislation, both statutory and constitutional, is enacted, it is true, from an experience of evils, but ... should not be necessarily confined to the form that evil had theretofore taken. Time works changes, brings into existence new conditions and purposes. Therefore, a principle, to be vital, must be capable of wider application than the mischief which gave it birth. This is peculiarly true of constitutions.... In the application of a constitution, therefore, our contemplation cannot be only of what has been, but of what may be. Under any other rule, a constitution would indeed be as easy of application as it would be deficient in efficacy and power. Its general principles would have little value, and be converted by precedent into impotent and lifeless formulas. Rights declared in words might be lost in reality.[389]

---

[389] Weems v. United States, 217 U.S. 349 (1910), quoted in Olmstead v. United States, 277 U.S. 438 (1928), accessed 6/16/18 at https://supreme.justia.com/cases/federal/us/277/438/case.html

Brandeis goes on to talk about the changes that have occurred since the creation of the Fourth (and Fifth) Amendment(s):

> Subtler and more far-reaching means of invading privacy have become available to the Government. Discovery and invention have made it possible for the Government, by means far more effective than stretching upon the rack, to obtain disclosure in court of what is whispered in the closet.... The progress of science in furnishing the Government with means of espionage is not likely to stop with wiretapping. Ways may someday be developed by which the Government, without removing papers from secret drawers, can reproduce them in court, and by which it will be enabled to expose to a jury the most intimate occurrences of the home. Advances in the psychic and related sciences may bring means of exploring unexpressed beliefs, thoughts and emotions.

Finally, Brandeis opines:

> The makers of our Constitution undertook to secure conditions favorable to the pursuit of happiness. They recognized the significance of man's spiritual nature, of his feelings, and of his intellect. They knew that only a part of the pain, pleasure and satisfactions of life are to be found in material things. They sought to protect Americans in their beliefs, their thoughts, their emotions and their sensations. They conferred, as against the Government, the right to be let alone - the most comprehensive of rights, and the right most valued by civilized men. To protect that right, every unjustifiable intrusion by the Government upon the privacy of the individual, whatever the means employed, must be deemed a violation of the Fourth Amendment.

ii. Katz v. U.S.

39 years later, the Supreme Court agreed with Brandeis and reversed their opinion on wiretapping in *Katz v. United States*. Charles Katz was convicted of transmitting wagering information after the U.S. government collected information by wiretapping a phone booth (without a warrant) that Katz was using. The Supreme Court found in favor of Katz, noting that "Wherever a man may be, he is entitled to know that the will

remain free from unreasonable searches and seizures."[390] Justice Stewart added:

> We conclude that the underpinnings of *Olmstead* ... have been so eroded by our subsequent decisions that the 'trespass' doctrine there enunciated can no longer be regarded as controlling. The Government's activities in electronically listening to and recording the petitioner's words violated the privacy upon which he justifiably relied while using the telephone booth, and thus constituted a 'search and seizure' within the meaning of the Fourth Amendment. The fact that the electronic device employed to achieve that end did not happen to penetrate the wall of the booth can have no constitutional significance.

iii. Berger v. New York (1967)

This Supreme Court case overturned a New York Statute which had been used to convict Ralph Berger of bribing a public official. The Supreme Court found that a warrant – relying on this law for issuance - wiretapping Berger's phone was overly broad and violated the Fourth Amendment. While the warrant demonstrated probable cause it, but was too broad in the describing the place and persons to be searched and seized. Justice Douglas in his opinion noted that electronic surveillance is "the greatest of all invasions of privacy. It places a government agent in the bedroom, in the business conference, in the social hour, in the lawyer's office - everywhere and anywhere a 'bug' can be placed."[391]

iv. United States v. United States District Court (1972)

This Supreme Court case presaged a lot of activity regarding the use of Presidential power exercised by the Attorney General to wiretap phones without judicial approval in cases concerning what we would now call "terrorism surveillance." It highlights the competing forces of "the Government's right to protect itself from unlawful subversion and attack and to the citizen's right to be secure in his privacy against unreasonable

---

[390] Katz v. United State, 389 U.S. 347 (1967), accessed 6/16/18 at https://supreme.justia.com/cases/federal/us/389/347/case.html

[391] Berger v. New York, 388 U.S. 41 (1967), accessed 6/`6/18 at https:// supreme .justia.com/cases/federal/us/388/41/case.html

Government intrusion."[392] The wiretaps were used as evidence against three defendants charged with conspiracy to destroy Government property. One defendant was charged with dynamite bombing of a Central Intelligence Agency office.

The Supreme Court ruled in favor of the defendants and the Fourth Amendment. Justice Powell opined that "The price of lawful public dissent must not be a dread of subjection to an unchecked surveillance power. Nor must the fear of unauthorized official eavesdropping deter vigorous citizen dissent and discussion of Government action in private conversation. For private dissent, no less than open public discourse, is essential to our free society."

b. House and Curtilage (property adjoining the house)

i. United States v. Karo (1984)

This Supreme Court case concerns whether the government has the right to monitor a beeper (intentionally planted by the Drug Enforcement Agency in a can of chemicals to be used for illegal drug production) once it has been transported into a private home. The court ruled that the government had violated the Fourth Amendment rights of the individual and should have obtained a warrant before monitoring the beeper within the private residence.[393]

ii. California v. Ciraolo (1986)

The Supreme Court case of *California v. Ciraolo* was a new kind of technology case. Law enforcement officers overflew Dante Carlo Ciraolo's backyard in a private plane to verify a tip that he was growing marijuana there. The yard was shielded from public view by two fences – one of six feet, the other of ten. Based on that evidence, the police obtained and executed a warrant for the house, seized the marijuana plants and prosecuted Ciraolo. While the California Court of Appeals subsequently

---

[392] United States v. United States District Court, 407 U.S. 297 (1972), accessed 6/16/18 at https://supreme.justia.com/cases/federal/us/407/297/case.html

[393] United States v. Karo 468 U.S. 705 (1984), accessed 6/16/18 at https://supreme.justia.com/cases/federal/us/468/705/

found in favor of Ciraolo, i.e. his Fourth Amendment rights had been violated, the U.S. Supreme Court reversed this.[394]

iii. Kyllo v. United States (2001)

In this Supreme Court case, law enforcement agents used thermal imaging technology without warrant to determine that parts of Danny Kyllo's residence were substantially hotter, indicating that grow lamps could be being used to grow marijuana. A warrant was issued on this evidence, marijuana plants were found and Kyllo was indicted. The Supreme Court ruled that the thermal imaging was a violation of Fourth Amendment rights. In his opinion, Justice Scalia opined:

> Where, as here, the Government uses a device that is not in general public use, to explore details of the home that would previously have been unknowable without physical intrusion, the surveillance is a 'search' and is presumptively unreasonable without a warrant.[395]

iv. United States v. Jones (2012)

This Fourth Amendment case concerned the constitutionality of law enforcement putting a GPS device on the vehicle of an alleged drug trafficker without a warrant. The Supreme Court found that this was a violation of the Fourth Amendment.[396]

v. Riley v. California (2012)

Stopped on a routine traffic stop, David Leon Riley's car was searched, resulting in his arrest on weapons charges. A police officer searching Riley found and seized Riley's cell phone, which contained numerous references to a local street gang. The police's subsequent search of Riley's cell phone provided sufficient evidence in their minds to charge Riley in connection with a shooting several weeks earlier. Riley argued that the evidence was inadmissible.

---

394 California v. Ciraolo, 476 U.S. 207 (1986), accessed 6/16/18 at https://supreme.justia.com/cases/federal/us/476/207/case.html

395 Kyllo v. United States, 533 U.S. 27 (2001). Accessed 6/16/18 at https://supreme.justia.com/cases/federal/us/533/27/case.html

396 United States v. Jones, 565 U.S. 400 (2012). Accessed 6/16/18 at https://supreme.justia.com/cases/federal/us/565/400/opinion.html

In upholding this as a Fourth Amendment violation, Supreme Court Chief Justice Roberts opined that whereas the search of an individual posed only limited privacy intrusions,

> modern cell phones have immense storage capacity… [which has] several interrelated privacy consequences. First, a cell phone collects in one place many distinct types of information that reveal much more in combination than any isolated record. Second, the phone's capacity allows even just one type of information to convey far more than previously possible. Third, data on the phone can date back for years. In addition, an element of pervasiveness characterizes cell phones but not physical records. A decade ago officers might have occasionally stumbled across a highly personal item such as a diary, but today many of the more than 90% of American adults who own cell phones keep on their person a digital record of nearly every aspect of their lives.[397]

He adds that

> The scope of the privacy interests at stake is further complicated by the fact that the data viewed on many modern cell phones may in fact be stored on a remote server. Thus, a search may extend well beyond papers and effects in the physical proximity of an arrestee, a concern that the United States recognizes but cannot definitively foreclose.

We'll dig into these ideas more in the second half of this book.

c. Medical Testing and Records (including alcohol, drug, disease and DNA)

i. United States v. Comprehensive Drug Testing, Inc. **(2009)**

This case involved a federal government investigation into the Bay Area Lab Cooperative (Balco), which was suspected of providing steroids to professional baseball players. The government obtained a warrant authorizing seizure of the records of ten players from the Comprehensive Drug Testing Inc. (CDT). When the government executed the warrant, they seized the medical records of 100's of baseball players as well as other individuals. CDT and the Players moved to have the seized

---

397 Riley v. California, 573 U.S. ___ (2014). Accessed 6/16/18 at https://supreme.justia.com/cases/federal/us/573/13-132/

property returned. Ultimately, Judge Kozinski of the Court of Appeals of the Ninth Circuit Court affirmed the lower court decisions in California (to return all the seized data) and Nevada (to return all the seized data except that about the 10 players). In his opinion, Judge Kozinski opined that

> We accept the reality that such over-seizing is an inherent part of the electronic search process and proceed on the assumption that, when it comes to the seizure of electronic records, this will be far more common than in the days of paper records. This calls for greater vigilance on the part of judicial officers in striking the right balance between the government's interest in law enforcement and the right of individuals to be free from unreasonable searches and seizures.[398]

He added that

> Everyone's interests are best served if there are clear rules to follow that strike a fair balance between the legitimate needs of law enforcement and the right of individuals and enterprises to the privacy that is at the heart of the Fourth Amendment.

ii. Maryland v. King (2013)

A Maryland law was passed which permitted DNA testing on all persons charged with a violent crime. The defendant Alonzo Jay King was identified as a rapist by running his DNA sample through Combined DNA Index System (CODIS) which links local, state, and national DNA laboratories. Found guilty, King appealed arguing his Fourth Amendment rights had been violated. The Supreme Court upheld his conviction. Justice Antonio Scalia wrote a notable dissention, arguing that "Solving unsolved crimes is a noble objective, but it occupies a lower place in the American pantheon of noble objectives than the protection of our people from suspicionless law-enforcement searches. The Fourth Amendment must prevail."[399]

Fifth Amendment

The Fifth Amendment case we will consider here concerns the individual right not to have to give testimony that incriminates oneself. In

---

[398] United States v. Comprehensive Drug Testing, Inc., 579 F.3d 989 (C.A. 9 (Cal.), 2009), in Allen and Rotenberg, 510.

[399] Maryland v. King, 569 U.S. ___ (2013). Accessed 6/16/18 at https://supreme.justia.com/cases/federal/us/569/12-207/dissent4.html

2010, John Doe's personal computer and several external hard drives were lawfully seized in the course of a child pornography investigation. When John Doe was served with a subpoena duces tecum, a legal writ ordering him to appear in Florida District Court and provide the decrypted version of the seized media. John Doe appeared in court but refused to decrypt the files, invoking his Fifth Amendment rights. The government granted Doe immunity limited to "the use [of Doe's] act of production of the unencrypted contents" of the hard drives. John Doe still refused to comply under the Fifth Amendment, arguing that the contents of the media could be used as testimony against himself. He also claimed he was unable to decrypt the files. He was held in contempt and jailed.

In John Doe's subsequent appeal[400], the U.S. Court of Appeals (11th District) reversed the lower court's decision, ruling that John Doe had correctly invoked his Fifth Amendment rights and that the district court had erred in finding him in contempt.

Eighth Amendment

This amendment prohibits the government from imposing cruel and unusual punishment, and is cited in privacy cases (e.g. related to isolation, modesty, and security) brought by prisoners, but they are beyond the scope of this book.

Ninth Amendment

This amendment states that "The enumeration in the Constitution, of certain rights, shall not be construed to deny or disparage others retained by the people." You can almost hear Alexander Hamilton here, right? This amendment was cited in *Griswold v. Connecticut*, a landmark 14th Amendment which we will talk about shortly.

Fourteenth Amendment

The Fourteenth Amendment prohibits any state from making any laws which prohibit any U.S. citizen's right to due process and equal rights under the law. Digging into this a bit, we see that the Fourteenth Amendment is used in constitutional cases involving decisional privacy.

---

[400] In Re Grand Jury Subpoena Duces Tecum, 670 F.3d 1335 (11th Cir, 2012), accessed 6/16/18 at https://caselaw.findlaw.com/us-11th-circuit/1595245.html

That includes many hot button issues, things like health care, marriage, procreation, education, sexuality, and the right to die.

a. Private Lives, Private Matters

In the case of *Meyer v. Nebraska* (1923), the Supreme Court was asked to consider whether the Nebraska law banning the teaching of modern foreign languages to schoolchildren. The schoolteacher Robert Meyer had been convicted of violating this law by teaching reading in German to a ten-year-old. The Supreme Court overturned the conviction on the grounds that it violated fundamental rights of the individual.[401]

b. Sterilization, Birth Control and Abortion

i. Griswold v. Connecticut (1965)

This and the next case are the landmark cases in reproductive rights. As members of Planned Parenthood of Connecticut, Estelle Griswold and Dr. C. Lee Buxton provided advice on how to avoid conception to married persons and provided birth control to the wife. They were convicted as accessories violating a Connecticut law prohibiting the use of any drug or article to prevent conception. The Supreme Court overturned this decision on 14th Amendment grounds.[402]

In his majority opinion, Justice Douglas cites *NAACP v. Alabama* (discussed above) where the Supreme Court affirmed the "freedom to associate and privacy in one's associations" as a "peripheral First Amendment right." Justice Douglas describes this as a First Amendment "penumbra where privacy is protected from governmental intrusion." He opines that "the specific guarantees in the Bill of Rights have penumbras, formed by emanations from those guarantees that help give them life and substance…. Various guarantees create zones of privacy." In this case, attempts by the state to regulate conception and contraceptives violates the marital zone of privacy. More about zones of privacy in Part 2.

Note that *NAACP v. Alabama* and *Griswold v. Connecticut* share a basic ideal of "every autonomous citizen having an individual right of

---

[401] Meyer v. Nebraska, 263 U.S. 390 (1923), accessed 6/17/18 at https://supreme.justia.com/cases/federal/us/262/390/case.html

[402] Griswold v. Connecticut, 381 U.S. 479 (1965), accessed 6/17/18 at https://supreme.justia.com/cases/federal/us/381/479/case.html

privacy to be free from unwanted monitoring and interference by the government."[403]

ii. Roe v. Wade (1973)

The most famous right to abortion case in U.S. judicial history. The Supreme Court upheld a woman's right to abortion. In his opinion, Justice Blackmun noted that throughout most of 19th century, abortion practices were far more liberal than today. They became more conservative, over time, perhaps because of Victorian mores against sexual promiscuity, the medical threats to a woman's life, and – given a belief that life begins at the moment of conception – the State's interest in protecting the rights to the unborn child.[404] The Supreme Court retained and reaffirmed in Planned Parenthood v. Casey (1992).

c. Marriage and Divorce

i. Loving v. Virginia (1967)

This Supreme Court decision struck down a Virginia law preventing intermarriage between races, citing violation of the equal protection and due process clauses of the Fourteenth Amendment. Chief Justice Warren reiterated that "The clear and central purpose of the Fourteenth Amendment was to eliminate all official state sources of invidious racial discrimination in the States."[405]

ii. United States v. Windsor (2013)

26 years later, the U.S. Supreme Court upheld lower court judgements that the surviving same-sex spouse was entitled to a federal estate tax exemption. This effectively struck down the federal Defense of Marriage Act which had defined marriage as something with existed only between a man and a woman. Justice Kennedy cited both the Fifth and Fourteenth Amendments in his opinion.[406]

---

403 Allen and Rotenberg, 317.

404 Roe v. Wade, 410 U.S. 113 (1973), accessed 6/17/18 at https://supreme. justia. com/cases/federal/us/410/113/case.html

405 Loving v. Virginia, 388 U.S. 1 (1967). Accessed 6/17/18 at https://supreme. justia. com/cases/federal/us/388/1/case.html

406 United States v. Windsor, 570 U.S. ___ (2013). Accessed 6/17/18 at https:// supreme.justia.com/cases/federal/us/570/12-307/opinion3.html

d. Informational Privacy

This will provide another meaty topic for privacy. We will consider two cases to illustrate some points to be used later.

i. Whalen v. Roe (1977)

This Supreme Court case concerned a New York law requiring the filing of a copy of Class II prescriptions with the State Health Department for inclusion in computerized records. Information required included the medication and dosage, the prescribing physician, the pharmacy, and the patient's name, address and age. This law was passed to combat the flow of controlled substances into illegal channels. In unanimous decision, the Supreme Court acknowledged that there is an implicit threat to privacy in the collection of information in government computerized repositories. But the very act of collecting the data bears with it a responsibility to avoid unintentional disclosure. Given that New York had taken these concerns about privacy and its protection seriously, the Court found that no violation of any Constitutional right had been violated.[407]

ii. NASA v. Nelson (2011)

The U.S. President order that all contract employees working for the National Aeronautics and Space Administration (NASA) should be subject to the same identification standards as NASA government employees. This translated into a requirement for all NASA employees to undergo background checks, whether or not this had been a requirement at their time of hiring. Failure to complete this process could lead to denial to NASA facilities and face termination. This policy was challenged by contract employees and an invasion of informational privacy. At issue was a question about recent illegal drug use, drug treatment or counseling, and a questionnaire sent to the referent's references with open ended questions. The Supreme Court found that all the challenged questions were "reasonable, employment-related inquiries that further the Government's interests in managing its internal operations." It also noted that under the Privacy Act, all the information is "shielded by statute from unwarranted

---

[407] Whalen v. Roes, 429 U.S. 589 (1977). Accessed 6/17/18 at https:// supreme .justia.com/cases/federal/us/429/589/case.html

disclosure." We will talk more about the Privacy Act in a subsequent chapter.[408]

In his opinion, Justice Scalia added:

> Like many other desirable things not included in the Constitution, "informational privacy" seems like a good ideawherefore the People have enacted laws at the federal level and in the states restricting the government's collection and use of information. But it is up to the People to enact those laws, to shape them, and, when they think it appropriate, to repeal them. A federal constitutional right to 'informational privacy' does not exist.

Justice Scalia believed in originalism, "the view that the Constitution should be interpreted in accordance with its original meaning-that is, the meaning it had at the time of its enactment."[409]

University of Chicago law professor William Baude defined originalism as "the view that law laid down by the framers in the Constitution remains binding until we legally change it, such as through the amendment process.... Or differently, ... that the words in the Constitution have the same meaning over time, even if modern circumstances change, and even if we wish the words meant something else."[410]

Twenty-first Amendment

This amendment repealed prohibition as enacted in the 18th Amendment. Allen and Rotenberg tell us that "The Twenty-first Amendment arguably protects to 'privacy' of the evening cocktail as a personal choice barred by formal prohibition of alcoholic beverages."[411] It

---

[408] NASA v. Nelson, 562 U.S. 134 (2011). Accessed 6/17/18 at https://supreme.justi a . com /cases/federal/us/562/134/

[409] Definition taken from Center for the Study of Constitutional Originalism at the University of California School of Law. Accessed 6/17/18 at https://www. sandiego. edu/law/centers/csco/

[410] Aaron Blake, "Neil Gorsuch, Antonio Scalia and originalism explained," Washington Post, 2/1/17. Accessed 6/17/18 at https://www.washingtonpost. com/ news/the-fix / wp/2017/02/01/neil-gorsuch-antonin-scalia-and-originalism-explained/ ?utm_term=.dcc8f03d077e

[411] Allen and Rotenberg, 286-287.

restored the individual the right to drink alcohol, and returned the power to the states to regulate alcohol. We will not discuss it further.

Today, we may see temperance as a laughable folly. Perhaps in another 100 years, our descendants will see our efforts to legislate marijuana use a similar folly. Times change, and the law evolves, albeit sometimes very slowly.

Conclusion

> What is there more holy, what is there more carefully fenced round with every description of religious respect, than the house of every individual citizen? Here are his altars, here are his hearths, here are his household gods: here are all his sacred rites, all his religious ceremonies are preserved. This is the asylum of every one, so holy a spot that it is impious to drag any one from it.[412]
>
> **Cicero**

Even from ancient times, the individual had the right to be secure in person and property. That included the person, his reputation, his home, his land, and the rest of his physical personal property. The land issue was a bit conflated during the feudal period in England since all the land (and many of the homes) belonged to the King and was only granted or leased to others. Issues regarding inheritance and other disputes about land became matters were handled by governmental authorities whereas personal property disputes were relegated to ecclesiastical authorities. Injury to reputation could be prosecuted by either/both church and state. After the printing press made vernacular language books readily available, and after Henry VIII declared himself the absolute monarch over both church and state, printed language began to be regulated by the English government with greater vigor. This gave rise to new legislative and judicial decisions on the crimes of libel and seditious libel which built upon precedents involving heresy, slander, and treason.

Allen and Rotenberg tell us that "privacy law could be summed up as a set of legal rules, principles and policies that regulate physical,

---

[412] Translated by C. D. Yonge, 1891. Accessed 6/2/18 at http://www.perseus.tufts.edu/hopper/text?doc=Perseus%3Atext%3A1999.02.0014%3Atext%3DDom.%3Asection%3D109

informational, decisional, proprietary, associational, and intellectual privacy."[413] Our rules regarding physical intrusion can be traced from the English jurist Coke through our Constitutional Third and Fourth Amendments. It touches upon the guarded sanctity of the home as the center of private life.

Informational privacy is by far the larger privacy issue we will address throughout the rest of this book. You may have given the information because it is required by law or by your contractual relationship with a service provider. Or you may have given the information voluntarily. The real issue is its protection. All information security policies have requirements to protect the confidentiality, availability, and integrity of the information it stewards. Data breeches are violations of confidentiality.

Decisional privacy issues concern the right to freedom from government interference in the personal lives of individuals, married couples, and families. While an absolutely fascinating subject, it is beyond the scope of this book and will not be discussed further.

Proprietary privacy has its origins in U.S. law with advertisers' use of photographs of individuals without permission. We talked about this as a violation of tort law. In the digital age, proprietary privacy has extended to the ubiquitous problem identity theft.

Associational privacy concerns the right to associate with whom you choose privately, and the right to seek membership in a closed group. In the first case, we talked NAACP v. Alabama, where the Supreme Court upheld the NAACP's right to not disclose its membership rolls to the State of Alabama. These cases frequently are premised on the exclusion of people of different races, religions, sexual orientations, or sexes. While also a fascinating topic, we will not discuss it further.

Intellectual privacy concerns mental repose, which Allen and Rotenberg argue is a kind of privacy. It is the right to think, express, and share one's own thoughts without fear of government intervention. It may be to think about mathematics, verbalize non-democratic view, write a poem, or to express oneself through pornographic art. Our founding fathers believed that freedom of expression was essential in a democracy.

---

[413] Allen and Rotenberg, 6.

It acknowledged that the individual should be free to investigate diverse ideas and as a rational being to make her own decisions about her own life, as long as it didn't hurt others. This is a huge big idea which we will come back to in Part II.

PART II
The Present

Part II looks at the privacy mechanisms which emerged in government and the commercial world in the late twentieth and early twenty-first centuries. Technology, perceived threats to national security, and individual rights all collided as the privacy discussion moved forward.

Let's begin by looking at privacy legislation. The Privacy Act of 1974 finally spelled out how the government was going to protect the private information it held about its citizenry. In fact, this privacy discussion had raged in Congress for twenty years before it became law. Congressional hearings in the 1970s, about government intrusions into communications privacy lead to the laws restricting government surveillance, like the Wiretap Act and the Foreign Intelligence Surveillance Act (FISA).

These laws applied only to the USG. It did nothing to curb the commercial usage of private consumer information. Congress approached privacy protection one commercial sector at a time. It passed the Fair Credit Reporting Act in 1970, which included privacy provisions. The Health Insurance Portability and Accountability Act (HIPAA) emerged in 1996 to protect the privacy of all medical patients in the United States. Today, privacy laws like the EU's General Data Protection Regulation (GDPR), the California Data Protection Act, and Utah's Electronic Information or Data Privacy bill are squeezing Washington legislators toward broader federal privacy legislation.

We'll then look at the perspective taken by U.S. financial institutions. Generally Accepted Accounting Principles - used by companies for decades – reassured companies, shareholders, and government regulators that the company is being run responsibly and within legal parameters. Unfortunately, these alone were insufficient to prevent the financial crises which spawned laws like Sarbanes-Oxley

(SOX), Dodd-Frank, and Gramm-Leach-Bliley. These acts set the bar higher, inducing companies to adhere to more formal frameworks of governance, risk management, and compliance (GRC). In situations where the government recommended a specific framework, companies adopted them to hedge their bets against future regulatory action.

After that, we'll see how the such frameworks and the resulting norms were adapted to manage the privacy and security risks associated computer systems and private information. Traditional frameworks were used to inform the NIST-originated Cybersecurity Framework, which addresses both information and computer security. NIST is currently working on a Privacy Framework for information privacy.

With all these elements, we'll then be ready to look at our way forward in the future.

Chapter 7
The Privacy Act

We're going to take a deep dive into the Privacy Act in this chapter. There are several reasons for that. First, it gives us an opportunity to take a look at the historical events related to technology, war, politics, and social movements that shaped the ramp-up to this act. Most notably, the perceived threat of Soviet aggression played largely on the American psyche throughout the 1950s, and early 1960s. This prohibited Congress from getting to "yes" on privacy legislation until 1974. Evolving U.S. judicial interpretation of privacy rights rounds out this discussion.

Second, a detailed look at the language in and reasoning associated with the Privacy Act helps us understand how we think about privacy today. Some very smart people thought long and hard about how computers and data repositories would challenge American privacy. Fortunately for us, they wrote their thinking down, and we'll get to take a look at it. An understanding of these thought processes is essential to understanding the language used to talk about privacy today.

Third, it's an excellent illustration of how difficult it is in the United States to correctly balance between national security and individual rights, particularly in highly turbulent times. The reader should have some appreciation for this by the conclusion of this chapter.

Historical Introduction

Governments exercise extraordinary powers during national security crises. In democracies, the tacit understanding is that defense of the nation trumps individual rights in a time of imminent threat. After the crisis subsides, the balance between the two needs to be restored. For example, U.S. entry into World War I in 1917 enabled passage of the 1918 Sedition Act, which effectively curtailed free speech against the government. The conclusion of the war lead to its repeal in 1920.

But before, during, and after World War I, communism posed an internal national security threat. Anti-communism had been born during the previous century, when abysmal working conditions spawned by rapid industrialization and urbanization popularized Marxist-style labor activism. World War I spawned nationalism and aroused suspicions towards foreign born immigrants. In 1917, the Russian Revolution reinflamed American suspicions towards Bolsheviks and anarchists. After the war, industry stepped down from wartime production, unemployment rose, membership in labor unions increased, and xenophobic attitudes towards immigrants persisted.

The first U.S. Red Scare – an American fear of spreading communism and anarchism - occurred from 1919 to 1920. Bombs exploded in several cities and Attorney General Palmer authorized the arrest of anarchists across the United States. Believing that immigrants brought communist thinking with them from abroad, Palmer deported as many of them as possible with minimal consideration of their civil rights. Immigration quotas in 1921 and 1924 took it a step further by limiting the number of "undesirables" that might immigrate to this country.

Anti-communism gave way to anti-fascism as Hitler rose to power. During World War II, the Soviet Union eventually joined the United States and its allies, in a marriage of convenience, to defeat Nazi Germany. Once victory was assured in Europe, however, the U.S. and Soviet Union became opponents again, racing to claim territorial dominance for democracy and communism in what had been Nazi Germany. In 1949, the Soviets tested their first nuclear device. It appeared that the USSR had technologically caught up with the United States. It was now a bi-polar world. The same year, Mao Zedong finally prevailed in the Chinese civil war, bringing yet another communist sphere of influence into the world.

This created the context for the 1950s, an era of dichotomies. After the grueling ordeal of World War II, everyone wanted to believe that everything was fine - wonderful in fact. The economy rebounded from its post-war letdown by the middle of the decade, and consumerism flourished. The GI Bill made it possible for many people to go to college. The standard of living increased. We wanted to believe that our world and our families were like those depicted in TV shows like "*Father Knows Best*," where every American family lived in a safe suburban home, dad worked outside the home, mom contentedly thrived as a homemaker, and the kids were well adjusted and happy.

But beneath this veneer lurked a reawakened fear of communism which would fuel the second U.S. Red Scare. In Congress, the House Un-American Activities Committee (HUAC) extended its investigations into communist influence in Hollywood. Many actors would be blacklisted as a result of these investigations.[414] Two additional Congressional acts, the 1950 Internal Security Act and the 1952 Immigration and Nationality Act, were passed to keep Communists out of the United States, to keep tabs on Communists within the United States, and to expedite deportation of Communists from the United States. Sensational trials of Soviet spies - like Julius and Ethel Rosenberg – confirmed that Americans living among us had supplied atomic secrets to the Soviet Union.

Senator Joseph McCarthy catalyzed communist fears in his "Enemies Within" speech of 1950 when he claimed: "I have in my hand 57[415] cases of [State Department] individuals who would appear to be either card-carrying members or certainly loyal to the Communist Party…." [416] McCarthyism would mark the peak of Congressional activities against communists and held the seeds of its decline.

But the 1950s, also marked a time when Americans began to be disillusioned with their government. The U.S. entered both the Korean and Vietnam wars to contain the spread of Soviet and Chinese communism. Neither war lead to a decisive victory. In 1954, Senator McCarthy was censored by his Congressional peers and castigated by the press. Also, in 1954, the Supreme Court ruled in *Brown v. Board of Education* that

---

[414] Many HUAC witnesses – taking the Fifth in lieu of answering incriminating questions - were held in contempt and subsequently lost their jobs. While in 1951 the Supreme Court upheld such convictions under the Alien Registration Act of 1940, by 1956 the tide began to turn.

[415] Allegedly, the figure originally used in the speech was 205, but the number 57 appears in the official version of the speech.

[416] Joseph McCarthy, "Enemies Within" Speech Delivered in Wheeling, West Virginia (1950), accessed 10/12/18 at https://liberalarts.utexas.edu/coretexts /files/ resources/ texts/1950%20McCarthy%20Enemies.pdf

public-school segregation violated the Fourteenth Amendment, sparking massive resistance to integration in the South.

The technology race between the U.S. and the USSR continued. In 1957, when the Soviets successfully launched Sputnik - the first artificial satellite to orbit the earth - we worried that this presaged an era when the Soviets could launch nuclear warheads from their sphere of influence against U.S. targets.

Communist influence spread to our own backyard – Cuba. CIA's ill-fated Bay of Pigs invasion in 1961 was intended to stem the tide of spreading communism to Cuba. The 1962 Cuban Missile Crisis, brought on by U.S. discovery that the Soviets had deployed ICBMs to Cuba, was resolved by their removal by the USSR after thirteen very nerve-wracking days of negotiation. Many believe it was as close to nuclear war as we ever came during the Cold War.

By the 1960s, the U.S. citizenry was in full and righteous rebellion. The Civil Rights Act of 1964 enforced the constitutional right for all U.S. citizens to vote, and prohibited "discrimination and segregation on the ground of race, color, religion or national origin" in places of public accommodation (e.g. hotels, restaurants, movie theaters). The Civil Rights movement exploded with full force. The American public protested against the Vietnam War. The sexual revolution challenged traditional mores. The assassinations of heroes associated with different constituencies – John F. Kennedy, Robert Kennedy, Martin Luther King Jr., and Malcolm X – fueled disillusionment and revolt. Rioting occurred across the nation. The American public was not happy with the way the country was being run.

Having swung very far to the right during the anti-Communism movement during the 1950s, America attempted to restore some balance internally with respect to liberty and individual rights in the 1960s. Communist claims in past decades that the U.S. majority oppressed disenfranchised minorities (who made up the working class) now found resonance and response with the Civil Rights Movement in America. This was the time when every citizen demanded the same rights everyone else had, regardless of race, gender, religion, and national origin. The restoration of individual rights had begun.

The citizenry was still unhappy in the 1970s. Protests against the Vietnam War continued. The Pentagon Papers - featured in a 1971 *New York Times* front page article - revealed that the government had misled the American public about U.S. involvement and success in Vietnam.[417] The Watergate break-in of 1972 became a full-fledged scandal -covered by the media, investigated by the FBI and Congress - which induced President Nixon to resign in 1974 before he could be impeached.[418] Rumors, hearsay, and evidence that U.S. intelligence committee had not respected the rights of U.S. citizens began to emerge in the early 1970s. These were fully investigated by the Congressional Church[419] and Pike committees in 1975, and many of the allegations were substantiated. The findings of the committees made the American public even more jaded about and suspicious of their government.[420]

Privacy Activities in Congress Before the Privacy Act

In his book *Privacy and Freedom*, Alan Westin tells us that many former military intelligence and law enforcement officers, trained in U.S. Government schools in electronic eavesdropping, became private detectives after World War II.[421] Technological advances made possible by wartime investments were rebranded in peacetime for customers in

---

[417] The Pentagon Papers contained portions of a DoD history of the role of the United States in Indochina from World War II until 1968. They raised some very thorny First and Fourth Amendment issues after they were leaked to the New York Times and the Washington Post. The entire DoD history is available at https://www.archives.gov/research/pentagon-papers. A description of the judicial record the Pentagon Papers spawned is available at http://topsecretplay.org/the-courts/. Both accessed 6/23/19.

[418] A collection of political scandals, resulting in the prosecution of several individuals with ties to the Re-election Committee for the President (Nixon), and the only resignation of a president (before likely impeachment). Investigated and leaked by the Washington Post, Time, and the New York Times. A long and complicated story involving unauthorized surveillance, burglary, conspiracy, executive privilege, and First and Fourth Amendment challenges. Many sources available.

[419]Accessed 5/22/19, see https://www.intelligence.senate.gov/resources/intelligence-related-commissions

[420] Accessed 5/22/19 , see article on Congressional investigation of US Army surveillance against U.S. citizens at https://www.repository.law.indiana.edu/cgi/viewcontent.cgi?referer=&httpsredir=1&article=3019&context=ilj

[421] Westin, 90.

private detective firms and the business world. Anyone could buy telephone wiretaps, radio bugs, miniature recording devices, and cameras for surreptitious surveillance. In the absence of effective laws and regulations governing the use of these devices, their usage snowballed among private eyes and businesses as well as federal, state, and local officials.

Such gadgets fueled the public's imagination in spy movies like *Dr. No* (1962) and successive James Bond films, and in TV shows like *The Man from U.N.C.L.E.* (1964-1968). *The Prisoner* (1967-8) was a dystopian TV show about a retired spy who spent all his time trying to escape from the prison village where he was held. His captors were eternally trying to extract information from him. Referred to as merely "Number Six," the prisoner was no longer entitled to a real name. This show provided a remarkable depiction of Orwellian fears about loss of identity, freedom, privacy, and anonymity.

Congressional efforts to pass wiretapping legislation in the early 1950s, included hearings in both the House and Senate Judiciary committees. Confounded by partisan politics and the national security churn over communists "in our midst," Congress was unable to pass any wiretapping legislation in 1955.[422]

From 1958-1964, there was renewed interest in the House and the Senate in looking at the surveillance question. The Senate Subcommittee on Constitutional Rights was active between 1958 and 1962. It failed to obtain any information about federal wiretapping or eavesdropping from any of its executive branch witnesses, nor any information about state and local use of physical surveillance.[423]

Congressman John E. Moss (D-CA) lead the Special Subcommittee on Government Information of the House, which substantiated that in at least thirty-three federal agencies, federal employees were using technologies to listen-in and/or record telephone conversations. While initially only eight of the agencies had any regulations concerning the use of this technology, by 1962 the Moss Subcommittee determined that forty additional agencies had monitoring

[422] Westin, 179-183.
[423] Westin, 194.

regulations. The Department of Justice was one of the nine agencies that refused to adopt any such regulations.[424]

In 1962, the Senate Judiciary Committee held hearings on government and private wiretapping. The brothers Kennedy (the President and the Attorney General) favored passage of a law limiting private wiretapping and limiting law enforcement taps. As previously, "the same factual and ideological confrontation arose as in … 1954-55 among opponents of all wiretapping, supporters of a limited court-ordered system, and those wanting executive control of law-enforcement taps," and no wiretapping legislation ever reached either house of Congress for debate.[425]

Increased media coverage and public awareness about wiretapping and eavesdropping lit the fire on the debate in the 1960s. Popular books, films, and television laid bare the threats to privacy. By the time Senator Edward V. Long (D-MO) began hearings on his Subcommittee on Administrative Practices and Procedures in 1964, the pump was primed for privacy legislation.

The Long hearings reviewed the catalog of commercial viewing and listening devices available from industry and available to the government. The miniaturization of such devices was dramatically demonstrated after a private detective delivered his Congressional testimony. He played back his opening statement, captured by a miniaturized device hidden in an olive in the martini glass he had pretended to sip throughout his testimony.[426]

Senator Long took on the use of such devices by Treasury in racketeering and income-tax-evasion cases. His hearings revealed the use of such technologies by the Food and Drug Administration investigators. The Post Office revealed that it copied the covers of first-class mail envelopes of watchlisted individuals at the behest of law enforcement. Their prying eyes extended to opening the first-class letters of some

---

424 Westin, 194-195.
425 Westin, 195.
426 Brian Hochman, "Eavesdropping in the Age of 'The Eavesdroppers; or, The Bug in the Martini", Post 45, 2/3/16. Accessed 12/27/19 at http://post45. research. yale.edu/ 2016/ 02 /eavesdropping-in-the-age-of-the-eavesdroppers-or-the-bug-in-the-martiniolive/#identifier_71_6796

individuals, and using surveillance technology against its own employees.[427]

Having achieved a modicum of success, Long began investigations into practices of the FBI in 1965. The FBI had secured telephone lines from the phone company to eavesdrop on organized crime cases. It had placed many electronic bugs, including one in the hotel room of a lobbyist who was being indicted on tax-evasion. The bug enabled them to hear the lobbyist's conversation with his attorney, and that information was passed on to the prosecution.[428]

In 1965 and 1966, the Senate and House respectively passed what is known today as the Freedom of Information Act (FOIA).[429] Eleven years after assuming the chairmanship of the House Special Subcommittee on Government Information, Congressman Moss argued that this bill looked to "balance between the public need to know and a necessary restraint upon access to information in specific instances." He added that "Inherent in the right of free speech and of free press is the right to know."[430] Exemptions included information required to be kept secret for national security and foreign policy purposes, investigatory files for law enforcement, and "personnel and medical files and similar files the disclosure of which would constitute a clearly unwarranted invasion of personal privacy."[431]

FOIA was a step forward in terms of transparency in government. It left plenty of ambiguity when it prohibited disclosure of "personnel and medical files and similar files. which would constitute … a clearly unwarranted invasion of personal privacy." It completely failed to address the wiretapping and surveillance issue.

---

[427] Westin, 197

[428] Westin, 197-198

[429] See excellent legislative history records from the National Archives accessed 10/31/18 at https://nsarchive2.gwu.edu//nsa/foialeghistory/legistfoia.htm

[430] 112 Congressional Record 13007, accessed 10/31/18 at https://nsarchive2.gwu.edu//nsa/foialeghistory/112%20Cong.%20Rec.%2013007%20(1966%20Source%20Book).pdf

[431] FOIA, 1966, accessed 10/31/18 at https://www.gpo.gov/fdsys/pkg/STATUTE-80/pdf/STATUTE-80-Pg250.pdf

The Privacy Act

Time passed. The civil rights movement and Vietnam War continued to fuel public unrest and disillusionment in government. In the middle of the swirl and scandal of the early 1970s, a call came to amend FOIA. The act had been written so that the government, not the individual, was the judge of what was a citizen's private information. It had also failed to spell out any legal recourse for citizens whose FOIA requests were denied.[432]

Relevant legislative action finally came in 1974 when FOIA strengthening measures were incorporated into the Privacy Act, giving the requesting individual the right to file a complaint in court when a FOIA request was denied. But the Privacy Act itself went much further. It specifically addressed protection of individual's private information held by U.S. government agencies in the executive branch.[433]

The Privacy Act opens with words to explain why such an act was necessary then:

"Sec. 2. (a) The Congress finds that –

1. the privacy of an individual is directly affected by the collection, maintenance, use, and dissemination of personal information by Federal agencies;
2. the increasing use of computers and sophisticated information technology, while essential to the efficient operations of the Government, has greatly magnified the harm to individual privacy that can occur from any collection, maintenance, use, or dissemination of personal information;
3. the opportunities for an individual to secure employment, insurance, and credit, and his right to due process, and other legal protections are endangered by the misuse of certain information systems;
4. the right to privacy is a personal and fundamental right protected by the Constitution of the United States; and
5. in order to protect the privacy of individuals identified in information systems maintained by Federal agencies, it is necessary and proper for the Congress to regulate the

---

432 Accessed 10/31/18 at http://www.loc.gov/rr/frd/Military_Law/pdf/FOIA-1974.pdf
433 Accessed 10/31/18 http://www.loc.gov/rr/frd/Military_Law/pdf/LH_privacy_act-1974.pdf

> collection, maintenance, use, and dissemination of information by such agencies."

These opening words are illustrative of Congressional thought in 1974. (1) acknowledges that federally held records of private information affect the privacy of individuals. (2) brings the context right up to (then) modern times, when the information age is emerging and beginning to magnify the threat to individual privacy. (3) makes the threat real. It is not just highfalutin language about dangers to privacy, but threats to employment, insurance, credit, due process, and other legal rights. (4) substantiates that privacy is "a personal and fundamental right protected by the Constitution of the United States." I spent all of Part One of this book explaining the origins of the U.S. right to privacy, so this should not come as news. Finally, (5) ties all the pieces together. In the information age, it is necessary for the Congress to step in and regulate the use of private information by government agencies. The subtext here might be something like "We know you're fed up with the mess that the Executive Branch has made of things, so as your elected representatives we're going to try to step in and ensure they do the right thing with your private information in the future."

So, what were the remedies? Congress intended this Act to "provide certain safeguards for an individual against an invasion of personal privacy by requiring Federal agencies, except as otherwise provided by law, to -

1. Permit an individual to determine what records about him are collected, maintained, used, or disseminated;
2. Permit an individual to prevent records pertaining to him obtained by such agencies for a particular purpose from being used or made available for another purpose without his consent;
3. Permit an individual to gain access to private information pertaining to him in Federal agency records, to have a copy made of all or any portion thereof, and to correct or amend such records;
4. Collect, maintain, use, or disseminate any record of identifiable personal information in a manner that assures that such action Is for a necessary and lawful purpose, that the information is current and accurate for its intended use, that

that adequate safeguards are provided to prevent misuse of such information;

5. Permit exemptions from the requirement with respect to records provided in this Act only in those cases where there is an important public policy need for such exemption as has been determined by specific statutory authority; and
6. Be subject to civil suit for any damages which occur as a result of willful or intentional action which violated any individual's right under this Act."

This law formalized the responsibility which federal agencies had to protect private information of individuals. It prohibited disclosure of private information contained in its records to any other individual or agency, except by written request from the person described. A few exceptions were allowed, such as sharing of information with law enforcement if it pertained to a civil or criminal law matter. It required federal agencies to account for all disclosures made to individuals and agencies for at least five years. Every individual had a right to review, get copies, and amend the record containing private information about him in a timely manner.

Federal agencies were thereafter required to maintain the minimal amount of information about an individual necessary for its purposes as specific by law or Executive Order; attempt to collect private information about an individual directly from the individual; and let the individual know under what authority the information is being collected, its purpose, the expected uses of the information, and the effects of not providing the information. They were required to maintain records with "such accuracy, relevance, timeliness, and completeness as is reasonably necessary to assure fairness to the individual" in agency decision-making. Agencies were specifically prohibited from maintaining any record "describing how any individual exercises rights guaranteed by the First Amendment unless expressly authorized by statue or by the individual about who the record is maintained or unless pertinent to and within the scope of an authorized law enforcement activity."

Furthermore, federal agencies were required to "establish rules of conduct for persons involved in the design, development, operation, or maintenance of any system of records, or in maintaining any record, and instruct each such person with respect to such rules and the … penalties for noncompliance."

Finally, the Privacy Act highlights the need to "establish appropriate administrative, technical, and physical safeguards to insure the security and confidentiality of records and to protect against any anticipated threats or hazards to their security or integrity which could result in substantial harm, embarrassment, inconvenience, or unfairness to any individual on whom information is maintained."

The Privacy Protection Study Commission

A feature of the Privacy Act frequently overlooked was the creation of the Privacy Protection Study Commission (PPSC), chartered to "make a study of the data banks, automated data processing programs, and information systems of governmental, regional, and private organizations, in order to determine the standards and procedures in force for the protection of personal information." The Commission's 1977 report is a tour de force, and worth examining as it will be instructive later in this book.

The Commission rightly attributes the basic tenets of the Privacy Act to a 1972 report by the Health, Education and Welfare (HEW) Secretary's Advisory Committee on Automated Personal Data Systems. Already at that time, the HEW Secretary (Elliot Richardson) was thinking about personal privacy in record-keeping systems within his purview – especially those that affect citizens' records related to health, education, and welfare (e.g. entitlements programs like social security, Medicaid, Medicare, etc.). The HEW report outlines five fair information practices for all record-keeping organizations:

1. "There must be no personal-data record-keeping systems whose very existence is secret."
2. "There must be a way for an individual to find out what information about his is in a record and how it is used."
3. "There must be a way for an individual to prevent information about him obtained for one purpose from being used or made available for other purposes without his consent."
4. "There must be a way for an individual to correct or amend a record of identifiable information about him."

5. "Any organization creating, maintaining, using, or disseminating records of identifiable personal data must assure the reliability of the data for their intended use and must take reasonable precautions to prevent misuse of the data."[434]

These five fair information practices (FIPS) are generally acknowledged as providing a framework for the subsequent Privacy Act. The Privacy Protection Committee studied the HEW report, and concluded that Congress had expanded them into eight Fair Information Practice Principles (FIPPS)[435]:

1. "There shall be no personal-data record-keeping system whose very existence is secret and there shall be a policy of openness about an organization's personal data recordkeeping policies, practices, and systems. (The Openness Principle)
2. An individual about whom [sic] information is maintained by a record-keeping organization in individually identifiable form shall have a right to see and copy that information. (The Individual Access Principle)
3. An individual about whom information is maintained by a record-keeping organization in individually identifiable form shall have a right to correct or amend the substance of that information. (The Individual Participation Principle)
4. There shall be limits on the types of information an organization may collect about an individual, as well as certain requirements with respect to the manner in which it collects such information. (The Collection Limitation Principle)
5. There shall be limits on the internal uses of information about an individual within a record-keeping organization. (The Use Limitation Principle)

---

[434] Health, Education and Welfare (HEW) Secretary's Advisory Committee on Automated Personal Data Systems, "Records, Computers and the Rights of Citizens." Washington: U.S. Government Printing Office, 1973, p. 41, accessed 10/12/18 at https://www.justice.gov/opcl/docs/rec-com-rights.pdf

[435] There are many versions of FIPs and FIPPs. FIPs became a generic term which does not necessary refer to a specific set of recommendations, but the overall intentions of them. While we cover some in the body of this chapter, a fuller description is given in appendix 7A.

6. There shall be limits on the external disclosures of information about an individual a record-keeping organization may make. (The Disclosure Limitation Principle)
7. A record-keeping organization shall bear an affirmative responsibility for establishing reasonable and proper information management policies and practices which assure that its collection, maintenance, use, and dissemination of information about an individual is necessary and lawful and the information itself is current and accurate. (The Information Management Principle)
8. A record-keeping organization shall be accountable for its personal-data record-keeping policies, practices, and system. (The Accountability Principle)" [436]

The National Institute of Standards and Technology formalized the description of the FIPPS in NIST 800-53[437] as:

1. Authority (to collect) and Purpose (of collection)
2. Accountability, Audit, and Risk Management
3. Data Quality and Integrity
4. Data Minimization and Retention
5. Individual Participation and Redress
6. Security
7. Transparency
8. Use Limitation

We will come back to these in chapter eleven.

Over the course of their study, the Commission made a number of insightful observations about the information age in 1977:

1. Historically, face-to-face relationships between individuals enabled them to establish a certain level of trust and share information. Should one of them violate that trust, the relationship could be severed. This is not true in the

---

[436] The Privacy Protection Commission, "Personal Privacy in an Information Society: the report of the Privacy Protection Commission." Washington: U.S. Government Printing Office, 1977, pp. 501-502, accessed 10/12/18 at pp. 501-502, accessed 10/12/18 at https://babel.hathitrust.org/cgi/pt?id=pur1.32754076046428;view=1up;seq=520;size=125

[437] NIST SP 800-53 Rev. 4, April 2013. Accessed 12/2/19 at https://nvlpubs.nist.gov/nistpubs/SpecialPublications/NIST.SP.800-53r4.pdf

information age. The relationship is between an individual and an impersonal record-keeping organization. While the information may have been collected for one purpose, it can be used for others. It can be shared with other organizations, including the U.S. Government.

2. Individuals are motivated to provide private information in exchange for benefits and services. These extend to consumer-credit relationships, banking, mailing lists, insurance, employment, medical services, education, government-citizen interactions (e.g. taxes, government assistance programs), and government access to personal records (e.g. for law enforcement purposes).
3. There is a trend towards verifying information about individuals through other information sources. Alternate information sources are generally considered at least as reliable as information obtained directly from the individual.
4. The information record about an individual chart her life events. Similar instantiations of the records are generated via multiple avenues. Some of the records are copies of the information derived from the information held by other organizations. This accumulation of records can exercise unprecedented influences on decisions that affect the individual.
5. Neither the law nor technology equip the individual to protect his legitimate interests in the records kept by organizations.

Looking a little more carefully at these trends, the Commission concluded that three objectives were necessary for an effective privacy protection policy:

1. "Create a proper balance between what an individual is expected to divulge to a record-keeping organization and what he seeks in return *(to minimize intrusiveness)*."[438]
   Specifically, organizations need to inform the individual why certain information is being collected, understand what information should not be collected, and limit methods of collection.

2. "Open up record-keeping operations in ways that will minimize the extent to which recorded information about an

---

[438] The Privacy Protection Commission, 14.

individual is itself a source of unfairness in any decision about him made on the basis of it (*to maximize fairness*)."[439] It should allow the individual access to records about herself "for the purpose of reviewing, copying, and correcting or amending them as necessary plus some control over the collection and disclosure about [said] information…."[440] The Privacy Act was one example of this.
The Commission recommended that authorization from an individual before disclosure to other organizations should be the norm.[441] We will discuss this more when we talk more about "opt-in" and "opt-out" options later.

3. "Create and define obligations with respect to the uses and disclosures that will be made of recorded information about an individual *(to create legitimate, enforceable expectations of confidentiality)*."[442]
The individual should be prohibited from improper actions with respect to the records about herself. The record keeper should be prohibited from voluntary disclosure of information about an individual. The individual should be able to assert legal rights over improper and unreasonable disclosure requests involving her records.

In order to implement policy recommendations, the Commission recommended

1. Creating incentives for systemic reform. For example, the individual should be able to compel compliance even if she has suffered little or no injury.
2. Leveraging existing regulatory and enforcement mechanisms. This can be accomplished at the federal or state level. The Committee noted that "National bankers, insurers, retailers, and other industries subject to Federal regulations have strongly urged the Commission to recommend that any mandatory requirements be exclusively Federal so that they and, indeed, their customers, do not have to struggle with 50 separate sets of rules."[443]

---

[439] The Privacy Protection Commission, 14.
[440] The Privacy Protection Commission, 18.
[441] The Privacy Protection Commission, 19.
[442] The Privacy Protection Commission, 14.
[443] The Privacy Protection Commission, 32.

3. Avoiding unnecessary costs. The Commission did not recommend that any organization seek prior approval regarding its record systems, thus minimizing the cost to government.

In the case of repeated or systemic violations, the Commission recommended that the appropriate government agency (e.g. Federal Trade Commission) be assigned responsibility on behalf of the public for enforcing record-keeping compliance measures.[444]

The Commission stated that three implementation choices existed for enhancing privacy in records systems which could be used singly or in combined fashion across the public and private sectors. These included voluntary compliance, creation of laws which could be used to enforce privacy rights, establishment of government entities to "investigate, study, and report on privacy protection issues."[445] As we will see later, all three were adopted.

The Commission's Verdict on the Privacy Act

The Commission also took a look at the Privacy Act itself. One of its seminal conclusions was that the Privacy Act should not be extended to organizations beyond the Federal Government. The Commission cited a number of reasons for this conclusion:

1. The commercial world can be economically incentivized to protect individuals' information. Vendors can collect, store, and share private customer information, but customers aware of these practices can "use the competition of the marketplace as an ally in securing compliance with privacy protection safeguards." Additionally, companies found legally liable can suffer prolonged negative publicity and loss of market share, expensive legal battles and hefty fines, and their executives may risk being fined and/or going to jail. It behooves all companies to ferret out suitable fair information practices and proactively subscribe to them.[446]
2. The commercial world exhibits a greater degree of variability in administrative processes and practices than the

[444] The Privacy Protection Commission, 32.
[445] The Privacy Protection Commission, 33.
[446] The Privacy Protection Commission, 497.

government. Whereas a one-size-fits-all Privacy Act may be suitable for the USG, no such claim can be made across all of the American commercial world.[447]

3. A requirement for the commercial world to subscribe the Privacy Act would generate the need for considerable regulation, "giving government an unprecedented role in channeling and monitoring flows of information throughout society." More government insight into private information is not a good trade-off for more privacy in the commercial data stores of the commercial world.[448]
4. Some of the provisions of the Privacy Act concern the individual's constitutional rights which are guaranteed by the government, not industry. As the Commission says: "the restriction the Privacy Act places on the collection of information on an individual's exercise of his First Amendment rights would be ill-considered, and perhaps unconstitutional, if it were to be applied to all private sector organizations without limitation."[449]

Another issue that the commission considered was FOIA versus the Privacy Act. Since FOIA directed public disclosure and the Privacy Act limited public disclosure, some argued that they are contradictory. The Commission took the view that "they mesh well" without statutory conflict. When FOIA was passed (before the Privacy Act), government agencies were given discretionary authority to withhold information which could violate personal privacy. After the passage of the Privacy Act, personal private information was protected from disclosure – including FOIA disclosure - by law, rather than by individual discretion alone. FOIA disclosure of information that could violate personal privacy was specifically prohibited by law.[450][451]

---

[447] The Privacy Protection Commission, 498.

[448] The Privacy Protection Commission, 498.

[449] The Privacy Protection Commission, 498.

[450] The Privacy Protection Commission, 520.

[451] Admittedly, there was no agreement about what types of information, individually or collectively, could or could not be released, so there was some latent discretionary power that remained. This is actually an extremely complex subject, and beyond the scope of this book.

Conclusion

The Privacy Act marks a turning point in our law and history. Technology, war, politics, and social movements all shaped the privacy debate that began in the 1950s. The debate dragged on through the 1960s, and culminated in 1974 with passage of a privacy law which applied only to the USG. The language and concepts we use to talk about privacy today owe a lot to this era, as we shall see in succeeding chapters.

We spent considerable time looking at the specific language of the Privacy Act itself. Finally, Congress acknowledged that "the right to privacy is a personal and fundamental right protected by the Constitution of the United States." Concluding that it was within its purview to "protect the privacy of individuals identified in information systems maintained by Federal agencies," Congress decided it was time to regulate "the collection, maintenance, use, and dissemination of information by such agencies."

The Privacy Protection Committee concluded that extending a generic privacy law over the private sector was ill-advised. Designing one-size-fits-all privacy law did not appear tractable at that point in time. In fact, the government was already using a sectoral approach to protect the private information of consumers. We will investigate this more when we talk about federal laws enacted to protect privacy in the credit and medical arenas.

The commercial world never wants more laws and regulations with which to comply. I imagine commercial interests lobbied hard to persuade the PPSC to recommend against a broad privacy law. When, however, businesses see that new laws are inevitable, they change tactics. Now they lobby for the new rules to impose the minimal burden on their commercial interests. This is the tipping point that we are coming to today with privacy. Faced with an inevitable outcome that there will be privacy laws, companies will lobby for one federal law as opposed to 50 separate state laws. We will talk more about this idea in section three.

In the next chapter, we will dig into the history of privacy in communications in America that lead to the well-known Foreign Intelligence Surveillance Act in 1978.

Appendix 7A

The Code of Fair Information Practices (FIPs, sometimes FIPPs)

As a generic term, fair information practices (FIPs) are "a set of internationally recognized practices for addressing the privacy of information about individuals." [452] There are multiple versions of them which have been defined by the USG, referred to as FIPs or FIPPs.

This appendix is intended merely to highlight some of the ideas associated with different versions of fair information practices. Deeper study is required to understand the different nuances associated with each version.

The idea for a code of fair information practices began with a US Department of Health, Education, and Welfare (HEW) in the early 1970s. Its name is said to have been inspired by the Code of Fair Labor Practices.[453] The report outlined five fundamental privacy principles:

1. No secret record keeping systems
2. Individual should be able to see his data in record
3. Usage should be limited to purpose for which the information was provided
4. Individual should be able to correct/amend record
5. Organization must ensure reliability and prevent misuse of data.

These principles were used as a privacy framework for the Privacy Act in 1974. The Privacy Protection Study Commission (PPSC) refined the original five principles into eight:

1. Openness: No secret record keeping systems
2. Individual Access: Individual should be able to see his data in record
3. Individual Participation: Individual should be able to correct/amend record
4. Collection Limitation: Limits on what and how information is collected

---

[452] Bob Gellman, "Fair Information Practices: A Basic History", p. 1. Accessed 12/27/19 at https://bobgellman.com/rg-docs/rg-FIPshistory.pdf [453]Gellman, 2.

[453] Gellman, 2.

5. Use Limitation: Limits on internal usage of data
6. Disclosure Limitation: Limits on disclosure
7. Information Management: Organizational responsibility for lawful / necessary / accurate information collection/ maintenance / usage/ dissemination
8. Accountability: Organization should be accountable for personal data record keeping policies/practices/systems.

Overseas, the Organisation for Economic Cooperation and Development (OECD) authored a document in 1980 which revised the FIP principles and became internationally influential. [454] The OECD FIPs were:

1. Collection Limitation
2. Data Quality
3. Purpose Specification
4. Use Limitation
5. Security Safeguards
6. Openness
7. Individual Participation
8. Accountability.[455]

We will talk more about the OECD in chapter 11.

In a 1998 report, the Federal Trade Commission (FTC) identified the "five core principles of privacy protection" which were common to "widely-accepted principles concerning fair information practices:"

1. Notice/Awareness
2. Choice/Consent
3. Access/Participation
4. Integrity/Security
5. Enforcement/Redress.[456]

---

[454] Gellman, 10, 12.

[455] "OECD Guidelines on Protection of Privacy and Transborder Flows of Personal Data", 1980. Accessed 12/6/19 at http://www.oecd.org/sti/ieconomy/oecdguidelines ontheprotectionofprivacyandtransborderflowsofpersonaldata.htm

[456] Federal Trade Commission, Privacy Online: A Report to Congress 7 (1998), p. 7. Accessed 12/27/19 at http://www.ftc.gov/sites/default/files/ documents/ public_ events/exploring-privacy-roundtable-series/priv-23a_0.pdf.

In 2000, the FTC recommended that commercial websites should adhere to the "four widely-accepted fair information practices" when collecting private information:

1. Notice
2. Choice
3. Access
4. Security.[457]

In 2008, the Secretary of Health and Human Services (HHS) outlines eight core privacy principles:

1. Individual Access
2. Correction
3. Openness and Transparency
4. Individual Choice
5. Collection, Use, and Disclosure Limitation
6. Data Integrity
7. Safeguards
8. Accountability.[458]

In 2008, HHS subsequently established its Privacy and Security Framework, with the following principles:

1. Individual Access
2. Correction
3. Openness and Transparency
4. Individual Choice
5. Collection, Use, and Disclosure Limitation
6. Data Quality and Integrity
7. Safeguards
8. Accountability.[459]

---

[457] Federal Trade Commission, Privacy Online: Fair Information Practices in the Electronic Marketplace 36-37, (May 2000), p. iii. Accessed 12/17/19 at http:// www.ftc.gov/sites/default / files / documents/reports/privacy-online-fairinfor mation practices-electronic-marketplace-federal-trade-commission-report/privac y2000.pdf.
[458] Speech by HHS Secretary Mike Leavitt, 12/5/08, accessed 12/28/19 at https:// www.govtech.com / dc / articles / HHSs-Leavitt-Announces-New-Privacy-Principle s.html
[459] Office of the National Coordinator for Health Information Technology, US Department of Health and Human Services, "Nationwide Privacy and Security

We will talk more about the HHS Privacy and Security Framework in chapter nine.

In 2011, the White House included a version of the FIPPS in a National Strategy for Trusted Identities in Cyberspace report:

1. Transparency
2. Individual Participation
3. Purpose Specification
4. Data Minimization
5. Use Limitation
6. Data Quality and Integrity
7. Security
8. Accountability and Auditing.[460]

The White House issued a report in 2012, prepared by the Department of Commerce, which included a Consumer Privacy Bill of Rights that "applies comprehensive, globally recognized Fair Information Practice Principles."[461] These are:

1. Individual Control
2. Transparency
3. Respect for Context
4. Security
5. Access and Accuracy
6. Focused Collection
7. Accountability.

The FTC issued a privacy report in 2012 which "urged companies to adopt the following practices, consistent with the Fair Information Practice Principles first articulated almost 40 years ago:"

Framework for Electronic Exchange of Individually Identifiable Health Information", 15 December 2008, accessed 12/28/19 at https://www.healthit.gov /sites/default/files/ nationwide-ps-framework-5.pdf

460 The White House, "National Strategy for Trusted Identities in Cyberspace: Enhancing Online Choice, Efficiency, Security, and Privacy", April 2011. Accessed 12/28/19 at https://obamawhitehouse.archives.gov/sites/default/files/ rss_viewer/ NSTICstrategy_041511.pdf

461 The White House, "Consumer Data Privacy in a Networked World: A Framework for Protecting Privacy and Promoting Innovation in the Global Digital Economy", February 2012. Accessed 12/28/19 at https://obamawhitehouse. archives.gov /sites/ default/files/privacy-final.pdf

1. Privacy by Design
2. Simplified Choice for Businesses and Consumers
3. Greater Transparency.[462]

[462] Federal Trade Commission, "Protecting Consumer Privacy in an Era of Rapid Change: Recommendations for Businesses and Policymakers", FTC Report, March 2012. Accessed 12/28/19 at https://www.ftc.gov/sites/default/files/ docum ents/ reports/federal-trade-commission - report-protecting-consumer-privacy-era-rapid-change-recommendations/120326privacyreport.pdf

Chapter 8
Privacy in Communications

Constitutional wrangling about communications privacy is nothing new in the United States.

But in order to understand the modern debate, you have to understand its heritage.

This chapter is devoted to illuminating this heritage. As in the previous chapter, we'll see the interleaving of law with technology, war, politics and social movements. By the middle of the twentieth century, we'll see the citizenry assert its civil rights and demand curtailment of government powers over individuals. This subsequently led to course corrections in government.

Along the way, we will talk about the 1934 Federal Communications Act. The reason to call this out is that ambiguous interpretation of this act became a pivotal issue for law enforcement investigations, and judicial proceedings and decisions. Congress would finally sort this out later in the century by passing new laws regarding electronic surveillance.

We will also look at how U.S. domestic intelligence activities grew in the twentieth century. This growth was largely hidden from public view until the Senate's Church Committee investigations put the whole story together for the American public in the 1970s, and what a story it was. The committee hearings revealed civil rights abuses by the U.S. government against citizens (and non-citizens) throughout the twentieth century. Public faith in the U.S. government was severely shaken. Congress responded with proactive legislative actions to put an end to these abuses. This included the Foreign Intelligence Surveillance Act (FISA) of 1978. Seen in this light, FISA was a positive step, a point that should be remembered.

We will close this chapter by talking about the evolution of FISA until the present. It was driven by technological advances, the war on terrorism, public revelations about classified government activities, and public opinion. Once again, we'll see that the government continued to try to thread the needle between national security and privacy concerns.

Law Regarding Privacy of the U.S. Mail

The first privacy provisions in communications appeared in the 1792 Post-Office and Post Road Act. Establishing a U.S. Post Office for the delivery of letters, the act added that should any person working for the post office "unlawfully detain, delay, or open any letter, packet, bag or mail of letters," he could be fined up to $300 or imprisoned for up to six months for each offense.[463] These provisions were reiterated in the Post Office Act of 1825.[464]

The privacy right of letters was affirmed by the Supreme Court in 1878 in Ex parte Jackson:

> … letters, and sealed packages subject to letter postage … are fully guarded against examination and inspection, except as to their outward form and weight…. The constitutional guaranty of the right of the people to be secure in their papers against unreasonable searches and seizures extends to their papers, thus closed against inspection, wherever they may be. Whilst in the mail, they can only be opened and examined under … warrant….[465]

While the 1917 Espionage Act specifically prohibited the transmission or communication of national defense information, it also affirmed that no one should open any letter except under "search warrant authorized by law." Privacy of the mail was still assured, despite the fact that the thrust of this law was to prohibit the sharing of any national defense information by any means, including the mail.

In 1921, the Supreme Court denied that senders of second-class mail (e.g. newspapers and magazines) should be guaranteed the same right

---

[463] Accessed 5/30/19 at http://njpostalhistory.org/media/pdf/postact1792.pdf

[464] Accessed 7/26/19 at http://memory.loc.gov/cgi-bin/ampage?collId=llsl&file Name =004/llsl004.db&recNum=154

[465] Ex parte Jackson, 96 U.S. 787 (1878), accessed 6/10/19 at https://supreme.justia.com/cases/federal/us/96/727/

to privacy. Supreme Court Justice Oliver Wendell Holmes dissented: "the use of the mails is almost as much a part of free speech as the right to use our tongues…."[466]

The privacy of the mail would become a hot topic for decades to come. In 1970, Congress unequivocally affirmed, in the Postal Service Act, that first-class mail originating in the United States could not be opened except under authority of a search warrant.[467] As we will see shortly, even this did not resolve the privacy issue in the mail.

Emerging Privacy Challenges to Wired Communications

First-class letters in a sealed envelope provided a private channel of communications, but no such expectation was associated with telegraph messages. Such messages had to be transmitted through at least two intermediaries in order to get from sender to receiver.

The law was aware of the privacy challenges associated with the telegraph. Even before the Civil War, state statutes had prohibited the cutting or tapping of telegraph lines and the interception of telegraph messages.[468] No federal law would address the privacy of telegraphic messages until the twentieth century.

Telegraph companies were in the habit of saving the originals of telegraph messages and copies of their replies. This made good business sense. It protected them from allegations of having sent inaccurate or false messages. Over time, these same messages started to be used in "court and before legislative bodies, as instruments of evidence."[469]

---

[466] The Supreme Court found in favor of the Postmaster General, who had rescinded the right for the Milwaukee Social Democratic Publishing Company to use second class mail to distribute its newspaper because it violated the 1917 Espionage Act. See Milwaukee Social Democratic Pub. Co. v. Burleson, 255 U.S. 407 (1921), accessed 6/10/19 at https://supreme.justia.com/cases/federal/us/255 /407/

[467] Accessed 5/22/19 at https://www.govinfo.gov/content/pkg/STATUTE-84/ pdf / STATUTE-84-Pg719.pdf

[468] Westin, 337

[469] T. M. Cooley, "Inviolability of Telegraphic Correspondence." University of Pennsylvania Law Review, v. 27, 1882. Accessed 7/26/19 at https:// scholarship. law.upenn.edu/penn_law_review/vol27/iss2/1/

During the Civil War, both the Union and Confederate armies relied on (wired) telegraphy to communicate between headquarters and the field.[470] The U.S. Government took over the public telegraph companies (then Western Union, the American, and the Southwestern) during the war with an act of Congress.[471] This law made no provision for privacy of civilians using these services.[472] Both the Union and Confederacy relied on codes and ciphers to provide secrecy.[473] Both sides tapped their opponents' telegraph lines.[474]

After the Civil War, the tapping of telegraph lines presented an irresistible commercial opportunity to many. Some were unemployed Civil War veterans, some had worked or currently worked for a telegraph company. The tapping of telegraph lines required expertise. The physical tapping had to be done astutely to avoid detection. The skilled tapper needed to use a supplementary battery ensure that a fluctuation in signal strength didn't given the game away. He needed to minimize service interruptions – like those associated with cutting the line to insert one's own signaling and receiving device – to avoid suspicion. A telegrapher operating a tap had to be able to read and send Morse code flawlessly, and minimize suspicion that he was an unauthorized transmitter. This was all the more challenging since every telegraphic operator had his own rhythmic "fingerprint" for Morse, and could recognize the fingerprints of other operators.

Criminal schemes were devised using the skills of telegraphers to exploit bookies taking bets on horse races. As early as 1883, newspapers reported how criminals - by changing or delaying the telegraphic race results delivered to the bookie - could cheat and place winning bets.[475] Wiretapping became commonplace, used by criminals, enterprising

---

[470] Center for Cryptologic History (CCH), National Security Agency (NSA), "The Friedman Legacy: A Tribute to William and Elizebeth Friedman", 1992, second printing, p. 84.
[471] Railroad and Telegraph Seizure Act 1862, accessed 5/22/19 at https://www.originalsources.com/Document.aspx?DocID=U2GVADDEAT4BRX9
[472] CCH, 77.
[473] CCH, 84
[474] CCH, 97.
[475] Kerry Segrave, Wiretapping and Electronic Surveillance n America, 1862-1920. Jefferson, NC: McFarland and Company, Inc., 2014, p. 24.

detectives, and local police forces. Many states enacted laws against wiretapping over the course of the late nineteenth and early twentieth century.

At the same time, the Western Union Telegraph Company empowered its own investigatory unit to look into wiretapping incidents on its lines. This was an astute business move. Why? Firstly, the company had an obligation to provide swift, accurate, and reliable telegraph services to all customers. Tappers could jeopardize this. Secondly, Western Union was especially motivated to provide sterling service for its most lucrative customers, e.g. bookies.[476] Tappers could interfere with that. Thirdly, current and former Western Union employees had the skills to tap telegraph lines and participate in all sorts of criminal schemes, and many did. In order to preserve its reputation, Western Union was obliged to root these bad apples out. Fourthly, the local law and law enforcement capabilities against wiretapping matured slowly. In the absence of effective government action, Western Union was forced to protect itself.[477]

The telephone proliferated as a technology from the time of its invention. Unlike the telegraph, it didn't require going to a specific office to get the assistance of a skilled telegrapher to send a message. The telephone was destined for individual's homes, and required no expertise to operate. Yes, at least one operator had to assist in placing and establishing the call. But as a service available from one's home, telephony offered the customer a sense of greater privacy than the telegraph.[478]

It quickly became evident that telephone lines could be tapped. In 1898, two men were arrested after the Metropolitan Telephone Company of New York found a wiretap which enabled an individual to obtain insider information and make lucrative stock sales/purchases on the New York Stock Exchange. This was just one of many cases where criminals used

---

[476] There were ambiguities in the law. It wasn't clear whether a company was legal liable if it provided services to someone breaking the law, including a bookie. On the other hand, some government officials declined to prosecute telegraph tappers, arguing it was an effective way to help break up illegal bookie establishments.

[477] Segrave, 24, 32, 41, 49.

[478] Segrave, 20.

wiretapping to obtain private stock and commodity information to exploit the markets.[479]

In these early days, many stories came to light of companies, law enforcement, and the federal government wiretapping the telegraph and telephone lines of labor unions. In a *New York Sun* newspaper article on June 13, 1916, the public learned that a consortium of labor leaders had asked a New York legislature investigative committee (the Thompson Commission) to make available the names of 350 individuals (not all of whom were labor union figures) who had been wiretapped on the authority of the New York Police Department, as well as the transcripts of their overhead conversations. The labor union's letter referred to the "'the Russianized secret service in New York at this time.'" Specifically, the letter asked the committee "'to make public the private understanding that permits the Police Department to allow these private detective agencies to tap wires and install dictographs and detectaphones, break into offices, smash desks and copy private correspondence.'"[480]

The dictograph appeared in 1911 as the world's first electronic bug (the detectaphone was a similar but competing model). The bug was basically a listening device about the size of a man's palm. It was to be hidden in the room where the conversation to be overheard took place. Attached to it were two wires to provide a wired connection to a battery and a receiver at some distance. Beginning life as an inter-office intercom several years earlier, the dictograph quickly became a surveillance device of choice for businesses, government, law enforcement, and detective agencies. The downside of course was that someone had to be at the receiving end to transcribe the conversation. The investigatory powers of the dictograph helped collect evidence against corruption in government, labor leaders planning strikes, spouses seeking divorce, and even innocent individuals being framed.[481]

---

[479] Segrave, 67.

[480] Accessed June 10, 2019 at http://nyshistoricnewspapers.org/lccn/sn83030272/1916-06-13/ed-1/seq-6/ [481]Segrave, 141-153.

[481] Segrave, 141-153.

A Useful Note on Terminology

It's worth noting that a subtle distinction arose in vernacular usage between the terms "wiretapping" and "eavesdropping." "Wiretapping" originally referred to unauthorized physical connection into a telegraph wire. This idea carried over cleanly into the early era of telephony, but the definition became muddied as telegraphy and telephony adopted wireless technologies. In the early twentieth century, the dictograph made it possible to conduct electronic "eavesdropping," listening in with a wired microphone to a conversation in another room. U.S. law actually evolved separately for wiretapping and electronic eavesdropping, as we will see.

Somewhere along the way, the term "electronic surveillance" came along. In 1968, Congress would pass the Wiretapping and Electronic Surveillance provisions of the Omnibus Crime Control Act (more about this later). The distinction between wiretapping and electronic surveillance was not defined in this act. However, the law did generically prohibit the interception and disclosure of wire and oral communications by electronic, mechanical or other devices. Today, electronic surveillance is used as a generic term for all such activities.

Law, Regulation, and Privacy in Wired and Wireless Communications Systems

In the late nineteenth century, the public services provided by telegraph and railroad companies proliferated, giving rise to government regulation. In 1887, Congress created the Interstate Commerce Commission to regulate the railroads. This act referred to the "common carrier," defined as any entity involved in the interstate "transportation of passengers or property by railroad, or partly by railroad … for a continuous carriage or shipment."[482] This law required every common carrier to offer each service at the same price to all persons.

While only the railroads were called out as common carriers subject to government regulation in this law, the handwriting was on the wall for telegraphy. The Supreme Court had already ruled in 1881 that with respect to commerce, a telegraph company was a "carrier of

---

[482] Accessed 6/13/19 at http://www.legisworks.org/congress/49/session-2/chap-104.pdf

messages" just as a railroad was a "carrier of goods."[483] Future federal regulation would refer to all telecommunications providers as "common carriers," a term still used today.

By the early twentieth century, wireless technology became a reality. In 1910, Congress amended the 1887 Interstate Commerce Act, extending the ICC's purview to include telegraph, telephone, and cable ("wired and wireless") companies, which were now also considered common carriers.[484] Regulation had come into being for telecommunications.[485]

The Radio Act 1912 applied to all "radio communication," meaning "any system of electrical communication by telegraphy or telephone without the aid of any wire connecting the points from and at which the radiograms, signals, or other communications are sent or received."[486] It established the first licensing of specific frequencies for users, a legal authority which the government exercises to the present day. It also included a privacy provision, requiring secrecy of radio messages be maintained. It said:

> No person or persons engaged in or having knowledge of the operation of any station or stations, shall divulge or publish the contents of any messages transmitted or received by such station, or their authorized agent, or to another station employed to forward such message to its destination, unless legally required so to do by the court of competent jurisdiction or other competent authority.

Any person found guilty of divulging the contents of a radio message to anyone besides the intended recipient would be subject to a fine and or imprisonment.

After the United States entered World War I, President Wilson seized control of all U.S. telegraph and telephone systems on the basis of

---

483 Telegraph Company v. Texas, 105 U.S. 460 (1881), accessed 6/10/19 at https://supreme.justia.com/cases/federal/us/105/460/

484 Accessed 5/30/19 at http://legisworks.org/sal/36/stats/STATUTE-36-Pg539. pdf

485 This was the anti-monopolistic era of the trustbusters, and the Federal Trade Commission (FTC) – the government's second regulatory body – would come into being in 1914. See the original law, accessed 5/30/19 at http://legisworks.org/congress/63/publaw-203.pdf

486 Accessed 5/30/19 at http://legisworks.org/sal/37/stats/STATUTE-37-Pg302b. pdf

national defense and security. He put them under the control of the Postmaster General.[487] Three months later, Congress passed an act to protect the users of the telephone and telegraph services and their properties during Government operation and control. It specifically stated that anyone who may

> without authority and without the knowledge and consent of the other users thereof, except as may be necessary for operation of the service, tap any telegraph or telephone line, or willfully interfere with the operation of such telephone and telegraph systems or with the transmission of any telephone or telegraph message, or with the delivery of any such message, or whoever being employed in any such telephone or telegraph service shall divulge the contents of any such telephone or telegraph message to any person not authorized or entitled to receive the same [shall be subject to fine and/or imprisonment].[488]

There are some subtle, yet crucial, points here. Firstly, this law authorized representatives of the telegraph/telephone company to have access to the system needed to assure its smooth operation. This operation included the successful transmission of messages for clients. To accomplish this, the representatives needed access not only to the message itself, but to the external physical and/or invisible electronic envelope used to route it and assess a charge to the customer.

That brings us to the second point. The law prohibited unauthorized personnel from divulging the contents of telephone/ telegraph messages. Later on, we will see that communications privacy will come to involve not only the contents of messages, but also the additional information used in delivery and billing. This will lead to a distinction being made between the contents of a message and its metadata. But we are getting ahead of ourselves.

Thirdly, "authority" could extend to the government. Federal government authorities could be authorized access for purposes of national security and law enforcement. This could include censorship, a typical

---

[487] See Wilson's proclamation of July 22, 1918, accessed June 10, 2019 at https:// cybertelecom.blogspot.com / 2016/08/aug-1-1918-pres-woodrow-wilson. html [48]

[488] Accessed 6/17/19 at https://www.loc.gov/law/help/statutes-at-large/65th-congress/session-2/c65s2ch197.pdf

government activity undertaken during wartime for national security and public morale purposes. Censorship was enacted during World War I, and the 1918 Sedition Act specifically permitted the Postmaster General to restrict delivery of letters which violated the 1917 Espionage Act.[489] Such behavior could and did extend to law enforcement, as we will see shortly.

Fourthly, the government could and did exercise these powers to gain complicity of the common carriers. In some cases, the government would rely on existing federal laws or court orders to get this assistance. In other cases, it relied on Attorney General certification, the exercise of Presidential privilege, or persuasion by government representatives.

The Radio Act of 1927 repealed and replaced the 1912 Radio Act. It created a Federal Radio Commission to license and regulate radio frequencies.[490] As the party responsible for licensing radio stations (to include broadcast stations), the government was careful to prescribe that the First Amendment right to free speech would not be impeded by its licensing process:

> Nothing in this Act shall be understood or construed to give the licensing authority the power of censorship over the radio communications or signals transmitted by any radio station, an no regulation or condition shall be promulgated or fixed by the licensing authority which shall interfere with the fright of free speech by means of radio communication.

The privacy provision of the 1912 Radio Act was echoed and enhanced in this act:

> No person receiving or assisting in receiving any radio communication shall divulge or publish the contents, substance, purport, effect, or meaning thereof except through authorized channels of transmission or reception [except to the intended recipient, or to] a telephone, telegraph, cable, or radio station employed or authorized to forward such radio communication to its destination….

---

[489] The law specifically stated that all such mail should be marked "Mail to this address undeliverable under the Espionage Act" and returned to local postmasters, who should in turn return the mail to senders "under such regulations as the Postmaster General may prescribe." Accessed 7/31/19 at http://www.legisworks. org/congress/65/publaw 150.pdf

[490] Accessed 5/30/19 at http://legisworks.org/congress/69/publaw-632.pdf

It prohibited the interception and divulging of such messages by unauthorized individuals. People who came unknowingly to be in possession of such interceptions were prohibited from divulging their contents when they became aware that the information had been obtained through such interception. The act made specific provisions to ensure fair methods of competition and anti-monopolization. Finally, it defined radio communication(s) as:

> any intelligence, message signal, power, pictures, or communication of any nature transferred by electrical energy from one point to another without the aid of any wire connecting the points from and at which the electrical energy is sent or received and any system by means of which such transfer of energy is effected [sic].

The 1934 Communications Act

The 1934 Communications Act was passed "For the purpose of regulating interstate and foreign commerce in communication by wire and radio so as to make available ... to all people of the United States a rapid, efficient, Nation-wide, and world-wide wire and radio communication service ... at reasonable charges, for the purpose of the national defense...."[491]

This act also created the Federal Communications Commission (FCC) to centralize regulatory authority for the regulation of communications services. Heretofore, the FCC would be responsible for the licensing and regulation of radio channels and wireline systems, to include broadcast radio stations, telegraphy, and telephony. It carefully defined terms for wire communication, radio communication, and common carriers:

> 'Wire communication' ... means the transmission of writing, signs, signals, pictures, and sounds of all kinds by aid of wire, cable, or other like connection between the points of origin and reception of such transmission, including all instrumentalities, facilities, apparatus, and services (among other things, the receipt, forwarding, and delivery of communications) incidental to such transmission.

[491] Accessed 5/30/19 at http://www.legisworks.org/congress/73/publaw-416.pdf

> 'Radio communication' … means the transmission by radio of writing, signs, signals, pictures, and the sounds of all kinds, including all instrumentalities, facilities, apparatus, and services (among other things, the receipt, forwarding, and delivery of communications) incidental to such transmission.
>
> 'Common carrier' … means any person engaged as a common carrier for hire, in interstate or foreign communication by wire or radio or in interstate or foreign radio transmission of energy… [and not including radio broadcasting entities].

The 1934 Act reiterated that antitrust laws still applied, and affirmed that the FCC would regulate in accordance with these (and all other) existing laws. Just as in the 1927 Radio Act, this law prohibited the government (now the FCC) from exercising any censorship or abridging free speech over radio communication.

Section 605 of the Federal Communications Act prohibited anyone receiving or transmitting "any interstate or foreign communication by wire or radio" (e.g. telephone or telegraph) from disseminating that communication to anyone besides the intended recipient except in response to subpoena or lawful authority. The whole of Section 605 is provided in appendix 8A for completeness. This provision, also adopted from the Radio Act of 1927, was upheld by the Supreme Court in 1937, and again in 1939.

We will talk more about this provision when we get to the Church Committee report later in this chapter. What we can say for now is that federal, state and local law enforcement disregarded Section 605 and these Supreme Court decisions, arguing that wiretapping and eavesdropping were indispensable tools for apprehending criminals. Congressional interest in passing any clarifying legislation would wane during the buildup, duration and aftermath of World War II.

The Omnibus Crime Control and Safe Streets Act of 1968

In the 1960s, the federal government still believed that the Soviet Union was trying to fuel the fires of the Civil Rights movement by encouraging white supremacist, black rights, and Vietnam anti-war unrest. Civil rights demonstrations which escalated into violence posed demonstrable challenges to internal security. The government reacted by calling out the national guard and /or federal troops repeatedly to quell civil unrest. As in other times of crisis, extraordinary powers were exercised by government which trumped civil rights.

In February, 1966, the FCC issued an order which prohibited the use of any radio device for eavesdropping on private conversations without the consent of all parties involved in the conversation. Now merely a footnote in history, Westin saw this in 1967 as "an important conceptual breakthrough in its official recognition of the threat to personal and group privacy through what we have called 'surveillance by reproducibility.'" [492] Around the same time, individual states were beginning to weigh in legislatively and judicially in favor of privacy.

FOIA had provided a first - but inadequate - step forward in terms of transparency in government in 1966. It failed to address ongoing concerns about wiretapping and surveillance issues. President Johnson publicly committed to addressing this in his 1967 State of the Union address, nothing that:

> We should protect what Justice Brandeis called the 'right most valued by civilized men' – the right to privacy. We should outlaw all wiretapping – public and private – wherever and whenever it occurs, except when the security of the national is at stake – and only then with the strictest safeguards. We should exercise the full reach of our Constitutional powers to outlaw electronic 'bugging' and 'snooping.'[493]

In 1968, the Omnibus Crime Control and Safe Streets Act spelled out the rules for wiretapping and electronic surveillance. Title III - containing the provisions for "Wiretapping and Electronic Surveillance" - would come to be known as the Wiretap Act.[494] Noting that wiretapping and microphone surveillance had been broadly used by private entities and the government without consent or legal sanction, it made unauthorized interception of wire and oral communications by the government and private parties illegal. It outlawed the sale of electronic, mechanical, or

---

492 Westin, 201.

493 Accessed 7/21/19 at https://millercenter.org/the-presidency/presidential-speeches/january-10-1967-state-union-address

494 Note that the language had evolved far enough by this point that the word "eavesdropping" is not used.

other communications intercepting equipment. It established procedures for government officials to obtain wiretapping warrants based on "probable cause … that an individual is committing, has committed, or is about to commit a particular offense," and regulated disclosure and use of intercepted communications by law enforcement and investigative officers. It also prohibited unauthorized interceptions from being used as evidence in any court.[495]

Finally, this law stated that none of its provisions, or those of the 1934 Communications Act,

> shall limit the constitutional power of the President to take such measures as he deems necessary to protect the Nation against actual or potential attack or other hostile acts of a foreign power, to obtain foreign intelligence information deemed essential to the security of the United States, or to protect national security information against foreign intelligence activities…. The contents of any wire or oral communication intercepted by authority of the President in the exercise of the foregoing powers may be received in evidence in any trial hearing, or other proceeding only where such interception was reasonable, and shall not be otherwise used or disclosed except as is necessary to implement that power.

This left enough wiggle room for warrantless electronic surveillance to continue on President Nixon's authority, which it did.[496]

The 1970s,

During the summer of 1973, the American public watched spellbound as the Senate hearings about the Watergate scandal were broadcast to televisions across the nation on public access stations. The message the public couldn't help but take away was that parts of the government were rotten all the way to the top. The complicity of executive branch agencies in the crime and the cover-up added fuel to the fire. While passage of the Privacy Act in 1974 was a positive move by government in the right direction, the constitutional crisis catalyzed by Watergate eclipsed it.

---

[495] Accessed 6/21/19 at https://www.govinfo.gov/content/pkg/STATUTE-82/pdf/STATUTE-82-Pg197.pdf

[496] Church, 79.

Congress had to act. It had to investigate exactly what was going on with respect to the use of intelligence resources and authorities which might abridge civil rights. And so, in 1975, the Senate created its Select Committee to Study Governmental Operations with Respect to Intelligence Activities, looking specifically at the FBI, CIA, and NSA. Chaired by Senator Frank Church (D-ID), it came to be known as the Church Committee. Even after Sen. Church's work was done, a permanent Senate committee – the Senate Select Committee on Intelligence (SSCI) - was created to provide continuing oversight on intelligence community activities.

The House created its own Permanent Select Committee on Intelligence. Chaired by Representative Otis G. Pike (D-NY), it came to be known as the Pike Committee. Again, even after Rep. Pike's work was done, the House Permanent Select Committee on Intelligence (HPSCI) was created to provide continuing oversight on intelligence community activities. The overall conclusions of both committees were that executive branch agencies had been taking liberties with citizens' privacy.

The Church and Pike committee reports are both fascinating reading.[497] For the purposes of brevity, we will focus on the Church Committee report which covered the rise of U.S. domestic intelligence in depth.

The Church Committee: The Rise of Domestic Intelligence in the United States

The Church Committee couched its findings about the civil-rights-abridging activities of the FBI, the CIA, and the NSA in the context of twentieth century history. Congress had access to information that the average citizen did not. The Church Committee delved into non-public records of the FBI, of the Attorney General, and others, in order to explain (not excuse) the government's heavy-handed actions to perceived threats

[497] The Pike Committee Report was not be publicly released by the government (it's a long story). Fortunately for the historian, its contents were leaked and ultimately printed. The report is complementary to the Church report, adding details on CIA covert action, intelligence failures, unwillingness of executive branch agencies to produce documents for the committee, etc. Accessed 7/31/19 at https://archive.org /details/PikeCommitteeReportFull

during hot wars and the Cold War. So now we will go back and synopsis the Church Committee's inside-baseball version of U.S. history, largely based on the government perceptions of the threat facing the nation during the twentieth century.

U.S. domestic intelligence programs of the twentieth century did not spring fully formed, like Athena, from Zeus's head. Their modern roots go back to World War I, and included the Department of Justice's Bureau of Investigation (BOI, later the FBI), other federal intelligence agencies, and the volunteer American Protective League. The BOI took part in the Palmer Raids and other activities against alleged "subversives."[498]

By 1924, the Great War and the First Red Scare were over. Upon assuming the role of Attorney General that year, Harlan Fiske Stone stated that the conduct of the BOI had been "lawless, maintaining activities which were without any authority in federal statutes, and engaging in many practices which were brutal and tyrannical in the extreme." He alluded to activities of the BOI as those of secret police abusing power, adding that:

> The Bureau of Investigation is not concerned with political or other opinions of individuals. It is concerned only with their conduct and then only with such conduct it is forbidden by the laws of the United States. When a police system passes beyond these limits, it is dangerous to the proper administration of justice and to human liberty, which it should be our first concern to cherish.[499]

Appointing J. Edgar Hoover as Acting Director of the BOI, Stone directed Hoover to adhere to the following standard:

> The activities of the Bureau are to be limited strictly to investigations of violations of law, under my direction or under the direction of an Assistant Attorney General regularly conducting the work of the Department of Justice.[500] [501]

---

[498] Church Committee (US Senate Select Committee on Intelligence Activities Within the United States, "Intelligence Activities and the Rights of Americans: 1976 US Senate Report on Illegal Wiretaps and Domestic Spying by the FBI, CIA and NSA." St. Petersburg, FL: Red and Black Publishing, 2007, p.24.

[499] Ibid.

[500] Church, 24.

[501] Stone left his post as Attorney General the following year for a seat on the Supreme Court.

In 1934, President Roosevelt asked the FBI to investigate the activities of the Nazi movement in the United States. In 1936, the president further tasked the FBI to investigate subversive – particularly Fascist and Communist – activities in the United States. Hoover's notes describe a request by FDR to take a look at the overall movement and its potential for having an impact on economic and political life. By late 1938, the president issued an order to investigate "all espionage, counter espionage, and sabotage matters," and entrusted it to FBI, military intelligence (Army), and the Office of Naval Intelligence. The president broadened the FBI's responsibilities to include "matters relating to espionage, sabotage, and violations of the neutrality regulations" after the outbreak of World War II.[502]

Although the Supreme Court had ruled in 1939 that wiretapping was illegal,[503] in 1940 the President instructed Attorney General Robert Jackson to wiretap suspected subversives and spies. FDR required the Attorney General to authorize each wiretap and limit wiretapping to aliens "insofar as possible."[504] Somewhere in these murky details lay the origins of the FBI's Custodial Detention List, a watchlist of pro-Axis sympathizers within the United States who could be rounded up in the event of war.

While the 1934 Communications Act had made it illegal to wiretap, Attorney General Jackson interpreted that to mean it applied to everyone except the federal government. He reasoned that Section 605 illegality to "intercept and divulge" communications did not apply if the information never left the federal government. This view was accepted by attorney generals until 1968, but never by the courts. Congress did consider legislating an exception to the 1934 act to codify Jackson's interpretation in law, but ultimately left the decision up to presidential discretion.[505]

Over the course of these developments, efforts were made by the President, Attorney General, and FBI Director to keep Congress in the

---

502 Church, 25-26.

503 Nardone v. United States, accessed 6/12/19 at https://supreme.justia.com/ cases/ federal/us/308/338/

504 Church, 25-27, 32.

505 Church, 32-33.

dark. When Congress became witting of any extraordinary powers being exercised by the FBI under presidential authority, it chose to ignore them. Instead, it passed wartime criminal statutes. The 1938 Voorhis Act required registration of individuals who were "agents of a foreign principal."[506] The 1940 Smith (or Alien Registration) Act made certain subversive activities unlawful, amended previous immigration acts to expedite detainment and deportation of aliens, and required registration and fingerprinting of all aliens seeking visas to enter the United States.[507]

After the United States entered World War II, President Roosevelt issued proclamations concerning the apprehension of German, Japanese, Italian, Romanian, Hungarian, and Bulgarian aliens in the United States.[508] These individuals were subsequently interned, paroled, released, or "repatriated." Hoover crowed about his successes in newspaper releases in October, 1943, admitting that the FBI had been investigating individuals with pro-Axis sympathies before the U.S. had entered the war. This had enabled the FBI to detain 1,771 suspicious individuals on 8 December 1941, the day after Pearl Harbor.[509]

FBI concerns about subversive infiltration also led the Bureau to investigate lawful groups and citizens, to include those in industry, youth groups, labor organizations, newspapers, African-American groups, church groups, political groups, and even the armed forces. This information was passed directly to the White House.[510]

In 1943, Attorney General Francis Biddle declared that the Custodial Detention List was "impractical, unwise, and dangerous" and ordered its abolition. He did not believe these actions were supported by existing laws nor justified by any other - including wartime - circumstances. Echoing former Attorney General (now Justice) Stone, Biddle stated that:

---

[506] Accessed 6/1/19 at http://legisworks.org/congress/75/publaw-583.pdf

[507] Accessed 6/11/19 at http://legisworks.org/congress/76/publaw-670.pdf

[508] Accessed 6/11/19 at https://vault.fbi.gov/Custodial%20Detention/Custodial%20Detention%20Part%201%20of%203/view#document/p5

[509] Accessed 6/11/19 at https://vault.fbi.gov/Custodial%20Detention/Custodial%20Detention%20Part%203%20of%203/view, pp. 8-9.

[510] Church, 29-30.

> The Department fulfills its proper function by investigating the activities of persons who may have violated the law. It is not aided in this work by classifying persons as to dangerousness.[511]

The FBI ignored the Attorney General's instruction. It changed the name of the Custodial Detention List to the Security Index and "continued to maintain an index of persons 'who may be dangerous or potentially dangerous to the public safety or internal security of the United States.'"[512]

Beginning in 1945, there were instances of wiretapping initiated by and against executive aides in the White House. Some involved private conversations suspected individuals had had with such prominent personages as Supreme Court Justice Felix Frankfurter and the journalist Drew Pearson.[513]

World War II ended, but the wartime mentality of domestic intelligence operations persisted. According to the Church Committee:

> The domestic intelligence programs of the FBI and the military intelligence agencies, established under presidential authority before World War II, did not cease with the end of hostilities. Instead they set the pattern for decades to come.[514]

This wartime mentality synergized Cold War hysteria. By 1946, the FBI had notified Attorney General Clark that it had compiled a Security Index of "potentially dangerous" individuals.[515] The Internal Security Act of 1950[516] called for registration of communist groups and their members, and legalized internment of spies/saboteurs during times of crisis.[517] The FBI chose to ignore the 1950 law because it was narrower than the program they already had in place. The Bureau would eventually

---

[511] Church, 32.
[512] Ibid.
[513] Church, 33.
[514] Church, 34.
[515] Church, 44.
[516] President Truman vetoed this bill, but Congress overrode his veto.
[517] Accessed 6/11/19 at http://legisworks.org/congress/81/publaw-831.pdf

shorten the Security Index, placing the removed names on a secret new Communist Index, which then became the Reserve Index in 1960.[518] [519]

Public statements by presidents Truman and Eisenhower [520] authorized FBI investigations into subversive activities. President Kennedy moved supervision of these investigations from the National Security Council to the Attorney General in 1962, and Attorney General Robert F. Kennedy reauthorized the FBI investigations in 1964.[521]

The FBI investigated the subversive activities of Communist, socialist and "New Left" groups like the Communist Party; infiltrated private groups such as the NAACP,[522] anti-war protesters, and civil rights movement groups; and investigated racial matters and hate groups, like the Ku Klux Klan and the John Birch Society.[523]

Church Committee: Domestic Intelligence Revelations

Times of national crisis require the government to exercise extraordinary powers. The censoring of international communications (letters, telegrams, telephone conversations) had been conducted during World War II. Mail censorship was discontinued after the war, but by the early 1950s, – given the Cold War atmosphere - both the FBI and the CIA felt it needed to be resumed.[524] From 1940 to 1973, the CIA and FBI "covertly and illegally opened and photographed first class letter mail within the United States."[525] These programs were initiated without prior authorization from any President, Attorney General, or Postmaster General. Many of them were initiated without prior authorization of the

---

[518] Church, 44-45.

[519] There were many such FBI lists. They included the 1967 "Rabble Rouser Index". A Rabble Rouser was "a person who tries to arouse people to violent action by appealing to the emotions, prejudices, etcetera; a demagogue." In 1968 this was renamed the "Agitator Index", which was then supplemented by the Key Activist List, and the Key Black Extremist Target List. See Church, 67-68.

[520] In 1950 and 1953 respectively.

[521] Church, 38.

[522] The FBI investigated the NAACP for at least 25 years, beginning in 1941. See Church, 128.

[523] Church, 39-41.

[524] Church, 295.

[525] Church, 294.

most senior agency officials.[526] Specifically,

> -Nearly a quarter of a million first class letters were open and photographed in the United States by the CIA between 19531973, producing a CIA computerized index of nearly one and one-half million names.[527]
>
> -At least 130,000 first class letters were opened and photographed by the FBI between 1940-1966 in eight U.S. cities.[528]

In 1945, the U.S. Army also wanted to continue its censorship of telegraph traffic, so it negotiated approval with Western Union, ITT, and RCA for interception of all telegraph traffic entering, leaving, or transiting the United States. The companies acquiesced, contingent on the fact that the Attorney General ruled that such programs were not illegal (e.g. under section 605). This program went forward, although no record of Attorney General approval exists. In 1948, the Department of Defense attempted but failed to get Congress to pass an act which would have made this program legal.[529] National Security Agency (NSA) – when created in 1952 - inherited the program and ran it until 1975. As the Church Committee Report tells us:

> -Millions of private telegrams sent from, to, or through the United States were obtained by the National Security Agency from 1947 to 1975 under a secret agreement with three United States telegraph companies.[530]

NSA also targeted international communications of U.S. citizens from the early 1960s, until 1973 using watch lists.[531] 1200 Americans' names appeared on NSA watchlists from the early 1960s, to 1973.[532] The report parenthetically added that "no statute or executive directive prohibits NSA's monitoring a telephone circuit with one terminal in the United States."[533]

---

[526] Church, 296.
[527] Church, 11.
[528] Ibid.
[529] Church 409-411.
[530] Church, 11. The committee misspoke. From 1947 until 1952, the telegrams went to the Army.
[531] Church, 386.
[532] Church, 144.
[533] Church, 401.

The FBI had continued to investigate individuals and organizations. It wiretapped, bugged, and performed surreptitious entries. The FBI passed political information on directly to the White House during the Truman, Eisenhower, and Kennedy administrations.[534] This effort "grew to unprecedented dimensions" under the Johnson and Nixon presidencies.[535] For example, at President Johnson's request, the FBI used their existing electronic surveillance to prepare a report of interactions between certain foreign officials, and Congress members and their staffs from July 1, 1964 to March 17, 1966.[536]

The FBI targeted civil rights leader Martin Luther King, Jr. for five years in an intensive FBI 'smear campaign' [537] intended "to 'neutralize' him as an effective civil rights leader."[538] The FBI used "nearly every intelligence-gathering technique at the Bureau's disposal in order to obtain information about the 'private activities of Dr. King and his advisors' to … 'completely discredit' them."[539]

Caught off-guard by the riots in Newark and Detroit in 1967, the Justice Department created the Interdivision Information Unit (IDIU). Leveraging information from the Army and Internal Revenue Service (IRS), and other agencies, the IIDU "developed a computer system which could generate lists of all 'members and affiliates' of an organization, their location and travel, 'all incidents' relating to specific issues', and 'all information' on a 'planned specific demonstration.'" Tapes containing these records were subsequently shared with the CIA and the IRS. This new list contained information about private individuals, public figures, journalists, actors, and private organizations.[540]

In 1969, the IRS – encouraged by the Senate and President Nixon - established its Special Service Staff to develop intelligence on special category of taxpayers defined by "political criteria." The Justice Department's IDIU provided names. Targets included a Nobel Prize

---

[534] Church, 42.
[535] Church, 86.
[536] Church, 88.
[537] Church, 100.
[538] Church, 14.
[539] Church, 14.
[540] Church, 60-61.

winning physicist, a Congressman, two Senators, journalists, political groups, religious groups, professional associations, private foundations, publications, and governmental institutions.[541]

This brings us to an interesting side note. During Senator Long's investigation into electronic surveillance and mail cover in the 1960s, Attorney General Katzenbach and other Bureau officials warned the senator that any investigation into FBI activities could lead into national security areas. Senator Long deferred, calling no FBI witnesses.[542] But perhaps there was more to the story.

The Church Committee Report revealed that there was a "widespread – and accurate – belief in Congress and the administration that the Bureau had available to it, derogatory information on politician and critics [which] created what the late Majority Leader of the House of Representative, Hale Boggs, called 'fear' of the Bureau:

> 'Freedom of speech, freedom of thought, freedom of action for men in public life can be compromised quite as effectively by the fear of surveillance as by the fact of surveillance.'"[543]

It's possible that Senator Long feared that unflattering details about him might emerge, courtesy of the FBI, if he probed further into Bureau activities. And it's likely that we'll never know.

Church Committee: Findings

The Church Committee acknowledged that the policies pursued by domestic intelligence programs

> grew out of a legitimate concern. Nazi Germany, Japan and the Soviet Union mounted intelligence efforts in this country before World War II; and Soviet operations continued after the war. In the 1960s, and 1970s, racist dissidents engaged in violence as a form of political protest, and there were large-scale protest demonstrations and major civil disorders in cities stemming from minority frustrations.[544]

They went on to say:

---

[541] Church, 71-72.
[542] Church, 82.
[543] Church, 157.
[544] Church, 121.

> Most of the activities exampled [sic] in this report occurred during periods of foreign or domestic crisis. There was substantial support from the public and all branches of government for some of the central objectives of domestic intelligence policy, including the search for 'Fifth Columnists' [545] before World War II; the desire to identify communist 'influence 'in the Cold War atmosphere of the 1950s; the demand for action against Klan violence in the early 1960s; and the reaction to violent racial disturbances and antiVietnam war activities in the late 1960s, and early 1970s. It was in this heated environment that President and Attorney General ordered the FBI to investigate 'subversive activities. Further, the Bureau's reputation for effectiveness and professionalism, and Director Hoover's ability to cultivate political support and to inspire apprehension, played a significant role in shaping the relationship between the FBI and the rest of the Government.'[546]

Nonetheless, the Committee listed seven overall findings.

1. Domestic intelligence activities had violated and ignored the law.[547]
2. Domestic intelligence activities were overly broad.[548] They had targeted: "'rightist' or 'extremist' groups in the anticommunist field;" "persons with 'anarchistic or revolutionary beliefs' or who were 'espousing the line of revolutionary movements;'" "'general racial matters,'" "'hate organizations;'" "'key activists;'" "'black nationalists;'" "'white supremacists;'" "'agitators;'" and, "'key black extremists.'"[549]

---

[545] According to Webster, a fifth columnist is a secret sympathizer or supporter of an enemy that engages in espionage or sabotage within defense lines or national borders.
[546] Church, 181.
[547] That is, "... domestic activities of the intelligence community at times violated specific statutory prohibitions and infringed the constitutional rights of American citizens." See Church, 98.
[548] "(1) many Americans and domestic groups have been subjected to investigation who were not suspected of criminal activity and (2) the intelligence agencies have regularly collected information about personal and political activities irrelevant to any legitimate governmental interest." See Church, 121.
[549] Church, 118.

3. Domestic intelligence activities used intrusive techniques excessively.[550]
4. Domestic intelligence activities used covert action to disrupt/discredit domestic groups.[551]
5. Domestic intelligence activities were involved in political abuse of intelligence information.
6. Domestic intelligence activities had inadequate controls on dissemination and retention.
7. Domestic intelligence activities had deficiencies in control and accountability.[552]

The Church Committee concluded that:

> "intelligence activities cannot be left to police themselves."[553]

Finally, alluding to the exercise of executive privilege, the report asserted that

> "Here, there is no sovereign who stands above the law."[554]

Recognition of the Power of New Technology

The Church Committee also noted that modern technology was enabling a "drift toward 'big brother government.'"[555] It added that

> The most extensive use of electronic surveillance has been by the National Security Agency. NSA has electronically monitored (without wiretapping in the traditional sense) international communication links since its inception in 1952; because of its sophisticated technology, it is capable of intercepting and recording an enormous number of

---

[550] Scientific and technological advances have rendered traditional controls on electronic surveillance obsolete and have made it more difficult to limit intrusions. Because of the nature of wiretaps, microphones and other sophisticated electronic techniques, it has not always been possible to restrict the monitoring of communications to the persons being investigated." See Church, 130.

[551] They "interfered with the First Amendment rights of citizens", and targeted Martin Luther King, Jr. with a smear campaign. They took actions to break up marriages, terminate funding or employment, and encourage gang warfare. See Church, 150, 152, 156.

[552] Church, 97.

[553] Church, 196.

[554] Church, 199.

[555] Church, 197.

> communications between the United States and foreign countries.[556]

Noting that NSA could now monitor any communications (telegrams, telephone calls) which propagate through the air (and most do at some point), the report stated:

> NSA's potential to violate the privacy of American citizens is unmatched by any other intelligence agency. Furthermore, since the interception of electronic signals entails neither the installation of electronic surveillance devices nor the cooperation of privacy communications companies, the possibility that such interceptions will be undetected is enhanced.[557]

Supreme Court Decisions on Communications Privacy Before 1975

The legislative result of this was FISA, among other things. But before we can consider that, we have to consider the opinions about communications privacy in the third branch of government, the judiciary. We will specifically look at Supreme Court cases, which always involve constitutional issues.[558]

A short synopsis of the key cases appears in appendix 8B. What we are most interested in are how Supreme Court rulings evolved over time.

First, the Supreme Court treated wiretapping and using a microphone to overhear a conversation as separate issues for a long time. For example, the Supreme Court found that wiretapping was prohibited by section 605 of the Federal Communications Act in 1937 and again in 1939. Three years later, it found that eavesdropping using a microphone was allowed by section 605 and did not violate any constitutional rights. By 1968, Congress would pass the Omnibus Crime Control and Safe Streets Act, which included provisions related to "Wiretapping and Electronic Surveillance."

---

[556] Church, 131.

[557] Church, 143.

[558] Recall that Supreme Court cases challenging state court decisions involve the Fourteenth Amendment, which prohibits state law from abridging any constitutional rights, including the First, Fourth and Fifth Amendments.

Second, the interpretation of what constituted an unconstitutional invasion of privacy evolved over time. In 1927, the Supreme Court said wiretapping was legal. In *Nardone v. U.S.* in 1937 and again in 1939, the Supreme Court said wiretapping was illegal. For years, the federal government would ignore the Nardone decision and continue its wiretapping and eavesdropping. It would not be until 1967 that the Supreme Court would finally affirm the privacy of communications from unauthorized electronic surveillance.

Third, Section 605 specified that electronic surveillance was legal when done "in response to a subpena [sic] issued by a court of competent jurisdiction, or on demand of other lawful authority…." It did not specifically say that information obtained this way had to be backed up by a warrant based on probably cause. It did not specify that the rules were the same for law enforcement investigating criminal matters, as opposed to federal investigations into subversives and national security threats. This, as we have seen, became a key issue.

Fourth, electronic surveillance did not always require physical trespass into an individual's physical property (e.g. home). There were arguments made that this absence of physical trespass precluded Fourth Amendment defenses. These complications were compounded when the government compelled common carriers to provide access. It would take decades to sort these thorny issues out. Eventually, an individual's communications would come to be seen as personal property protected from search and seizure under the Fourth Amendment, and by freedom of speech under the First Amendment.

Fifth, the Supreme Court was judicious about overstepping its bounds into the Congressional arena of lawmaking. In *Olmstead v. United States*, the majority opinion delivered by Chief Justice Taft specifically stated that it was up to Congress to specify when evidence could be excluded, not the court. "Without the sanction of an Act of Congress, federal courts have no discretion to exclude evidence, the admission of which is not unconstitutional, because it was unethically procured." Congressional dissatisfaction with the Olmstead ruling would lead to passage of section 605 of the Federal Communications Act. [559]

[559] See Justice Brennan's dissent in Lopez v. US.

Unfortunately, section 605 of the federal law was disregarded in many cases by law enforcement, the courts, and even the executive branch.

Sixth, there was a sincere concern that making electronic surveillance illegal would remove one of the most powerful weapons in law enforcement's arsenal. The majority opinion in *Olmstead v. United States* succinctly stated this:

> A standard which would forbid the reception of evidence if obtained by other than nice ethical conduct by government officials would make society suffer and give criminals greater immunity than has been known heretofore. In the absence of controlling legislation by Congress, those who realize the difficulties in bringing offenders to justice may well deem it wise that the exclusion of evidence should be confined to cases where rights under the Constitution would be violated by admitting it.

Seventh, a huge debate arose about whether illegally obtained evidence (like that obtained by a wiretap or eavesdropping device) was admissible in court. After passage of the Federal Communications Act, the Supreme Court ruled twice in *Nardone v. U.S.* that evidence illegally obtained by federal agents was inadmissible as evidence in federal court. Of course, we've already seen that the executive branch largely ignored these rulings, and the legislature and judiciary let them get away with it for some time.

If, however, the illegal evidence was collected by state officials and presented in state court, the rules could be completely different. In *Wolf v. Colorado* (1949), and again in *Irvine v. California* (1954), the Supreme Court ruled that illegally obtained evidence was admissible in state court. In the latter case, the court noted that about two-thirds of state courts allowed admission of "illegally obtained evidence," declining to rule on something it saw as a states' rights issue. By the time of *Berger v. New York* (1967), the Supreme Court went so far as to rule that that the eavesdropping laws of New York were too broad, and violated constitutional rights.

A Supreme Court View on Surveillance and Privacy

It is instructive to look at Supreme Court Justice Brennan's 1963 dissent in *Lopez v. US*, which neatly summarizes most of the salient issues regarding electronic surveillance and privacy. Brennan started by noting that since 1789, "search" had included looking and listening:

> … we find references in the Bible to 'searching' the Scriptures (John V, 39); in literature to a man 'searching' his heart or conscience; in the law books to 'searching' a public record. None of these acts requires a manual rummaging for concealed objects. . .. [J]ust as looking around a room is searching, listening to the sounds in a room is searching. Seeing and hearing are both reactions of a human being to the physical environment around him - to light waves, in one instance, to sound waves, in the other. And, accordingly, using a mechanical aid to either seeing or hearing is also a form of searching. The camera and the dictaphone both do the work of the end-organs of an individual human searcher - more accurately.

Brennan disagreed with the Supreme Court's ruling in *Olmstead v. US*, viewing it as "deviant in the law of the Fourth Amendment, and not a harbinger of decisional revolution." He added that:

> The Constitution would be an utterly impractical instrument of contemporary government if it were deemed to reach only problems familiar to the technology of the eighteenth century; yet the Court, in *Olmstead,* refused to apply the Fourth Amendment to wiretapping, seemingly because the Framers of the Constitution had not been farsighted enough to foresee the invention of the telephone.

He noted that past Supreme Court rulings regarding Fourth Amendment cases had been based on two factors "not often articulated in the decisions." The first was "the pervasive fear that, if electronic surveillance were deemed to be within the reach of the Fourth Amendment, a useful technique of law enforcement would be wholly destroyed, because an electronic 'search' could never be reasonable within the meaning of the Amendment." Brennan found this argument "unconvincing," and noted that there had been many suggestions on how "electronic searches could be made to comply with the other requirements of the Fourth Amendment." Either which way, Brennan affirmed that "[e]lectronic searches cannot be tolerated in the name of law enforcement if they are inherently unconstitutional."

The second factor noted by Brennan was a concern that such rulings would ban all deceptive methods used by law enforcement during investigations, like confidential informants, undercover agents, plain clothes officers, etc. Brennan dismissed this concern as unfounded. As he saw it in this case, it was not the deception but the using of electronic surveillance that violated the defendant's rights. As Brennan notes about new technology:

> Electronic aids add a wholly new dimension to eavesdropping. They make it more penetrating, more indiscriminate, more truly obnoxious to a free society. Electronic surveillance, in fact, makes the police omniscient, and police omniscience is one of the most effective tools of tyranny.

Taking it one step further, Brennan noted that:

> Under Hitler, when it became known that the secret police planted dictaphones in houses, members of families often gathered in bathrooms to conduct whispered discussions of intimate affairs, hoping thus to escape the reach of the sending apparatus.

Brennan also cautioned that electronic surveillance "[struck] deeper than the ancient feeling that a man's home is his castle; it strikes at freedom of communication [expected in] the privacy of home and office." Not only were the First Amendment right to freedom of speech threatened, but its "obverse," the right to "anonymity" (and the associated freedom of association). "The passive and the quiet, equally with the active and the aggressive, are entitled to protection when engaged in the precious activity of expressing ideas or beliefs. Electronic surveillance destroys all anonymity and all privacy; it makes government privy to everything that goes on."

Brennan concluded that Supreme Court enforcement of Fourth Amendment rights "against physical intrusions into person, home, and property by law enforcement officers" had now "been outflanked by the technological advances of the very recent past."

The Foreign Intelligence Surveillance Act

The Church Committee report provided an authoritative history of U.S. domestic intelligence activities for the United States citizenry. Not everything they had to say was unexpected and/or unsuspected. There had been early Congressional proceedings that suggested that privacy was being endangered by modern technology. Books and media reported instances where the government had misled its citizenry, the FBI had overreached, the CIA had run rogue, etc. But things were not black and white. There was a lot of gray area. The muddle of conflicting facts and sensationalized versions of the truth lead to many suspicions, but at the end of the day, people were left confused.

The Church Committee illuminated one very important fact: how anachronistic the wartime mentality of the government was with the modern civil rights priorities of the American public. The report acknowledged that FOIA and the Privacy Act "provide important mechanisms by which individuals can gain access to information on intelligence activity directed against them."[560] But public disillusionment with government had been growing for over a decade, and Watergate marked its zenith. Congress had to do something more.

The committee report also raised several important issues about privacy and electronic surveillance against national security threats. Are the communications of a US citizen protected when they call someone overseas? Does the citizen have to be suspected of being an agent of a foreign power? Is it enough for the call to be to a foreign country, or does the recipient have to be a suspected agent of a foreign power? What if a US citizen abroad calls a citizen or non-citizen in the United States? The line between foreign threats and national security authorities had become hopelessly confounded with domestic threats and law enforcement authorities.

The Foreign Intelligence Surveillance Act (FISA) of 1978[561] was a direct consequence of the findings of the Church and Pike committees. FISA authorized electronic surveillance - which now encompassed all

---

[560] Church, 234.
[561] Accessed 6/20/19 at https://www.govinfo.gov/content/pkg/STATUTE-92/pdf/STATUTE-92-Pg1783.pdf

"electronic, mechanical, or other surveillance device of the contents of any wire or radio communication" - to collect foreign intelligence information within the United States. "Foreign intelligence information" was defined in Title I as:

1. information that relates to, and if concerning a United States person is necessary to, the ability of the United States to protect against-
   (a) actual or potential attack or other grave hostile acts of a foreign power or an agent of a foreign power;
   (b) sabotage or international terrorism by a foreign power or an agent of a foreign power; or
   (c)clandestine intelligence activities by an intelligence service or network of a foreign power or by an agent of a foreign power; or
2. information with respect to a foreign power or foreign territory that relates to, and if concerning a United States person is necessary to-
   (a) the national defense or the security of the United States; or
   (b) the conduct of the foreign affairs of the United States.

A foreign power was defined as (any part of) a foreign government, "a faction of a foreign nation ... not substantially composed of United States persons," any entity directed and/or controlled by a foreign government, "a group engaged in international terrorism or activities in preparation therefor," or "a foreign-based political organization, not substantially composed of United States persons." With FISA, a much tighter definition of foreign intelligence information – including that which may concern US citizens - was finally codified.

FISA permitted the President to authorize electronic surveillance without a court order, given the consent of the Attorney General under specific circumstances. Alternatively, a federal officer could prepare an application for FISA which had to be confirmed by a defense or national security executive official, approved by the Attorney General, and approved by one of eleven judges of the Foreign Intelligence Surveillance Court (FISC). The FISC was created by FISA to grant orders for collection of communications of a foreign power within the United States. In both cases, the minimization procedures to be followed must be specified. Minimization procedures were provisions which minimized acquisition and retention, and prohibited the dissemination of information collected under FISA.[562] The act specified rules for disclosure and use of FISA information as evidence in legal proceedings, ensuring that the civil rights of any defendant were not abridged. Congress required the Attorney General to report to the HPSCI and SSCI on compliance with minimization procedures. FISA did not preclude the collection of communications against U.S. citizens who were acting as agents of a foreign power.

FISA affirmed citizens' constitutional rights by establishing a procedure for legally obtaining foreign intelligence information. FISA is reminiscent of the Wiretap Law, which had been enacted specifically for law enforcement purposes. For foreign intelligence purposes, FISA required a FISC court order, or a presidential authorization with Attorney General approval. Interested readers are encouraged to read the original FISA in order to understand the nuances not covered here.[563]

While warrants issued under the 1968 Wiretap Law required probable cause of a particular offense, FISA court orders required probable cause that the individual is a "foreign power or agent of a foreign power; provided that no United States person may be considered a foreign power or an agent of a foreign power solely upon the basis of activities protected by the first amendment to the Constitution of the United States…." This latter provision, of course, was intended to prevent the kind of targeting that had occurred in the past, when individuals exercising their first amendment rights had ended up on watch lists.

Title II of FISA authorized communications common carriers to assist "persons authorized by law to intercept wire or oral communications, or to conduct electronic surveillance" in support of FISA, assuming such assistance was directed by a court order or the Attorney General. Title II finally codified the conduct of electronic

---

[562] The Church Committee report established the foundation for this. It had talked about the need to "minimize the extent to which communications of Americans are intercepted, selected, or monitored." It had also talked about the need for any judge approving electronic surveillance to "adopt procedures to acquisition and retention of non-foreign intelligence information about Americans." See Church, pp. 211, 228.

[563] Accessed 5/22/19 at https://www.govinfo.gov/content/pkg/STATUTE-92/pdf/STATUTE-92-Pg1783.pdf

surveillance for foreign intelligence purposes, thus smoothing another wrinkle that had existed since passage of section 605[564] of the 1934 Communications Act.

Title III - added under the 1995 Intelligence Authorization Act – empowered the FISC to grant orders for physical searches within the United States of "the premises or property … owned, used, possessed by, or … in transit to or from a foreign power or an agent of a foreign power."[565] The procedures to be followed were quite similar to those already mentioned for electronic surveillance.

Title IV was added under the 1999 Intelligence Authorization Act.[566] Section 402 extended FISA to the use of pen registers[567] and trap and trace devices[568] for telephone and email surveillance "for any investigation to gather foreign intelligence information or information

---

[564] And section 606, which specified special Presidential powers over communications during times of war.

[565] Accessed 6/20/19 at https://www.govinfo.gov/content/pkg/BILLS-103hr4299eas/pdf/BILLS-103hr4299eas.pdf

[566] Accessed 6/20/19 at https://www.govinfo.gov/content/pkg/PLAW-105publ 272/pdf/PLAW-105publ272.pdf

[567] Pen register: A device that captures the dialed numbers and related information to which outgoing calls or communications are made by the subject. Described most precisely in U.S. Code: "…the term 'pen register' means a device or process which records or decodes dialing, routing, addressing, or signaling information transmitted by an instrument or facility from which a wire or electronic communication is transmitted, provided, however, that such information shall not include the contents of any communication, but such term does not include any device or process used by a provider or customer of a wire or electronic communication service for billing, or recording as an incident to billing, for communications services provided by such provider or any device or process used by a provider or customer of a wire communication service for cost accounting or other like purposes in the ordinary course of its business." See 18 U.S.C. section 3127 (2015), accessed 6/20/19 at https://law.justia.com/codes/us/2015/title-18/part-ii/chapter-206/sec.-3127/

[568] 568Trap and trace device: A device that captures the numbers and related information from which incoming calls and communications coming to the subject have originated. Defined most precisely in U.S. Code: "… the term 'trap and trace device' means a device or process which captures the incoming electronic or other impulses which identify the originating number or other dialing, routing, addressing, and signaling information reasonably likely to identify the source of a wire or electronic communication, provided, however, that such information shall not include the contents of any communication…." See 18 U.S.C. section 3127 (2015), accessed 6/20/19 at https://law.justia.com / codes/us / 2015/ title-18/part-ii/ chapter-206/sec.-3127/

concerning international terrorism which is being conducted by the Federal Bureau of Investigation under such guidelines as the Attorney General approves…."

Executive Orders and Additional Laws

Presidents after Nixon also responded to the findings of the Church and Pike Committees by issuing executive orders (EO's) on foreign intelligence activities. President Ford issued EO 11905 (1976),[569] President Carter issued EO 12036 (1978),[570] and President Reagan issued EO 12333 (1981).[571] These EO's addressed intelligence community control and oversight, and progressively formalized the distinct roles and authorities of each agency more and more precisely. Subsequent presidents would enact additional relevant executive orders.[572]

The 1986 Electronic Communications Privacy Act (ECPA) updated the 1968 Wiretap Law, extending its protections to include electronic communications, and making it unlawful to access stored wire and electronic communications and transactional records without a warrant.[573] Through subsequent amendments (including the USA PATRIOT Act of 2001) discussed below), ECPA today protects wire, oral, and electronic communications while they are being made, are in transit, and when stored on computers. It applies to email, telephone conversations, and data stored electronically.[574]

The 1994 Communications Assistance for Law Enforcement (CALEA), also known as the Digital Telephony Act set off a tempest of controversy.[575] This law required telecommunications carriers to ensure that their equipment, facilities, and services were capable of assisting federal, state and local government with "facilitating authorized

---

[569] Accessed 8/4/19 at https://www.fordlibrarymuseum.gov/library/speeches/760 110e .asp

[570] Accessed 8/4/19 at https://fas.org/irp/offdocs/eo/eo-12036.htm

[571] Accessed 6/12/19 at https://www.archives.gov/federal-register/codification/ execut ive-order/12333.html

[572] See EO 13284 (2003), EO 13355 (2004), EO 13470 (2008).

[573] Accessed 6/20/19 at https://www.govinfo.gov/content/pkg/STATUTE-100/ pdf/ STATUTE-100-Pg1848.pdf

[574] Accessed 6/21/19 at https://it.ojp.gov/PrivacyLiberty/authorities/statutes/1285

[575] Accessed 8/4/19 at https://www.epic.org/privacy/wiretap/calea/calea_law. html

communications interceptions and ... call-identifying information." CALEA was passed to help authorized electronic surveillance undertaken for both national security and law enforcement purposes. This act also amended the 1934 Communications Act, making the FCC responsible for prescribing the rules by which CALEA requirements would be implemented.

The Telecommunications Act of 1996 also amended the 1934 Communications Act, specifying in section 222 that telecommunications carriers have a "duty to protect the confidentiality" of customer proprietary information, defined as:

> (a) information that relates to the quantity, technical configuration, type, destination, and amount of use of a telecommunications service subscribed to by any customer of a telecommunications carrier, and that is made available to the carrier by the customer solely by virtue of the carrier-customer relationship; and
>
> (b) information contained in the bills pertaining to telephone exchange service or telephone toll service received by a customer of a carrier....[576]

Now both the content of a customer's communications, as well as information about his associated proprietary information, were protected by law.

9/11 and its Aftermath

Before 9/11, international terrorism had affected United States interests and citizens primarily overseas.[577] In 1979, U.S. hostages had

---

[576] Accessed 6/22/19 at https://www.govinfo.gov/content/pkg/STATUTE-110/ pdf/ STATUTE-110-Pg56.pdf

[577] The Church Committee had had enough insight to define terrorist activities as "acts or conspiracies, which (a) are violent or dangerous to human life; and (b) violate federal or state criminal statutes concerning assassination, murder, arson, bombing, hijacking, or kidnapping; and (c) appear intended to, or are likely to have the effect of:

1.Substantially disrupting federal, state or local government; or

2.Substantially disrupting interstate or foreign commerce between the United States and another country; or

3.Directly interfering with the exercise by Americans, of Constitutional rights protected by the Civil Rights Act of 1968, or by foreigner, of their rights under the laws or treaties of the United States." See Church, 238.

been taken from the U.S. Embassy in Iran. In 1988, Libyans blew up a Pan-Am flight bound for New York over Lockerbie, Scotland, killing 270 individuals, the majority of whom were Americans. In 1998, the terrorism group Al-Qaeda bombed the U.S. embassies in Tanzania and Kenya. Al-Qaeda struck again in 2000, inflicting substantial damage on the U.S. Navy destroyer *USS Cole* in Yemen and killing seventeen sailors.

The increase threat posed by terrorists caused Title IV of FISA to be added in 1999.

9/11 marked a "new kind of war,"[578] when international terrorism struck on American soil. The website of the 9/11 Memorial and Museum in New York succinctly describes 9/11 in the following way:

> On the morning of September 11, 2001, 19 terrorists from Al-Qaeda hijacked four commercial airplanes, deliberately crashing two of the planes into the upper floors of the North and South towers of the World Trade Center complex and a third plane into the Pentagon in Arlington, Va. The Twin Towers ultimately collapsed because of the damage sustained from the impacts and the resulting fires. After learning about the other attacks, passengers on the fourth hijacked plane, Flight 93, fought back, and the plane was crashed into an empty field in western Pennsylvania about 20 minutes by air from Washington, D.C.
>
> The attacks killed nearly 3,000 people from 93 nations. 2,753 people were killed in New York, 184 people were killed at the Pentagon and 40 people were killed on Flight 93."[579]

FISA after 9/11

In 2004, the National Commission on Terrorist Attacks on the United States (known as the 9/11 Commission) published its findings and recommendations. The Commission observed that "In wartime, government calls for greater powers, and then the need for those powers recedes after the war ends." Terrorist attack on our homeland changed the rules of the game. Terrorism reawakened the wartime mentality, and the

---

[578] 9/11 Commission Report, p. 48, accessed 6/22/19 at http://govinfo.library.unt.edu/911/report/911Report.pdf

[579] 9/11 Memorial and Museum website, accessed 6/22/19 at https://www.911memorial.org/faq-about-911

government would once again exercise enhanced powers to effectively protect the homeland.[580]

As a result of 9/11, Congress created the Department of Homeland Security in 2002, and the Office of the Director of National Intelligence in 2004. It also caused changes to FISA. For example, section 402 was modified by the 2001 USA PATRIOT (Uniting and Strengthening America by Providing Appropriate Tools Required to Intercept and Obstruct Terrorism) Act to read:

> for any investigation to obtain foreign intelligence information not concerning a United States person or to protect against international terrorism or clandestine intelligence activities, provided that such investigation of a United States person is not conducted solely upon the basis of activities protected by the first amendment to the Constitution….[581]

Also, under the 2001 Patriot Act, Title V of FISA was amended by adding Section 501, granting "Access to Certain Business Records for Foreign Intelligence and International Terrorism Investigations." Known as section 215 of the Patriot Act, this extended the FISA procedures to orders "requiring the production of any tangible things (including books, records, papers, documents, and other items) for an investigation to protect against international terrorism or clandestine intelligence activities, provided that such investigation of a United States person is not conducted solely upon the basis of activities protected by the first amendment to the Constitution."[582]

Under the FISA Amendment Act of 2008, Congress added Title VII, "Additional Procedures Regarding Certain Persons Outside the United States." [583] Specifically, section 702 permitted the Attorney General and the Director of National Intelligence to authorize surveillance

---

[580] National Commission on Terrorist Attacks, The 9/11 Commission Report: Final Report of the National Commission on Terrorist Attacks Upon the United States (Authorized Edition). New York: W.W. Norton & Company, 2004, p. 394.

[581] Accessed 6/20/19 at https://www.govinfo.gov/content/pkg/PLAW-107pub l56/ pdf/ PLAW-107publ56.pdf

[582] Accessed 6/20/19 at https://www.govinfo.gov/content/pkg/PLAW-107publ56 / pdf/ PLAW-107publ56.pdf

[583] Accessed 6/22/19 at https://www.govinfo.gov/content/pkg/STATUTE-122/ pdf/ STATUTE-122-Pg2436.pdf

for foreign intelligence purposes of non-U.S. persons believed to be outside the United States. This surveillance was accomplished with the assistance of electronic communications service providers as described in the statute itself.[584] It also required the Attorney General and DNI to file a certification with the FISC.

Public Revelations

There were many other amendments and reauthorizations to FISA after 9/11.[585] For our purposes, they are not essential to the story. What is essential is an understanding of how public awareness of FISA rose after 9/11.

In 2005, the *New York Times* published an article with the sensational headline "Bush Lets U.S. Spy on Callers Without Courts." This got the privacy issue front and center (again) for the American public. The article revealed that the president had signed a presidential order "months after the Sept. 11 attacks" authorizing NSA "to eavesdrop on Americans and others inside the United States to search for evidence of terrorist activity without the court-approved warrants ordinarily required for domestic spying, according to government officials." [586] The article goes on to say that the program was suspended and revamped after legal experts raised concerns about it in 2004.

In 2013, Edward Snowden leaked classified information from NSA about its global surveillance program. The public discussion about surveillance and privacy exploded again. Public attention initially focused on the "warrantless wiretapping" allowed under section 702 of FISA. In response to these revelations, the Office of the Director of National Intelligence (ODNI) and the National Security Agency issued a joint statement stating that "Press reports … mischaracterize aspects of NSA's

---

[584] See also https://icontherecord.tumblr.com/topics/section-702, accessed 7/29 /19.

[585] See the 2004 Intelligence Reform and Terrorism Prevention Act, the 2005 USA PATRIOT Improvement and Reauthorization Act, the 2006 PATRIOT Act Additional Reauthorizing Amendments Act, the 2007 Protect America Act, the 2011 FISA Sunsets Extension Act, and the 2012 FAA Reauthorization Act.

[586] James Risen and Eric Lichtblau, "Bush Lets U.S. Spy on Callers Without Courts." New York Times, December 16, 2005.

data collection activities conducted under section 702 of the Foreign Intelligence Surveillance Act." [587] The original *Wall Street Journal* article claimed that the NSA had "the capacity to reach roughly 75% of all U.S. internet traffic in the hunt for foreign intelligence…."[588] The ODNI and NSA replied that that was "simply not true," adding that "In its foreign intelligence mission, and using all its authorities, NSA 'touches' about 1.6%, and analysts only look at 0.00004%, of the world's internet traffic." The joint statement also made mention that assistance from providers (meaning telecommunications common carriers and Internet Service Providers) "is compelled by law" and "has been previously revealed."

Edward Snowden's leaks also revealed section 215 of FISA had been used to justify "bulk collection of domestic metadata."[589] What is bulk collection? Bulk collection is the collection of data without using a discriminant or identifier for a specific target. What's metadata? Glibly described as "data about data," metadata is the information about the communications. For telephone calls, it's the phone number called from and to, the name of the person who called, the name of person who was called, the date, time, duration of the call, etc. In other words, it's all the information the phone company needs to bill you (the client) and to successfully provide the desired telephone service. In the case of internet service providers (ISPs), metadata can include the originating and destination email addresses, IP addresses, and other technical details. Again, the ISP requires this information to ensure that they are able to successfully provide the service they contracted with you to provide and charge you any appropriate fees. The Snowden leaks made the public aware that both content and metadata could be of interest to the

---

[587] Accessed 6/22/19 at https://www.nsa.gov/news-features/press-room/Article/1 6187 54/

[588] Accessed 6/22/19 at https://www.wsj.com/articles/new-details-show-broader-nsasurveillance-reach-1377044261?tesla=y

[589] This is a very complex subject. Interested readers are encouraged to take a look at the National Research Council report entitled "Bulk Collection of Signals Intelligence: Technical Options" published by the National Academy in 2015. Accessed 7/21/19 at https://www.nap.edu/read/19414/chapter/12#100

government.[590] The Uniting and Strengthening America by Fulfilling Rights and Ensuring Effective Discipline over Monitoring Act (USA Freedom Act) of 2015 would subsequently ban section 215 collection by requiring the use of a "specific selection term" in "any requests for phone records."[591]

The American public was and today remains divided about Snowden and his leaks. Some see him as a traitor who should be prosecuted to the full extent of the law, if he ever returns to the United States. Others see him as a patriot, a sentiment captured in a magazine cover showing him clutching the American flag.[592] NSA Deputy Director John C. "Chris" Inglis, when asked in 2014 if the Snowden revelations hadn't brought about a healthy public debate, replied: "In the same way that somebody who burned my house down has given me the opportunity to perhaps build it in a way that I would prefer."[593]

FISA and Cyber Actors

FISA was subsequently amended to include cyber activities in the 2017 FISA Amendments Reauthorization Act.[594] This law enhanced the definition of "agent of a foreign power" to include any person who:

> engages in international malicious cyber activity that threatens the national defense or security of the United States, or activities in preparation therefor, for or on behalf of a foreign power, or knowingly aids or abets any person in the conduct of such international malicious cyber activity or activities in preparation therefor, or knowingly conspires with any person to engage in such international malicious cyber activity or activities in preparation therefor....

---

[590] The terms "metadata" and "content" were new, but the ideas had been exercised in earlier U.S. domestic intelligence programs which reviewed the outside envelope (metadata) and internal correspondence (content) of letters entrusted to the U.S. Postal Service.

[591] Lawfare Blog, accessed 6/22/19 at https://www.lawfareblog.com/topic/fisa-215-collection

[592] Wired Magazine, September 2014. See https://time.com/3107153/edward-snowden-embraces-american-flag-on-wired-cover/ accessed 6/22/19.

[593] National Public Radio Interview, January 10, 2014, accessed 3 November 2018 at https://www.npr.org/ 2014 / 01 / 10 / 261282601/transcript-nsa-deputy-director-john-inglis

[594] Accessed 6/21/19 at https://www.govtrack.us/congress/bills/115/hr4478/text

Furthermore, it defined "international malicious cyber activity" as:

"activity on or through an information system

1. originating from, or directed by persons located, in whole or in substantial part, outside the United States;
2. that seeks to compromise or impair the confidentiality, integrity, or availability of computers, information systems or communications systems, networks, physical or virtual infrastructure controlled by computers or information systems, or information resident thereon; and
3. that is not authorized by the United States Government or otherwise carried out in accordance with Federal law."

It also amended 702 authorities to adopt querying procedures "consistent with the requirements of the Fourth Amendment to the Constitution of the United States for information collected pursuant to an authorization.... Such procedure shall include a technical procedure whereby a record is kept of each United States person query term used for each query." A query is defined as "any instance in which information the United States Government has acquired is searched using one or more specific terms for the purpose of discovering or retrieving unminimized contents to noncontents of the communications of United States persons."

The Privacy and Civil Liberties Oversight Board

The 9/11 Commission report stated the additional powers granted to government after 9/11 "calls for an enhanced system of checks and balances to protect the precious liberties that are vital to our way of life."[595] Having learned that "there is no office within the government whose job it is to look across the government at the actions we are taking to protect ourselves to ensure that liberty concerns are appropriately considered," the Commission recommended the creation of what is now called the Privacy and Civil Liberties Oversight Board (PCLOB).[596] Today, the PCLOB is responsible for ensuing privacy and civil liberty protection by overseeing executive branch policies, procedures, regulations, and information sharing practices related to protecting the nation from terrorism. It also

---

595 9/11 Report, 394.

596 9/11 Report, 395.

provides advice on proposed legislation, regulations and policies related to counter-terrorism, ensuring a conscious balance with privacy and civil liberties.[597] The PCLOB provided important precedents that we will talk about in a subsequent chapter.

Conclusion

The first-class letter set the expectation for privacy in communications. Unfortunately, when the telegraph came along, it did not naturally afford any such privacy. There was no sealed envelope around the electronic telegraphic message.

The telegraph set the stage for the telephone. It acclimatized people to the idea they could communicate more quickly than by letter or in-person visits. The creation of a national network to support telegraphy - eased by post roads and railroad right-of ways – established a precedent which a national telephone system could naturally inherit. These technologies brought tremendous benefits, and tremendous privacy challenges in the form of wiretapping and eavesdropping.

The United States faced threats to its national security before, during and after declared international hostilities. These combined with threats to internal security, creating a permissive climate for the rise of domestic intelligence. With this came liberal rules about the usage of electronic surveillance.

The subtle effects of technologies on privacy slowly emerged, evolved, and coalesced. Societal awareness of these changes came even more slowly. There was no popular consensus on how these technologies might threaten privacy. Nor was there a consensus in Congress, the courts, or the executive branch on how to address the privacy issues. Citizens had been willing to sacrifice individual freedoms when a threat to their way of life lurked large from abroad, whether it be Nazis or Communists. However, when these fears were supplanted by the internal threats to privacy - reminiscent of the police states America condemned in totalitarian regimes - the citizenry finally became enraged and demanded a response to restore its faith in government.

---

[597] The Privacy and Civil Liberties Oversight Board website, accessed 3 November 2018 at https://www.pclob.gov/about/

Congress finally responded to the technological threats to communications privacy with the 1968 Wiretapping Law and FISA in 1978. The former applied to law enforcement while the latter applied to foreign intelligence. The two shared a common heritage. They possessed similar attributes. They have continued to evolve, amended to address new technological capabilities, emerging and receding threats, and wavering public opinion on the right balance between privacy and national security.

Today's technology continues to turbocharge functionality which can be used to enhance national security and undermine privacy. The issues are complex, elusive, and ever evolving. We can consult the experts, but must critically assess each point of view. To quote former Chairman of the Joint Chiefs of Staff and Secretary of State Colin Powell, "Don't be buffaloed by experts and elites. Experts often possess more data than judgment. Elites can become so inbred that they produce hemophiliacs who bleed to death as soon as they are nicked by the real world."[598]

At the end of the day, we have to understand enough to make our own decisions about our privacy preferences. We must remain vigilant about how technology challenges our privacy, and speak out so our government hears us.

Appendix 8A

Section 605 of the Federal Communications Act

UNAUTHORIZED PUBLICATION OF COMMUNICATIONS

No person receiving or assisting in receiving, or transmitting, or assisting in transmitting, any interstate or foreign communication by wire or radio shall divulge or publish the existence, contents, substance, purport, effect, or meaning thereof, except through authorized channels of transmission or reception, to any person other than the addressee, his agent, or attorney, or to a person employed or authorized to forward such communication to its destination, or to proper accounting or distributing officers of the various communicating centers over which the communication may be passed, or to the master of a ship under whom he is serving, or in response to a subpena [sic] issued by a court of competent jurisdiction, or on demand of other lawful authority ; and no person not being authorized by

---

[598] Oren Hariri, "Quotations from Chairman Powell: A Leadership Primer", 1996. Accessed 12/29/19 at https://govleaders.org/powell.htm

the sender shall intercept any communication and divulge or publish the existence, contents, substance, purport, effect, or meaning of such intercepted communication to any person ; and no person not being entitled thereto shall receive or assist in receiving any interstate or foreign communication by wire or radio and use the same or any information therein contained for his own benefit or for the benefit of another not entitled thereto; and no person having received such intercepted communication or having become acquainted with the contents, substance, purport, effect, or meaning of the same or any part thereof, knowing that such information was so obtained, shall divulge or publish the existence, contents, substance, purport, effect, or meaning of the same or any part thereof, or use the same or any information therein contained for his own benefit or for the benefit of another not entitled thereto : Provided, That this section shall not apply to the receiving, divulging, publishing, or utilizing the contents of any radio communication broadcast, or transmitted by amateurs or others for the use of the general public, or relating to ships in distress.[599]

Appendix 8B

Key Supreme Court Decisions Regarding Communications Privacy before 1975

1. Boyd v. United States, 116 U.S. 616 (1886): Supreme Court upheld right of individual not to produce his private papers for fear of self-incrimination after government seized alleged fraudulently imported goods. Established precedent linking Fourth Amendment rights with Fifth Amendment rights.[600]
2. Weeks v. United States, 232 U.S. 383 (1914): Supreme Court found that evidence (papers, letters, and other items) seized by federal agents without warrant and presented in federal court violated Fourth and Fifth Amendment rights.
3. Olmstead v. United States, 277 U.S. 238 (1928); Supreme Court found that wiretapping without trespass by federal officials was constitutional and admissible as evidence in federal court, i.e. it did not violate the Fourth nor the Fifth Amendments. "The policy of protecting the secrecy of telephone messages by making them, when intercepted, inadmissible as evidence in federal criminal trials may be

---

599 Accessed 7/31/19 at http://www.legisworks.org/congress/73/publaw-416.pdf

600 Accessed 7/27/19 at https://supreme.justia.com/cases/federal/us/116/616/

adopted by Congress through legislation, but it is not for the courts to adopt it by attributing an enlarged and unusual meaning to the Fourth Amendment."[601]

4. Nardone v. United States, 302 U.S. 379 (1937): Supreme Court ruled that based on section 605 of the 1934 Communications Act, "evidence obtained by federal agents by wiretapping telephone wires and intercepting messages is not admissible in a criminal trial in the federal district court." The court noted that the legality of wiretapping by federal agents is an issue for Congress. Alluded to Section 605 has having been perhaps adopted to preserve Fourth and Fifth Amendment rights.[602]
5. Nardone v. United States, 308 U.S. 338 (1939): Supreme Court concluded that wiretapping evidence was inadmissible in federal court because it violated section 605 of the Federal Communications Act.[603]
6. Goldman v. United States, 316 U.S. 129 (1942): Supreme Court held that detectaphone surveillance without trespass by federal agents was constitutional and admissible as evidence in a federal court. It did not violate section 605 of the Federal Communications Act nor the Fourth Amendment. The court specifically stated they were unwilling to overrule Olmstead v. U.S.[604]
7. Wolf v. Colorado, 338 U.S. 25 (1949): Supreme Court held that the Fourteenth Amendment did not prohibit the admissibility of evidence obtained through unreasonable search and seizure in a state court for a state crime. "While the doctrine of *Weeks v. United States* ... making evidence secured in violation of the Fourth Amendment inadmissible in federal courts, is adhered to, it is not imposed on the States by the Fourteenth Amendment."
8. On Lee v. United States, 343 U.S. 747 (1952): The Supreme Court ruled that a federal agent's collection of evidence against a defendant using a hidden radio transmitter did not

601 Accessed 6/12/19 at https://supreme.justia.com/cases/federal/us/277/438/
602 Accessed 7/27/19 at https://supreme.justia.com/cases/federal/us/302/379/
603 Accessed 6/12/19 at https://supreme.justia.com/cases/federal/us/308/338/
604 t https://supreme.justia.com/cases/federal/us/316/129/

violate the defendant's Fourth Amendment rights, nor section 605 of the Federal Communications Act.[605]

9. Irvine v. California, 347 U.S. 128 (1954): The Supreme Court ruled that illegally obtained evidence was admissible in California state court. The evidence had been obtained by installation of a microphone by a police officer without a warrant in the defendant's home. The Supreme Court ruled that such evidence neither violated the Fourteenth Amendment nor section 605 of the Federal Communications Act. It noted that about two-thirds of state courts allowed admission of "illegally obtained evidence." [606]
10. Mapp v. Ohio, 367 U.S. 642 (1961): "All evidence obtained by searches and seizures in violation of the Constitution is inadmissible in a criminal trial in a state court." [607] Furthermore, "there is an intimate relation between the Fourth and Fifth Amendments." Overturned Wolf v. Colorado.
11. Lopez v. United States, 373 U.S. 427 (1963): Supreme Court ruled (among other things) that a secret tape recording made by a federal agent during a conversation with the defendant in the latter's place of business was admissible in federal court. The court ruled this was not "eavesdropping." The federal agent was there at the defendant's invitation, and therefore this was also not an unlawful physical invasion in violation of the Fourth Amendment.
12. Berger v. New York, 388 U.S. 41 (1967): Supreme Court ruled that New York state law was too broad in authorizing eavesdropping orders and violated the Fourth and Fourteenth Amendments.[608]
13. Katz v. U.S., 389 U.S. 347 (1967): Supreme Court rules that eavesdropping by federal agents without warrant using an electronic listening and recording device attached to the outside of a telephone phone booth is a violation of the Fourth Amendment. The decisions affirmed that the Fourth

[605] An undercover federal agent collected evidence using a hidden radio receiver against the defendant who was out on bail. The agent was a past friend and former employee of the defendant, and collected the evidence in the defendant's place of business and on the sidewalk outside. Accessed 7/27/19 at https://supreme. justia. com/cases/federal/us/343/747/

[606] Accessed 6/12/19 at https://supreme.justia.com/cases/federal/us/347/128/

[607] Accessed 7/27/19 at https://supreme.justia.com/cases/federal/us/367/643/

[608] t https://supreme.justia.com/cases/federal/us/388/41/

Amendment "extends ... to the recording of oral statements."[609] This decision finally overturned Olmstead v. U.S. and Goldman v. U.S.

14. United States v. United States District Court (the Keith Case), 407 U.S. 297 (1972): Supreme Court ruled that Presidentially authorized warrantless electronic surveillance conducted for domestic security purposes violated the Fourth Amendment. While acknowledging "the President's constitutional power to protect against overthrow of the Government," the court ruled that Congressional failure "to define presidential powers in matters affecting national security ... is not a grant of authority to conduct warrantless national security surveillances." [610]

---

[609] Accessed 6/12/19 at https://supreme.justia.com/cases/federal/us/389/347/

[610] t https://supreme.justia.com/cases/federal/us/407/297/

Chapter 9
Privacy Law Comes to the Commercial World

Should there be a generic law to protect our private information in the commercial world? We cannot understand the question, much less address its answer, without considering how the law has addressed this subject up until now.

The Privacy Act of 1974 provides a precedent for a privacy debate in the arena of government repositories. It was the culmination of two decades of Congressional wrangling about how the government should protect citizens' information, precipitated by the enhanced capabilities that computers brought to the task. Departments enacted regulations, policies, and procedures which reflected passage of this law.[611]

Truth be told, the United States Government had been collecting information about its residents since 1790, when the first census was conducted to apportion Congressional representation and taxes. More government records about individuals were generated when people paid their taxes. During the New Deal, the usefulness of the census was extended to the apportionment of federal entitlements. Mainframe computers, developed as urgent endeavors during World War II, migrated in peacetime to non-military customers; the Census Bureau received Univac 1, the first non-military computer, in 1951. Computer use proliferated across the government.

Computers also migrated to the commercial world, empowering businesses to aggregate, correlate, and disseminate private information about individuals as never before. This affected the privacy of individuals

---

[611] For example, see notices in the Federal Register, retrieved 11/8/19 at https://www.govinfo.gov/content/pkg/FR-1975-10-08/pdf/FR-1975-10-08.pdf

in such diverse areas as consumer-credit relationships, banking, mailing lists, insurance, employment, medical services, and education.

Over time, individuals became increasingly accustomed to giving up private information to government and businesses in exchange for benefits and services. The Privacy Act curbed what the government could do with this information. Three years later, the Privacy Protection Study Commission concluded that a generic privacy law for the commercial world was intractable at that time.

But legally binding privacy provisions had already been – and would continue to be - introduced in specific sectors. This chapter briefly explores two areas – consumer credit and medical services - in which Congress brought privacy laws to the commercial world. They illustrate how Congress attempted to thread a path between commercial interests and individual rights. It also provides an essential backdrop for our discussion about the future of U.S. privacy in chapter twelve.

Privacy and Consumer Rights in Credit Reporting

The Rise of Credit, Credit Cards, and Consumer Rights

Consumer reporting in the United States began after the Civil War. Post-war industrialization brought urbanization. New arrivals in cities found themselves far from home and from friends. In order to afford the things they needed, they had to rely on third party individuals for credit. A need to assess an individual's creditworthiness became necessary.[612]

In 1914, retailers began giving credit cards to their wealthier clients for use within the store. Possession of such a credit account in those days was prestigious. It also built customer loyalty, and allowed employees to identify the store's best customers. Over time, cooperatives of retailers in cities began offering a single credit account that could be used across all participating stores. By the early 1920's, after the automobile came into vogue, gasoline stations began distributing paper courtesy cards, the forerunner of the gasoline credit card. These could be used to purchase gasoline from across stations that sold fuel from a

[612] Lewis Mandell, The Credit Card Industry: A History. Boston; Twyne Publishers, 1990, 18-20.

specific oil company. In 1931, the first airline offered the first airline travel card.[613]

After World War II, the economic conditions were ideal for an industry built around credit to emerge. As Lewis Mandell tells us:

> For the first time in the country's history, the majority of Americans were earning income in excess of what it took to pay for their basic needs. In addition, the necessities of war had produced a massive U.S. industrial base, which was prepared to produced consumer durables at a tremendous pace: stoves, refrigerators, automobiles – the more goods consumers purchased, the more goods industry produced, in ever increasing variety and number.[614]

In 1949, the Diners Club card emerged as the first credit card that could be used to make purchases at a variety of businesses, all dining establishments. In 1958, American Express and Carte Blanche launched credit card operations to compete with Diners Club. Also in 1958, the two largest U.S. banks, Bank of America and Chase Manhattan Bank, began credit card operations. By 1960, there were four basic types of credit cards: retail cards, gasoline cards, travel and entertainment cards, as well as bank issued cards.[615]

Credit cards and Consumer Reporting Agencies (CRAs) grew into an industry. Increasingly empowered by computer technology, CRAs were able to accumulate and organize all sorts of information about individual consumers. Localized credit reporting over time evolved into nationwide CRAs empowered by nationwide communications and computing. They became essential elements of the modern economy, providing efficiencies for customers and creditors, as well as "social and even physical mobility."[616]

The evolution of credit from across many types of businesses – department stores, gasoline companies, hotels, restaurants, airlines, and banks – meant that many different federal laws and regulators had de facto jurisdiction. This ambiguity – and the growth of the industry - induced

---

[613] Mandell, 18-20.
[614] Mandell, xiii.
[615] Mandell, 28-30.
[616] Chris Jay Hoofnagle, Federal Trade Commission Privacy Law and Policy. New York: Cambridge University Press, 2016, p. 271.

Congress to step in in 1968 with the Consumer Credit Protection Act.[617] Title I of this contains the original Truth in Lending Act, designed to "assure a meaningful disclosure of credit terms so that the consumer will be able to compare more readily the various credit terms available to him and avoid the uninformed use of credit." Intended for the private consumer, it covered such things as determination of finance charges and annual percentage rates. It granted regulatory authority to the Federal Reserve Board. It granted administrative enforcement to the Federal Trade Commission (FTC), except in those areas in which it has been granted to other government agencies by prior laws.[618] Finally, consumers were starting to have rights.

In the late 1960s, banks initiated huge campaigns to increase their credit card customers by mass mailing unsolicited credit cards to individuals. This predictably led to an explosion of fraudulent credit card charges and customer complaints. In 1970, the issuance of unsolicited credit cards was temporarily banned by the FTC, and then permanently banned by Congress in by amending the Truth in Lending Act.[619] The amendment also clarified the procedure to be followed by the cardholder and the card issuer to minimize the credit customer's liability. In cases of disputed liability, Congress added that the burden of proof was on the issuer, not the user. More rights had been accorded the consumer.

The Fair Credit Reporting Act

The Fair Credit Reporting Act (FCRA)[620] of 1970 was Congress' first law to address information privacy issues across a single industry.[621]

---

[617] Accessed 9/28/19 at https://www.govinfo.gov/content/pkg/STATUTE-82/pdf/STATUTE-82-Pg146.pdf

[618] Just to illustrate how confusing this all was, the other agencies included: the Comptroller of the Currency, the Federal Reserve Board, the Federal Deposit Insurance Corporation, the Federal Home Loan Bank Board, the Federal Savings and Loan Insurance Corporation, the Director of Bureau of Federal Credit Unions, the Interstate Commerce Commission, the Civil Aeronautics Board, and the Secretary of Agriculture.

[619] Accessed 9/28/19 at https://www.govinfo.gov/content/pkg/STATUTE-84/pdf/STATUTE-84-Pg1114-2.pdf

[620] Accessed 9/28/19 at https://www.govinfo.gov/content/pkg/STATUTE-84/pdf/STATUTE-84-Pg1114-2.pdf

[621] See Hoofnagle, 46.

FCRA acknowledged that the banking system relies on fair and accurate credit reporting provided by CRAs. It defined a CRA as "any person [who] ... regularly engages in ... the practice of assembling or evaluating consumer credit information or other information on consumers for the purpose of furnishing consumer report to third parties...." In performing this critical function, CRAs must "exercise their grave responsibilities with fairness, impartiality, and a respect for the consumer's right to privacy." Congress felt this was important because consumer reports could contain personal information about a "consumer's credit worthiness, credit standing, credit capacity, character, general reputation, personal characteristics, or mode of living" which could impact an individual's ability to obtain credit, insurance, or employment. We've already seen how the Privacy Act picked up on and reiterated such concerns.

FCRA stated that CRAs could prepare consumer reports in response to judicial order or written request from the consumer, or to a person who is using the information to decide whether to extend credit, employment, insurance, etc. to the consumer. In cases when public record information incorporated in a consumer report was likely to have an adverse effect on employment opportunities, the CRA must (1) make sure that the information is complete and up to date, and (2) notify the consumer. Investigative consumer reports – those which focused on noncredit issues like character, general reputation, personal characteristics, or mode of living – were prohibited from being prepared or procured unless the consumer was informed.

CRAs were required to ensure that the information contained in any consumer report was as accurate - complete and up-to-date - as possible. Upon request by the consumer, every CRA had to disclose the nature and substance of all information in the consumer's file to the consumer, as well as the sources of the information, and the recipients of any report on the consumer. The consumer had the right to dispute any information held by the CRA. The latter was obliged to investigate disputed information, and correct inaccuracies.

In this era before the Privacy Act and FISA, it is interesting to note that FCRA specifically stated that CRAs could "furnish identifying information respecting any consumer, limited to his name, address, former addresses, places of employment, or former places of employment, to a governmental agency."

Administrative enforcement authority was given to the FTC, again excepting those areas in which it has been granted to other government agencies by prior laws. Consumer rights progressed.

FCRA was subsequently amended in 1996 and 2003, resulting in permanent preemption of state law by federal legislation "under the theory that the states would create conflicting obligations that could harm a national consumer reporting system."[622] This was a boon to CRAs who did not want state and local laws to interfere with their national credit reporting operations. As long as the CRAs ensured accuracy of the records and limited disclosures, "they enjoy limited immunity from state defamation, privacy, and negligence cases."[623]

FCRA imposes limitations on the use of public record information by CRA's to protect individual privacy. But judicial decisions today favor almost-unlimited reporting of the same information as a First Amendment right of the commercial world, challenging privacy. Hoofnagle suggests that such challenges to FCRA could be deterred by tying immunity from state privacy law to right preservation under FCRA.[624]

Subsequent Laws Concerning Credit and Consumer Rights

In 1974, a few months before the Privacy Act was passed, Congress passed the Fair Credit Billing Act (FCBA).[625] With this act, Congress updated the Truth in Lending Act to "protect the consumer against inaccurate and unfair credit billing and credit card practices," and empowered the Federal Reserve Board as the credit billing regulator. FCBA set forth the right of individuals to request corrections to their billing statements, and to have the creditor respond within a fixed amount of time. Should the charge be erroneous, the creditor had to make corrections to the customer's account, including any finance charges, within a fixed time. The creditor could not "threaten to report to any person

---

[622] Hoofnagle, 276.
[623] Ibid.
[624] Hoofnagle, 286, 289.
[625] Accessed 9/28/19 at https://www.ftc.gov/sites/default/files/fcb.pdf

adversely on the obligor's credit rating or credit standing because of the obligor's failure to pay the [disputed] amount … until the creditor has met the requirements" outlined in this law.

In 1977, Congress passed the Fair Debt Collection Practices Act (FDCPA),[626] further amending the Consumer Credit Protection Act. This law was intended to reign in the "use of abusive, deceptive, and unfair debt collection practices by many debt collectors [which] contribute to the number of personal bankruptcies, to marital instability, to the loss of jobs, and to invasions of individual privacy." FTC was given the authority for administrative enforcement of FDCPA, except in cases in which the enforcement authority had already been granted by law to another government entity.

In 1978 – the same year that FISA passed – Congress passed the Right to Financial Privacy Act (RFPA).[627] This law prohibited the government from getting access to financial information, including from credit card companies, about an individual unless it was previously authorized by the individual, or judicially sanctioned.

The 1999 Gramm-Leach-Bliley Act[628] repealed Depression-era legislation to permit greater integration of financial institutions, now big players in the credit card industry. A financial institution was defined as "any institution engaged in the business of providing financial services to customers who maintain a credit, deposit, trust, or other financial account or relationship with the institution." Title V entitled "Privacy" affirmed that financial institutions had an obligation "to respect the privacy of its customers and to protect the security and confidentiality of those customers' nonpublic personal information [NPI]." NPI meant personally identifiable financial information "(i) provided by a consumer to a financial institution; (ii) resulting from any transaction with the consumer or any service performed for the consumer; or (iii) otherwise obtained by the financial institution."

---

[626] Accessed 9/28/19 at https://www.govinfo.gov/content/pkg/STATUTE-91/pdf/STATUTE-91-Pg874.pdf#page=1

[627] Accessed 9/28/19 at https://www.govinfo.gov/content/pkg/STATUTE-92/pdf/STATUTE-92-Pg3641.pdf#page=1

[628] Accessed 10/6/19 at https://www.govinfo.gov/content/pkg/STATUTE-113/pdf/STATUTE-113-Pg1338.pdf

It authorized all government authorities with jurisdiction to "establish appropriate standards for financial institutions relating to administrative, technical, and physical safeguards - (1) to insure the security and confidentiality of customer records and information; (2) to protect against any anticipated threats or hazards to the security or integrity of such records; and (3) to protect against unauthorized access to or use of such records or information which could result in substantial harm or inconvenience to any customer." In general, it restricted the release of NPI private to nonaffiliated third parties without providing prior notice and an "opt out" opportunity to the customer. Financial institutions could still provide NPI to third parties which provided services for the former, to include marketing. It limited the release of NPI by third parties to other parties. Fraudulent access to customer financial information was prohibited, and punishable with criminal penalties.

Health Information

Health Insurance Portability and Accountability Act (HIPPA)

The 1970 amendment to the Consumer Credit Protection Act had defined medical information as "information or records obtained, with the consent of the individual to whom it relates, from licensed physicians or medical practitioners, hospitals, clinics, or other medical or medically related facilities." It would take until 1996 before Congress was ready to tackle legislation of privacy in the medical industry.

The Health Insurance Portability and Accountability Act (HIPAA)[629] enacted provisions to protect the "privacy of [all] individuals receiving health care services." Now the privacy of patients' "individually identifiable medical information" (IIMI) was protected by law. All entities involved in the healthcare industry - doctors, nurses, hospitals, medical insurance companies, medical laboratories. etc. – would be held responsible.

---

[629] Accessed 9/28/19 at https://www.govinfo.gov/content/pkg/BILLS-104hr3103enr/pdf/BILLS-104hr3103enr.pdf

Congress directed the Secretary of Health and Human Services (HHS)[630] to adopt security standards that accounted for the technical capabilities of all systems containing health information, the costs associated with implementing security measures, the training required for the personnel who have access to the system, "the value of audit trails in computerized record systems," and the needs and capabilities of small health care providers. The law required safeguards to protect the integrity and confidentiality of IIMI. HIPAA also included provisions for civil and criminal penalties for violations of the law.

Informed by the 1973 HEW report and the 1977 Privacy Protection Study discussed in Chapter 7, HHS implemented these as the HIPAA Privacy Rule and the HIPAA Security Rule.

The HIPAA Privacy Rule[631] provides "Standards for Privacy of Individually Identifiable Health Information" (IIHI) which includes information related to:

1. "The individual's past, present or future physical or mental health or condition,
2. The provision of health care to the individual, or
3. The past, present, or future payment for the provision of health care to the individual…."

It also includes common information that can be used to identify the individual, like name, birth date, and Social Security Number. The Privacy Rule does not restrict the use of health information which has gone through a de-identification process so it no longer identifies the identify of an individual. This process can be completed by the removal of specific identifiers in the individual's records.

The Privacy Rule limits uses and disclosures of IIHI to the individual; to treatment, payment, and health care operations; and, for the public interest and benefit activities (as required by law, e.g. in the event of serious threat to health and safety). Limited data sets (from which specific identifiers have been removed) are available for research, health care operations, and public health purposes. All other uses require the

---

[630] HEW we split into the Department of Education and the Department of Health and Human Services in 1980.

[631] Retrieved 5/7/19 at https://www.hhs.gov/sites/default/files/privacysummary. pdf

individual's authorization. Furthermore, the Privacy Rule prohibits use of IIHI for marketing of health-related products or services.

The health care industry is required under the Privacy Rule to request, use, and disclose the "minimum necessary" information about the individual. Furthermore, all IIHI record keepers must have policies and procedures in place which restrict the access and use of IIHI, and identify the individuals in their workforce who require access to this information. Regular policies and procedures should also be implemented to handle "routine, recurring disclosure, or requests for disclosures" of IIHI.

As we all have experienced, the Privacy Rule requires the health care industry to provide a notice of its privacy practices to individuals. Individuals have the right to review, obtain a copy of, and amend their health records. They have a right to an accounting of the disclosures of IIHI, as well as the right to restrict use of disclosure of IIHI. Individuals have the right to confidential communications from their health care providers and health plans.

An entity subject to the Privacy Rule must designate a privacy official who develops and implements the required privacy policies and procedures. The workforce must be trained on the entity's privacy policies and procedures. A covered entity must mitigate against the effects of inappropriate disclosures or use of IIHI. A covered entity must apply reasonable and appropriate safeguards to protect IIHI. A covered entity must have procedures in place to handle complaints, and is prohibited from taking retaliatory action against an individual for exercising her Privacy Rule rights. The Privacy Rule enumerates civil and criminal penalties to which may be subject as a result of non-compliance.

The Security Rule [632] applies to electronic protected health information (e-PHI), that is, the "individually identifiable health information a covered entity creates, receives, maintains or transmits in electronic form." It requires entities to:

1. "Ensure the confidentiality, integrity, and availability of all ePHI they create, receive, maintain, or transmit;

---

[632] Accessed 5/6/19 at https:// www.hhs.gov / hipaa / for-professionals / security/ lawsregulations/index.html?language=es

2. Identify and protect against reasonable anticipated threats to the security or integrity of the information;
3. Protect against reasonably anticipated, impermissible uses of disclosures; and
4. Ensure compliance by their workforce."

Compliance with the Security Rule is explicitly expected to be tempered by the size, complexity, capability of the organization; its technical infrastructure; the costs associated with security measures; and the likelihood and potential impact to e-PHI associated with the risks.

The entity is required to perform risk analysis as part of their security management processes. The Security Rule emphasizes that "Risk Management should be an ongoing process, in which a covered entity regularly reviews its records to track access to e-PHI and detect security incidents, periodically evaluates the effectiveness of security measures put in place, and regularly reevaluates potential risks to e-PHI." It should also include physical safeguards and technical safeguards, like access control, audit, controls, integrity controls, and transmission security. In the event of a breach, the entity "must take reasonable steps to cure the breach or end the violation."

Concerns about the privacy of medical information even crossed over into the financial sector. Congress specifically called out protection, and limitation of the use and sharing of medical information in the financial system in its 2003 Fair and Accurate Credit Transactions Act.

The Health Information Technology for Economic and Clinical Health (HITECH) Act

The ''Health Information Technology for Economic and Clinical Health Act'' or HITECH Act was enacted in 2009 to promote a nationwide health information technology infrastructure. It was envisioned that such an infrastructure would allow electronic use and exchange of information to improve health care while also securing and protecting each patient's health information and reducing health care costs.

Congress defined the term 'qualified electronic health record' as an electronic record of health-related information on an individual that-

1. includes patient demographic and clinical health information, such as medical history and problem lists; and

2. has the capacity to provide clinical decision support; to support physician order entry; to capture and query information relevant to health care quality; and to exchange electronic health information with, and integrate such information from other sources.

Congress also defined a breach as the "unauthorized acquisition, access, use, or disclosure of protected health information which compromises the security or privacy of such information, except where an unauthorized person to whom such information is disclosed would not reasonably have been able to retain such information." Any covered entity that "accesses, maintains, retains, modifies, records, stores, destroys, or otherwise holds, uses, or discloses unsecured protected health information" is required to notify each affected individual in the case of a breach. Furthermore, HITECH prohibited the sale of electronic health records or protected health information.

Conclusion

This chapter reviewed some of the earliest federal privacy provisions enacted in law which applied to specific industries. The popularization of credit cards throughout the 1960s, brought Congressional legislation in 1968 and FTC regulatory action by 1970. In 1970, FCRA was enacted to protect the private credit information of citizens. This information was seen as something which could affect an individual's ability to get credit, insurance, or employment. We now understand that FCRA also helped pave the way for the Privacy Act in 1974. Subsequent laws continued to clarify the individual rights of consumers. The 1978 Right to Financial Privacy Act prohibited the government from getting financial information (including from credit card companies) about an individual unless authorized by the individual, or judicially sanctioned. By 1999, the Gramm-Leach-Bliley Act affirmed that financial institutions had an obligation to protect the security, confidentiality, and integrity of customer records containing NPI, and protect them from unauthorized use.

Considerable time has elapsed since the initial FCRA framework was enacted. It was built on a hodgepodge of different laws regulating different industries, implementing a complicated system of legal authorities and regulatory jurisdictions. When FCRA was passed, only large corporate players could afford the technology that allowed the derivation of important information from big data stores. Such capabilities are far more accessible to far more of the commercial world today, and pose threats to privacy the framework of existing consumer protection laws. Looking forward, FCRA can only go two ways. FCRA may be given the boot by Congress as obsolete. Alternatively, FCRA may receive a new lease on life from Congress. Law scholar Chris Hoofnagle suggests that the FCRA privacy framework could be leveraged in new legislation intended to implement FCRA's privacy intentions across commercial entities which commoditize consumers' private information.[633]

Whereas the Privacy Act talked about but never defined "personal information," the HIPAA Privacy Rule finally pinned down what was meant by IIHI. A definition for "Personally Identifiable Information" (PII) would finally emerge from the National Institute of Standards and Technology (NIST) in 2010, and we'll talk about that shortly.

These examples provide a necessary context for understanding how to approach privacy in a modern world of cyber threats and information system security. But before we can get to that in chapter eleven, we have to make one brief, but essential, excursion to talk about how public corporations evolved to manage risk – including that posed by government intervention – at an enterprise level.

---

[633] See Hoofnagle, 285-286.

Chapter 10
Governance, Risk Management, and Compliance

The multiplicity of issues and interests around U.S. commercial businesses makes it difficult for Congress to create generic laws. In the previous chapter, we saw how Congress used a sectoral approach to enact privacy provisions to cover credit reporting and medical entities. In this chapter, we're going to focus on the law of governance, risk management, and compliance (GRC), "the body of rules, regulations and best practices that … are intended to ensure that organizations are managed effectively and … to enhance social welfare."[634] These three intertwined concepts form an overlapping armor designed to protect both the organization and the public interest.

GRC evolved in the context of large companies and financial institutions. With huge investments at stake, large organizations needed GRC to ensure usage of sound business practices, and to remain on the right side of the law. Government regulators and prosecutors also needed GRC. It helped establish standard formats for financial reporting, and made it easier to track how well businesses were complying with the letter and spirit of the law.

GRC necessarily changed over time, evolving to accommodate risks associated with updates in the law and emerging technologies. Given no inherent concern about protecting the privacy of consumers, corporations only applied GRC to privacy when laws and regulations forced the issue.

It is the purpose of this chapter to familiarize ourselves with the basic concepts of GRC. We will look at its corporate origins, and how

---

[634] Geoffrey Parsons Miller, The Law of Governance, Risk Management, and Compliance. New York: Wolters Kluwer Law & Business, 2014, p.3.

financial crises, new legislation, and innovative technologies caused its practices to evolve.

This background on GRC provides a necessary perspective for chapter eleven, which focuses on how GRC was used to frame the privacy debate in cyberspace.

Evolution of Regulation and GRC

Until the time of the railroads, American industry was regulated by judicial action. If a company adopted an unfair practice, the courts adjudicated. This created a lot of work for the court system, and finally in 1887, the Interstate Commerce Act created the first regulatory body – the Interstate Commerce Commission (ICC) – which focused on the regulation of railroad fares.

The trend toward administrative regulation continued as the size and interconnectedness of corporations grew, and as their impact on and risk to the public good increased. Anti-monopoly legislation appeared with the 1890 Sherman Anti-Trust Act, and was made more substantive with the 1914 Clayton Anti-Trust Act. The Federal Trade Commission (FTC) was created in 1914 to prevent the usage of "unfair methods of competition in commerce."[635]

The 1929 stock market crash and resulting depression brought serious financial woes to the United States. The Banking (Glass-Steagall) Act of 1933 was enacted "To provide for the safer and: more effective use of the assets of banks, to regulate interbank control, to prevent the undue diversion of funds into speculative operations."[636] The Securities Act of 1933[637] introduced a federal registration system for securities and security exchanges, and specified the information to be contained in the registration application This included a financial statement, as well as signatures by the principal executive officers, the principal accounting officer, and the majority of the board of directors. The balance sheet had to be certified by

---

635 Federal Trade Commission Act of 1914, accessed 11/19/19 at https://uscode.house.gov/statviewer.htm?volume=38&page=717

636 The Banking (Glass-Steagall) Act of 1933, accessed 11/24/19 at https://fraser.stlouisfed.org/title/991

637 The Securities Act of 1933, accessed 11/19/19 at https://govtrackus.s3.amazonaws.com/legislink/pdf/stat/48/STATUTE-48-Pg74.pdf

an independent public or certified accountant. The 1934 Securities Exchange Act created the Securities and Exchange Commission (SEC) to regulate securities and exchanges.[638] It authorized the SEC to collect annual reports from regulated entities to protect investors and ensure fair dealing. The SEC could prescribe the rule and regulations for such filing, to include the forms and methods to be followed, and even certification by independent public accountants.

In 1930, the American Institute of Accountants (AIA, today the American Institute of Certified Public Accountants or AICPA) began working with the New York Stock Exchange (NYSE) to improve financial disclosures made by publicly held entities. There was a belief that "inferior accounting and reporting practices had contributed to the stock market decline and depression."[639] The NYSE felt that the variability in accounting methods had permitted questionable practices. Reform would come "to make financial statements more informative and authoritative, to clarify the authority and responsibility of auditors, and to educate the public about the conventional nature of accounting and the limitations of accounting reports."

After its creation, the SEC became increasingly involved in accounting practices and reporting. AIA was careful to foster a working relationship with the SEC, leading to a co-evolution of accounting practices. Over time, cooperation between the accountants, accounting professional organizations, and the SEC would lead to what we today Generally Accepted Accounting Principles (GAAP).

In 1977, bribery of foreign officials by American companies induced Congress to pass the Foreign Corrupt Practices Act (FCPA).[640] It prohibited bribery of foreign officials, and required the use of transparency in accounting practices. It also required companies "to devise and maintain

---

[638] Securities and Exchange Commission Act, of 1934, accessed 11/19/19 at https://govtrackus.s3.amazonaws.com/legislink/pdf/stat/48/STATUTE-48-Pg88 1a.pdf

[639] Read K. Storey & Sylvia Storey, "FASB Special Report: The Framework of Financial Accounting Concepts and Standards," No. 181-C, January 1998, p. 4, accessed 11/21/19 at https://www.fasb.org/jsp/FASB/Document_C/DocumentPage?cid=1176171746896&acceptedDisclaimer=true

[640] https://www.gpo.gov/fdsys/pkg/STATUTE-91/pdf/STATUTE-91-Pg1494.pdf

a system of internal accounting controls sufficient to provide reasonable assurances that-

1. Transactions are executed in accordance with management's general or specific authorization;
2. Transactions are recorded as necessary
   a. to permit preparation of financial statements in conformity with generally accepted accounting principles or any other criteria applicable to such statements, and
   b. to maintain accountability for assets;
3. Access to assets is permitted only in accordance with management's general or specific authorization; and
4. The recorded accountability for assets is compared with the existing assets at reasonable intervals and appropriate action is taken with respect to any differences."

The act was amended in 1988 and 1998.

The Savings and Loan (S&L) Crisis of the 1980s, and 1990s, led to the passage of new laws for financial institutions. The Financial Institutions Reform, Recovery, and Enforcement Act of 1989 (FIRREA)[641] to "reform, recapitalize, and consolidate the Federal deposit insurance system, to enhance the regulatory and enforcement powers of Federal financial institutions, regulatory agencies...." FIRREA also includes civil and criminal penalties. The word "compliance" appears 58 times in this law. The Federal Deposit Insurance Corporation Improvement Act of 1991 (FDICIA) specified the need for federal regulation regarding internal controls to ensure compliance with law and regulations. It further specified that bank's financial statements be audited by an independent accountant in accordance with GAAP, and required each bank to establish an Independent Audit Committee for improved accountability.

The next financial crisis was set off by the Enron scandal. Details about fraudulent accounting practices began emerging in 2001, and Enron stock prices collapsed. The SEC launched an investigation, and Enron filed for bankruptcy protection. Enron was ultimately dissolved, and several Enron officials went to jail. Enron's independent auditor, the then-

---

[641] Accessed 11/24/19 at https://www.govinfo.gov/content/pkg/STATUTE-103/ pdf/ STATUTE-103-Pg183.pdf#page=1

prestigious accounting firm Arthur Andersen, was indicted for obstruction of justice and went out of business. Enron was but one of the "several spectacular corporate failures"-others included WorldCom, Global Crossing, and Adelphia - which led to "one of the most important governance and compliance statutes in American history," the 2002 Sarbanes-Oxley (SOX) Act. We will look more deeply into SOX shortly.

The 2008-2009 financial crisis was set off by a cascade of financial institution failures like Bear Stearns, Lehman Brothers, IndyMac, and AIG. In response, Congress passed the 2010 Dodd-Frank Wall Street Reform and Consumer Protection Act "To promote the financial stability of the United States by improving accountability and transparency in the financial system, to end 'too big to fail', to protect the American taxpayer by ending bailouts, to protect consumers from abusive financial services practices…." This law is considered "the most significant piece of financial regulation since the Great Depression, which contains many provisions relevant to compliance."[642] It enacted corporate governance reforms, extended SEC regulatory power, created an SEC Office of Credit Ratings to oversee credit rating agencies, and established rewards for whistleblowers in SEC enforcement actions resulting in sanctions over one million dollars.

These events contextualize modern GRC based on its evolution in the big business sector. We are now ready to talk about the principles of governance, which today hold executive teams and boards of directors responsible for corporate behavior, including wrongdoing.

The Elements of Governance

Governance: "the processes by which decisions relative to risk management and compliance are made within an organization."[643]

In publicly held corporations, governance is executed by its owners and the controllers. The owners are the shareholders, whose involvement in the corporation is limited. Their total liability is restricted to the price of the shares they hold. The "public good" the government

---

[642] Miller, 140.
[643] Miller, 2.

seeks to protect through law, regulation, and policy includes shareholder interests.

The controllers are the Board and Directors (BOD) and the senior executives that work for them. The BOD operates at a high level, delegating day to day management to the senior executive team. Its leader, the Chief Executive Officer (CEO), makes key decisions for the organization, serves as the public face of the organization, and is responsible for setting the tone at the top.[644]

SOX started to hold governance controllers increasingly responsible for the corporation. It holds senior executives directly accountable for the activities of their organizations. Section 302 of SOX requires the CEO and Chief Financial Officer (CFO) to certify any quarterly or annual reports about the company as truthful. They are responsible for establishing and maintaining internal controls for the company. Section 802 outlines criminal penalties for anyone – including the CEO and CFO – who alters or falsifies documents. SOX Section 401 requires all financial reports to be accurate and prepared according GAAP. Transparency is key. The SEC reviews the filing to ensure that it presents its case to investors in a transparent fashion. SOX Section 404 requires an internal control report be part of the annual report to the SEC. The corporation must describe its internal control structure and procedure.

Publicly held corporations are required to conduct audits. An audit is defined in SOX as an "examination of the financial statements" of any publicly held corporation "by an independent public accounting firm" in accordance with SEC rules. Such audits are aided by internal audit processes within the corporation that "independently and objectively evaluate and report on the effectiveness of an institution's risk management, control and governance processes."[645] The internal audit consists of an audit plan, audit findings which identify problems, the causes and consequences of the problems, and recommendations and/or remediation.[646] Audit plans must be customized to account for the greatest risk areas, and cannot consist solely of a list of checkboxes.

---

[644] Miller, 107-108.
[645] Miller, 117-118.
[646] Miller, 113-114.

The Elements of Compliance

Compliance: "the processes by which an organization polices its own behavior to ensure that it conforms to applicable rules and regulations."[647]

Compliance is a function undertaken within an organization to ensure that its corporate norms are enforced. These norms should align with all applicable laws, regulations, and policies. A big part of the compliance function is ensuring that the organization is minimizing its risk with respect to civil and criminal liability so as to maximize its profits.

Corporate Compliance Players

A corporation's senior leadership is responsible for setting and modeling the values to which it expects every employee to subscribe. For example, Google's is "Don't be evil." The compliance policy also comes from the top. It addresses how the organization will deal with compliance issues, to include compliance with values, standards, and all applicable laws and regulations.

Compliance programs are mechanisms to ensure compliance, and procedures to follow when alleged incidents of non-compliance occur. Compliance values and standards are not just about financial misdeeds, but about fair hiring practices, training, and almost everything else, including privacy.[648] U.S. companies which operate overseas must also comply with foreign laws and regulations, like the European Union's General Data Protection Regulation (GDPR).[649]

In 2004, the SEC began requiring each investment company and investment adviser to identify a Chief Compliance Officer responsible for administering policies and procedures designed to prevent federal security law violations. The compliance officer is required to meet with the independent directors of the organization at least one a year.[650]

In the 2001 Patriot Act, the government described an early version of a compliance program, requiring "each financial institution ... [to]

---

[647] Miller, 2.
[648] Miller, 187-188.
[649] Miller, 190-191.
[650] Accessed 11/19/19 at https://www.sec.gov/rules/final/ia-2204.htm

establish anti-money laundering programs, including, at a minimum-

1. the development of internal policies, procedures, and controls;
2. the designation of a compliance officer;
3. an ongoing employee training program; and
4. an independent audit function to test programs."[651]

Regulators

Government regulators are in a tricky position. They need to draft regulations which maximize detection of compliance violations, while simultaneously guarding against over-regulation. The regulations also have to be sophisticated enough to identify improprieties even when the regulated organization might be trying to evade detection of wrongdoing.

Regulators have extremely limited resources. As Miller tells us: "By increasing their access to information and substituting administrative for judicial enforcement, the regulators reduce their costs and administering the law because it is easier for them to detect violations and, if they detect a violation, it is cheaper for them to enforce the rules. Regulators also reduce the cost of enforcement by increasing the severity for sanctions."[652]

While it is true that regulators have broad access to information about business firms, it is important to note that companies are recognized as legal persons protected by the Bill of Rights. We ran into the First Amendment rights of CRAs in the previous chapter, and we will pick up this thread in the concluding chapter.

Prosecutors

The US Department of Justice investigates and brings changes of criminal misconduct against corporations to protect the public interest. These interests include:

1. "protecting the integrity of our economic and capital markets by enforcing the rule of law;
2. protecting consumers, investors, and business entities against competitors who gain unfair advantage by violating the law;

[651] Accessed 11/19/19 at https://www.gpo.gov/fdsys/pkg/PLAW-107publ56/pdf/PLAW-107publ56.pdf
[652] Miller, 167-168.

3. preventing violations of environmental laws; and
4. discouraging business practices that would permit or promote unlawful conduct at the expense of the public interest."[653]

Prosecutors consider and weigh several factors before they proceed with prosecution. These can include the type, severity, and/or pervasiveness of the alleged crime; a company's prior history of similar offenses, timely and voluntary disclosure of the offense, cooperativeness during the investigation, whether a prior compliance program exists and its effectiveness, any remedial actions taken by the corporation, the impact of the offense on others (e.g. shareholders, employees, etc.).[654] The existence of a previously existing compliance program is a good thing, but will not necessary preclude prosecution. Nor can it be a program on paper only; it has to have been designed to detect the most likely forms of misconduct.[655]

The Federal Sentencing Guidelines for Organizations (1991, 2004) called for leniency in some cases against corporate defendants if an effective compliance and ethics program was in place. An organization is said to have such a program if it "(1) exercise[s] ... due diligence to prevent and detect criminal conduct; and (2) otherwise promote[s] an organizational culture that encourages ethical conduct and a commitment to compliance with the law."[656]

Gatekeepers

A gatekeeper is "someone whose certification or support is needed before an organization can meet a goal."[657] Gatekeepers include the attorneys. SOX spells out a code of conduct for attorneys appearing before the SEC, "requiring an attorney to report evidence of a material violation of securities law or breach of fiduciary duty or similar violation by the

---

[653] Accessed 11/24/19 at https://www.justice.gov/usam/usam-9-28000-principles-federal-prosecution-business-organizations [654]Miller, 253-254.

[654] Miller, (248-249).

[655] Miller, 253-254.

[656] Accessed 11/19/19 at https://www.ussc.gov/guidelines/2016-guidelines-manual/2016-chapter-8 [656]Miller, 293.

[657] Miller, 293.

company of any agent thereof to the chief legal counsel or the chief executive officer [CEO] of the company…."[658]

Gatekeepers include the accountants who must act "with integrity, objectivity, due professional care, and a genuine interest in serving the public," as described in the Code of Professional Conduct of the American Institute of Certified Public Accountants.[659]

Gatekeepers include the auditors, who perform an independent review of financial controls and statements. Whereas accountants owe their allegiance to the company, the auditors owe their allegiance to the investors. Auditors were self-regulating, until SOX created the Public Company Accounting Oversight Board (PCAOB) "to oversee the audit of public companies that are subject to the securities laws, and related matters, in order to protect the interests of investors and further the public interest in the preparation of informative, accurate, and independent audit reports for companies the securities of which are sold to, and held by and for, public investors."[660] The PCAOB was empowered to register all public accounting firms that perform audits, establish auditing standards, conduct inspections and investigations of public accounting firms, impose disciplinary actions and sanctions against public accounting firms, and enforce SOX compliance.[661] SOX also authorizes the SEC to establish the rules for the internal control part of the annual report required to be filed with the SEC annually. The auditor must use a framework for this evaluation. Generally, American accounting firms use the internal control framework of the Committee of Sponsoring Organizations of the Treadway Commission (COSO).

Finally, gatekeepers also include external consultants which may be called in to help a corporation. For example, consider the Independent Private Sector Inspector General (IPSIG), which according to their website

---

[658] Accessed 11/19/19 at https://www.congress.gov/107/plaws/publ204/PLAW-107 publ204.pdf

[659] Accessed 11/19/19 at https://www.aicpa.org/content/dam/aicpa/research/ standards/codeofconduct/downloadabledocuments/2014december15contentasof2016august31codeofconduct.pdf

[660] Accessed 11/19/19 at https://www.congress.gov/107/plaws/publ204/PLAW-107 publ204.pdf

[661] Ibid.

is "an independent, private sector firm with legal, auditing, investigative, management and loss prevention skills, employed by an organization (voluntarily or by compulsory process) to ensure compliance with relevant law and regulations, and to deter, prevent, uncover and report unethical and illegal conduct by, within and against the organizations. The IPSIG may, in addition, be a major participant with management in enhancing the economy, efficiency and effectiveness of the organization."[662]

How Compliance Programs Buy Good Will

We previously discussed the FCPA, which boiled down to a law against bribing foreign officials, and a requirement for accurate accounting books and controls. The associated penalties for violating this law can include severe reputational impact, monetary fines, suspension and/or disbarment, a criminal record, and jail time. However, DOJ and the SEC are inclined to look more favorably upon such transgressions if a strong compliance program has been implemented in good faith by the company, and is being continually improved. In point of fact, the DOJ and SEC released an FCPA Resource Guide in 2012 which included ten hallmarks of an effective compliance program:

1. Commitment from Senior Management and a Clearly Articulated Policy Against Corruption
2. Code of Conduct and Compliance Policies and Procedures
3. Oversight, Autonomy, and Resources
4. Risk Assessment
5. Training and Continuing Advice
6. Incentives and Disciplinary Measures
7. Third-Party Due Diligence and Payments
8. Confidential Reporting and Internal Investigation
9. Continuous Improvement: Periodic Testing and Review
10. Mergers and Acquisitions: Pre-Acquisition Due Diligence and Post-Acquisition Integration.[663]

The Elements of Risk Management

Risk Management: "the processes by which risk is identified, analyzed, included in strategic planning, and

---

[662] http://www.iaipsig.org/

[663] Accessed 11/19/19 at https://www.sec.gov/spotlight/fcpa/fcpa-resource-guide.pdf

> **either reduced through risk mitigation tactics or accepted as inherent activities that the organization wishes to conduct."[664]**

Risk management is the usage of strategies to manage uncertainties. The uncertainties are associated with future outcomes which can have positive or negative impacts on the organization. Compliance reduces risk by measuring adherence to best financial practices, and applicable laws and regulations. Non-compliance can lead to financial losses, prosecution, and loss of reputation.[665]

The risk management function is centralized today. It focuses on analyzing the risk appetite of the organization - the level of risk an organization is comfortable taking to achieve its strategic objectives. This includes financial and non-financial risks. Enterprise Risk Management (ERM) looks at risks across the entire enterprise, and emphasizes transparency for internal review and external regulation. ERM also elevates the importance of risk management to the senior governance level. Generally, organizations look to the COSO guidelines and the risk management white paper of the International Standards Organization (ISO 31000) to implement ERM.[666] We will look at risk management methodologies in the next chapter in more detail.

The effective performance of risk management requires all the following:

1. Access to and analysis of accurate and complete information is essential to risk management.
2. An understanding of the risk appetite of the organization - how much risk the organization is willing to take.
3. An implementation of the risk appetite by compiling a risk inventory, assessing inherent risk (the risk an activity poses in the absence of any prevention or mitigation efforts), assessing controls and mitigation options, assessing residual risk (the remaining an activity poses after prevention or mitigation efforts have been implemented), and acceptance of the residual risk.

---

[664] Miller, 2.
[665] Miller, 531-532.
[666] Miller, 537-538.

4. The use of sophisticated computer models to simulate possible outcomes based on ordinary and extraordinary events occurring.
5. An appreciation for the behavioral economics of the situation. Daniel Kahneman received the Nobel Prize for his work describing the predictable ways in which individuals behave "irrationally" when making financial decisions.[667]

Conclusion

Organizations rely on governance, compliance, and risk management to ensure they use sound business practices and remain on the right side of the law. Laws passed in the wake of financial crises enhanced government regulatory authorities and increased the personal accountability of corporate executives. This encouraged corporate entities to adopt ERM to enumerate, understand and manage risks across the enterprise more transparently and effectively. Such risk management investments also hedged against adverse regulatory outcomes in the future. Consumer privacy only became a corporate concern when laws and regulations insisted.

The essential point here is that GRC became very useful for framing the privacy debate in cyberspace, to which we turn next.

[667] Miller, 547-572.

Chapter 11
Privacy Frameworks Emerge for Cyberspace

Introduction

The cyber age irrevocably shaped governance, risk management, and compliance (GRC). Cyberspace made the world spin faster. Its connectivity permitted global markets to proliferate. Commerce now transcended international borders with ease, and transaction times accelerated to milliseconds. GRC principles evolved to meet the challenges of a cyberized world, and new privacy concerns led us back to the concept of personally identifiable information (PII).

Widespread adoption of information technology (IT) in the commercial world brought tremendous benefits, and unforeseen risks. Businesses already knew that effective risk management helped them maximize return on investment. Nudged by Sarbanes-Oxley (SOX), publicly-held companies began using one of the earliest internal control frameworks for risk management, COSO. Commercial interest in managing IT risks – now just another flavor of corporate risk - grew. Other frameworks, specifically designed to address IT challenges, emerged to complement COSO.

Computer security became a discipline, but addressing security concerns at just the computer level was not enough. It was really the interrelated network of computers that needed to be protected. And since computers contained information, there was a realization that we needed to talk about information system security, which included protecting private information about individuals. We will broadly call all these security efforts cybersecurity.

And just like that, we are back to privacy. The accountants developed the first privacy framework for the business world in 2003 and called it the Generally Accepted Privacy Principles (GAPP). We've already met the grandfather of all privacy frameworks, the fair information practices (FIPs) described in the Health, Education, and Welfare (HEW) report, which were used to frame the 1974 Privacy Act. The bottom line is that privacy frameworks can frame new laws.

Such US precedents are significant on the world stage. We will see how the rest of the world picked up on FIPs, and how that shaped what would become the most significant international privacy regulation thus far, General Data Protection Regulation (GDPR).

Congress instructed the executive branch to adopt best business practices, like enterprise risk management, while still preserving citizens' individual rights, like privacy. Government standards promulgated such business practices, and formalized understanding of the privacy issues. At the heart of the privacy issue was PII. This would lead to the National Institute of Standards and Technology (NIST) Cybersecurity and Privacy frameworks. The NIST Privacy Framework will surely help frame any new US privacy law.

Historical Context: European Privacy

World War I did not turn out to be the "the war to end all wars." The punitive Treaty of Versailles, the rise of Hitler and totalitarianism, and the failure of the League of Nations all set the stage for World War II. The new war spread death and destruction across Europe, Russia, and Asia. It reset world attention on creating an international body to maintain the peace. The United Nations was born in 1945.

In 1948, the United Nations passed its Universal Declaration of Human Rights. Article Twelve specifically called out a right to privacy, stating: "No one shall be subjected to arbitrary interference with his privacy, family, home or correspondence, nor to attacks upon his honour and reputation. Everyone has the right to the protection of the law against such interference or attacks."[668]

In the same year, the Organization for European Economic Cooperation (OEEC) was created to run the US-funded Marshall Plan for

---

[668] "Universal Declaration of Human Rights", 1948, accessed 12/6/19 at https://www.un.org/en/universal-declaration-human-rights/index.html

reconstruction after World War II. Shoshana Zuboff tells us that Europe was committed to a post-war "free-market creed...[undertaken] as a sweeping defense against the threat of totalitarian and communist collectivist ideologies." [669] Encouraged by the positive effects of considering economic interdependencies among countries, the organization widened its scope to a global scale with the Organisation for Economic Cooperation and Development (OECD) Convention of 1960.[670]

In 1980, the OECD also spoke out about privacy. Its "Guidelines on the Protection of Privacy and Transborder Flows of Personal Data" contained eight underlying principles:

1. Collection Limitation Principle: "There should be limits to the collection of personal data and any such data should be obtained by lawful and fair means and, where appropriate, with the knowledge or consent of the data subject."
2. Data Quality Principle: "Personal data should be relevant to the purposes for which they are to be used, and, to the extent necessary for those purposes, should be accurate, complete and kept up-to-date."
3. Purpose Specification Principle: "The purposes for which personal data are collected should be specified not later than at the time of data collection and the subsequent use limited to the fulfilment of those purposes or such others as are not incompatible with those purposes and as are specified on each occasion of change of purpose."
4. Use Limitation Principle: "Personal data should not be disclosed, made available or otherwise used for purposes other than those specified ... except: a) with the consent of the data subject; or b) by the authority of law."
5. Security Safeguards Principle: "Personal data should be protected by reasonable security safeguards against such risks as loss or unauthorised access, destruction, use, modification or disclosure of data."
6. Openness Principle: "There should be a general policy of openness about developments, practices and policies with

---

[669] Shoshana Zuboff, The Age of Surveillance Capitalism: The Fight for a Human Future at the New Frontier of Power. New York: Public Affairs, 2019, p. 38.

[670] Today, many countries worldwide participate in the OECD, working together to solve economic, social, and environmental problems.

respect to personal data. Means should be readily available of establishing the existence and nature of personal data, and the main purposes of their use, as well as the identity and usual residence of the data controller."

7. Individual Participation Principle: "An individual should have the right: a) to obtain from a data controller, or otherwise, confirmation of whether or not the data controller has data relating to him; b) to have communicated to him, data relating to him within a reasonable time; at a charge, if any, that is not excessive; in a reasonable manner; and in a form that is readily intelligible to him; c) to be given reasons if a request made under subparagraphs(a) and (b) is denied, and to be able to challenge such denial; and d) to challenge data relating to him and, if the challenge is successful to have the data erased, rectified, completed or amended."
8. Accountability Principle: "A data controller should be accountable for complying with measures which give effect to the principles stated above."[671][672]

The die was cast. The HEW report had framed the privacy principles for the United States which were incorporated into the Privacy Act, and now the OECD created an international (and more easily internationally sanctioned) version of the FIPs. From now on, privacy principles for personal data were dominated by democratic mindsets committed to individual rights. These rippled worldwide through laws, regulations, policies, and standards.

In 1995, the EU enacted its Directive on Data Protection.[673] This directive recognized that data processing of citizens' information could

---

[671] "OECD Guidelines on Protection of Privacy and Transborder Flows of Personal Data", 1980. Accessed 12/6/19 at http://www.oecd.org/sti/ieconomy/ oecdguidelines ontheprotectionofprivacyandtransborderflowsofpersonaldata.htm

[672] A 2013 revision to these guidelines left these principles intact. Revisions were intended to address the changes wrought by technology, globalization, the variety of analytics being applied to personal data, and the variety of new threats to personal privacy. See the "OECD Privacy Framework", accessed 12/6/19 at http://www.oecd.org/sti/ieconomy/oecd_privacy_framework.pdf

[673] Directive 95/46/EC of the European Parliament and of the Council of 24 October 1995 on the protection of individuals with regard to the processing of personal data and on the free movement of such data, accessed 12/6/19 at https://eurlex.europa.eu/legal-content/EN/TXT/HTML/?uri=CELEX:31995L0046

impinge on their "fundamental freedoms or privacy," and required such data processing to be lawful, fair, consensual, and "not excessive in relation to the purposes for which they are processed." The Directive also recognized that:

1. "cross-border flows of personal data are necessary to the expansion of international trade;"
2. "the protection of individuals guaranteed in the [EC]… does not stand in the way of transfers of personal data to third countries which ensure an adequate level of protection;"
3. "the adequacy of the level of protection afforded by a third country must be assessed in the light of all the circumstances surrounding the transfer operation or set of transfer operations;"
4. "the transfer of personal data to a third country which does not ensure an adequate level of protection must be prohibited…;"
5. "particular consideration shall be given to the nature of the data, the purpose and duration of the proposed processing operation or operations, the country of origin and country of final destination, the rules of law, both general and sectoral, in force in the third country in question and the professional rules and security measures which are complied with in that country."

In response to this EU directive, the US Department of Commerce issued the Safe Harbor Privacy Principles in 2000, a self-certifying legal framework for use by US organizations intended to demonstrate compliance with the EU Directive. Its principles were: notice, choice, onward transfer, security, data integrity, access, and enforcement.[674] In 2015, the Court of Justice of the EU (CJEU) invalidated the Safe Harbor agreement after Facebook Ireland transferred its users' personal data to the United States. Safe Harbor was not invalidated because of its selfcertification process, but because the Snowden revelations had raised doubts about whether the United States could ensure adequate privacy protection for EU citizens' data.[675] Safe Harbor as enacted has not been

---

[674] Safe Harbor Privacy Principles, accessed 12/6/19 at https://build.export.gov/main/safeharbor/eu/eg_main_018475

[675] CJEU case C-362-14, accessed 12/22/19 at http://curia.europa.eu/juris/document/document.jsf;jsessionid=9ea7d0f130d563c41d2d2c20460a85dffc9844dfe5cd.e34Ka

sufficient to resolve American and European differences regarding the safe handling of personal data, a problem which remains with us today.

In 2012, the EU passed its Charter of Fundamental Rights.[676] Article seven states that "Everyone has the right to respect for his or her private and family life, home and communications."

Article eight specifically addresses the protection of personal data:

1. "Everyone has the right to the protection of personal data concerning him or her."
2. "Such data must be processed fairly for specified purposes and on the basis of the consent of the person concerned or some other legitimate basis laid down by law. Everyone has the right of access to data which has been collected concerning him or her, and the right to have it rectified."
3. "Compliance with these rules shall be subject to control by an independent authority."

The EU General Data Protection Regulation (GDPR)

These events and documents establish the context for EU passage of the General Data Protection Regulation (GDPR) in 2016.[677] GDPR superseded the 1995 data protection directive, but echoes many of its sentiments. It opens by reiterating that the "protection of natural persons in relation to the processing of personal data is a fundamental right."[678] This right must be balanced with the overall interests of society, which include:

> respect for private and family life, home and communications, the protection of personal data, freedom of thought, conscience and religion, freedom of expression and information, freedom

[676] Charter of Fundamental Rights of the European Union, 2012/C 326/02, 2012. Accessed 12/6/19 at https://eur-lex.europa.eu/legal-content/EN/TXT/PDF/?uri=CELEX:12012P/TXT&from=EN

[677] REGULATION (EU) 2016/679 OF THE EUROPEAN PARLIAMENT AND OF THE COUNCIL of 27 April 2016 on the protection of natural persons with regard to the processing of personal data and on the free movement of such data, and repealing Directive 95/46/EC (General Data Protection Regulation), accessed 12/6/19 at https://eur-lex.europa.eu/legal-content/EN/TXT/PDF/?uri=CELEX:32016R0679

[678] GDPR, L-119/1.

> to conduct a business, the right to an effective remedy and to a fair trial, and cultural, religious and linguistic diversity.[679]

GDPR affirms these individual rights whenever their "processing activities are related to offering goods or services to such data subjects irrespective of whether connected to a payment."[680] We will see that extending privacy protections to transactions not involving payment will become a big issue for US companies like Google and Facebook.

Just as in the case of the 1995 Directive on Data Protection, the GDPR reserved the EU's right to determine the adequacy of data protection in a non-EU country. The invalidation of Safe Harbor posed further impediments for US entities desiring to compete in the European market.

The GDPR language reflects a more sophisticated understanding of threats posed to individual rights by the tools of cyberspace. It notes that citizens can now be

> associated with online identifiers provided by their devices, applications, tools and protocols, such as internet protocol addresses, cookie identifiers or other identifiers such as radio frequency identification tags. This may leave traces which, in particular when combined with unique identifiers and other information received by the servers, may be used to create profiles of the natural persons and identify them.[681]

The GDPR also includes the aspirational right to be forgotten:

> A data subject should have … a 'right to be forgotten' where the retention of such data infringes this Regulation…. In particular, a data subject should have the right to have his or her personal data erased and no longer processed where the personal data are no longer necessary in relation to the purposes for which they are collected or otherwise processed, where a data subject has withdrawn his or her consent or objects to the processing of personal data concerning him or her, or where the processing of his or her personal data does not otherwise comply with this Regulation.[682]

---

[679] GDPR, L/119-2.
[680] GDPR, L/119-5.
[681] GDPR, L/119-6.
[682] Ibid.

This provision is strengthened by requiring the controller of the data who released it to other controllers "to inform the [other] controllers …to erase any links to, or copies or replications of those personal data."[683]

GDPR requires objective assessment of the risks to individual rights and freedoms associated with the processing of citizens' data. The regulation states that it is critical to identify processing risks, their "origin, nature, likelihood and severity," and associated risk mitigation strategies.[684] GDPR suggests that "approved codes of conduct" and "approved certifications" can provide guidance in developing internal policies and implementing measures which can demonstrate compliance.[685] In anticipation of data breaches, GDPR suggests that data controllers should have already completed data protection impact assessments.[686]

So now we understand where the Europeans are "coming from" with GDPR. We next turn back to internal control frameworks designed to manage risk in big for-profit businesses.

The COSO Frameworks: Steering Corporate Internal Control

The Committee of Sponsoring Organizations of the Treadway Commission (COSO)[687] issued its original internal control framework in 1992. In response to Section 404 of SOX, the SEC began requiring publicly traded companies to use internal control frameworks for financial reporting in 2004. While the SEC did not require usage of any specific framework, COSO was the only one specifically mentioned as satisfying

---

683 GDPR, L/119-13.

684 GDPR, L/119-15.

685 Ibid.

686 GDPR, L 119/17.

687 COSO provides thought leadership, guidance, and frameworks on Enterprise Risk Management (ERM), internal control, and fraud deterrence. Initially formed in 1985, COSO is sponsored by five non-profit organizations: the Institute of Internal Auditors (IIA), the America Accounting Association (AAA), the American Institute of Certified Public Accountants (AICPA), Financial Executives International (FEI), and the Institute of Management Accountants (IMA).

the SEC criteria.[688] Not surprisingly, COSO was widely adopted by publicly traded companies.

COSO updated this framework in 2013, highlighting its continuing applicability to external/internal financial/non-financial reporting objectives, including operations and compliance.[689] The revision was designed to help corporations "adapt to changing business and operating environments, mitigate risks to acceptable levels, and support sound decision making and governance of the organization." [690] Risk analysis and anti-fraud measures were central to its continuous improvement strategy.

The 2013 Framework document defined internal control as:

> a process, effected by an entity's board of directors, management, and other personnel, designed to provide reasonable assurance regarding the achievement of objectives … [of] operations, reporting, and compliance.[691]

The document went on to describe how its objectives could be achieved through use of the five integrated components: control environment, risk assessment, control activities, information and communication, and monitoring activities. It captured the multiplicity of these dimensions in the COSO cube, shown here.

---

688 Security and Exchange Commission, "Final Rule: Management's Report on Internal Control Over Financial Reporting and Certification of Disclosure in Exchange Act Periodic Reports", SEC Release No. 34-55929. Accessed 12/28 19 at https://www.sec.gov/rules/final/33-8238.htm#iia

689 J. Stephen McNally, "The 2013 COSO Framework & SOX Compliance", Strategic Finance magazine, June 2013. Accessed 11/26/19 at https://www.coso.org/documents/COSO%20McNallyTransition%20Article-Final%20COSO%20Version%20Proof_5-31-13.pdf

690 Miles E.A. Everson et al, "Committee of Sponsoring Organizations of the Treadway Commission (COSO), Internal Control – Integrated Framework: Executive Summary", May 2013, p. iii. Accessed 11/26/19 at https://www.coso.org/Documents/990025P-Executive-Summary-final-may20.pdf

691 COSO Internal Control 2013, 3.

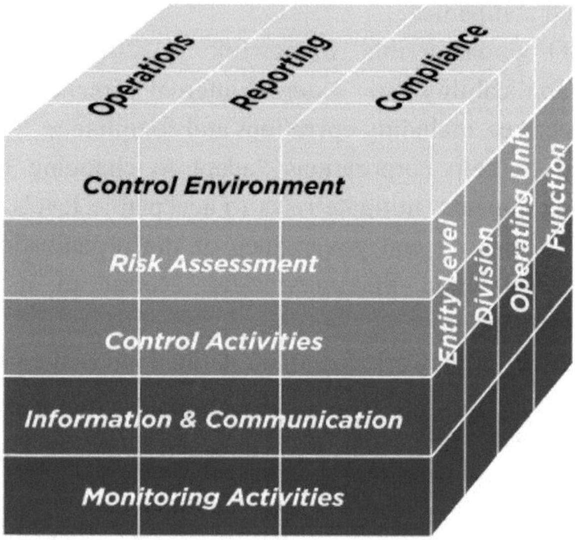

The 2013 COSO Cube.[692]

COSO acknowledged that limitations could result from: poor alignment between corporate objectives and internal control; judgement clouded by such things as error, bias, or nefarious intent; and external events. Everyone associated with the entity has a role in the framework, including the board of directors, the senior managers, other managers and personnel, and internal and independent auditors.[693]

The 2013 framework did not incorporate COSO's 2004 ERM framework, but referred to it as complementary. Its ERM framework paper had defined ERM as

> a process, effected by an entity's board of directors, management and other personnel, applied in strategy setting and across enterprise, designed to identify potential events that may affect the entity, and manage risk to be within its risk appetite, to provide reasonable assurance regarding the achievement of entity objectives.[694]

---

[692] COSO Internal Control 2013, 6.

[693] COSO Internal Control 2013, 9-10.

[694] Committee of Sponsoring Organizations of the Treadway Commission (COSO), "Enterprise Risk Management – Integrated Framework: Executive Summary",

COSO acknowledged that "the underlying premise of enterprise risk management is that every entity exists to provide value for its stakeholders."[695] Uncertainties are unavoidable. The purpose of COSO's ERM is to provide tools "to effectively deal with uncertainty and associated risk and opportunity, enhancing the capacity to build value."[696]

In January 2015, COSO issued a white paper addressing application of its framework for information system risks.[697] COSO had previously defined an information system as

> the set of activities, involving people, processes, data and/or technology, which enable the organization to obtain, generate, use and communicate transactions and information to maintain accountability and measure and review of the entity's performance or progress towards achievement of objectives.[698]

In the 2015 paper, COSO identified the specific types of cyber actors who introduce such risks: nation states and spies, organized criminals, terrorists, hacktivists, and insiders. COSO noted that new technologies – things like cloud computing, social networking, and mobility devices – increase an organization's potential cyber-attack surface. In the retail sector, COSO acknowledged that PII and credit card numbers were particularly attractive targets.

The 2015 white paper emphasized the need to evaluate all objectives – operations, internal reporting, external reporting, compliance – during the cyber assessment process. COSO argued that in order to protect themselves, entities needed to present data as quality information, that is, accessible, correct, current, protected, retained, sufficient, timely, valid, and verifiable.[699] COSO also made explicit mention of cyber focused standards and frameworks, including COBIT, ISO, and NIST, which we will about shortly.

September 2004, p. 2. Accessed 12/11/19 at https://www.coso.org/Documents/COSO-ERM-Executive-Summary.pdf

695 COSO ERM, 1.

696 Ibid.

697 Mary Galligan & Kelly Rau, "COSO in the Cyber Age" (January 2015), accessed 11/19/19 at https://www.coso.org/documents/COSO%20in%20the%20Cyber%20Age_FULL_r11.pdf

698 COSO cyber, 2.

699 COSO cyber, 12.

The 2015 COSO paper acknowledged that since publication of the original framework in 1992, internet connectivity has brought tremendous innovations to the business world. Then it gets interesting:

> However, the internet was designed primarily for sharing information, not protecting it. On any given day, there are numerous media reports about significant cyber incidents. While cyber-attacks in certain industries have dominated coverage in the news, all industries are susceptible to cyberattacks. Which data, systems, and assets are of value at any particular point in time depends on the cyber attacker's motives. As long as cyber incidents continue to have a negative impact on the financial well-being of victim companies and continue to draw additional regulatory scrutiny, cyber breaches will continue to be high profile events that draw a substantial amount of press.[700]

The 2015 white paper listed the keys to effectively control the environment and monitor cyber risks as:

1. "Clear tone from the top regarding the importance of protecting information systems;"
2. "A program of ongoing and separate evaluations to assess the design and operating effectiveness of controls that are intended to reduce potential cyber exposures;"
3. "Assistance and involvement of qualified cyber risk professionals;"
4. "Appropriate monitoring of cyber risk and controls related to outsourced service providers;"
5. "Proper and timely communication of cyber deficiencies;" and
6. "Holding control owners accountable to help protect information systems."

COSO updated its ERM recommendations in June 2017, citing lessons learned since 2004 and the "increasing volatility, complexity and ambiguity of the world."[701] It noted that boards of directors were now

---

[700] COSO cyber, 1.

[701] COSO was quoting the World Economic Forum. See Committee of Sponsoring Organizations of the Treadway Commission (COSO) "Enterprise Risk Management: Integrating with Strategy and Performance Executive Summary" (June 2017), accessed 11/19/19 at https://www.coso.org/Documents/2017-COSO-ERM-Integrating-with-Strategy-and-Performance-Executive-Summary.pdf

expected to exercise greater oversight over ERM, and emphasized the need for corporate adaptability, transparency and accountability. It also concluded that management's explicit understanding of risks could influence strategic choices. In other words, the risk tail could wag the strategy dog.

As for future trends, the 2017 report noted that ERM must continue to consider the impact of new technologies and leverage them as appropriate. For example, data continues to proliferate, and data analytics provides new ways to understand risks and their impact. An ongoing concern remains the management of risk management associated costs. As ERM evolves, GRC expenditures must be titrated to provide the best return on investment.

COSO published a white paper on the application of internal control to the healthcare provider industry in January 2019.[702] It is particularly instructive as it was not written for COSO's typical audience, the publicly-held company. A brief synopsis appears in appendix 11A.

COBIT Frameworks: Steering Information & Technology (I&T) as an Enterprise

The first Control Objectives for Information and Related Technologies (COBIT) framework was released in 1996 by the ISACA (formerly known as the Information System Audit and Control Organization).[703] [704]The COBIT 5 framework - released in 2012 - was

---

[702] Annette Schandl & Philip L.Foster, "COSO Internal Control –Integrated Framework: An Implementation Guide for the Healthcare Provider Industry" January 2019), accessed 11/19/19 at https://www.coso.org/Documents/COSO-CROWE-COSO-Internal-Control-Integrated-Framework.pdf

[703] Accessed 11/29/19 at http://www.isaca.org/COBIT/PublishingImages/20th/COBIT-Timeline-lg.jpg

[704] 703ISACA began in 1967 as an organization of individuals concerned with audit controls in computer systems which were becoming more critical to operations. Today, ISACA is a worldwide organization composed of professionals in I&T-related positions, like information system auditors and security professionals, internal auditors, consultants, and CIOs. They work across industry categories, to include "financial and banking, public accounting, government and the public sector, utilities and manufacturing." ISACA provides professional certifications, including Certified Information Systems Auditor (CISA), and Certified Information Security Manager (CISM).

adapted by enterprises worldwide as a framework to govern and manage enterprise IT assets. This framework was recently succeeded by the COBIT 2019 framework.

Acknowledging that "Digitized enterprises are increasingly dependent on I&T [information and technology] for survival and growth," [705] COBIT 2019 emphasizes the need for governance stakeholders (Board of Directors, executive team, etc.) to adapt Enterprise Governance of Information and Technology (EGIT). COBIT 2019 relies on six principles for a governance system:

1. Providing the stakeholders with value;
2. Using a holistic approach;
3. Dynamism of the governance system;
4. Distinguishing between governance and management;
5. Tailoring to the enterprise's needs; and
6. System governance from end-to-end.

COBIT 2019 relies on three principles for a governance framework: a conceptual model of components and their relationships should underlie the framework; openness and flexibility of the framework; and framework alignment with major relevant standards, and regulations. Implicit in COBIT is risk optimization via explicit understanding of the threat landscape and risk assessment. Risks include both business risks and those associated with failure to comply with external laws and regulations.

ISO Standards for Information Security and Risk Management

The international standards organization known as ISO [706] has been publishing standards since 1951. Its standards are cited in frameworks regularly, so a passing familiarity with them is useful.

In 2005, ISO and IEC Electronics Corporation published ISO/IEC 27001, an information system security management system standard. This popular standard focused on making information systems secure and

---

[705] See COBIT 2019 Framework: Introduction and Methodology, Accessed 11/30/19 at https://www.isaca.org/bookstore/Pages/COBIT-2019.aspx

[706] ISO was formed in 1947 and today has members from 164 national standards bodies.

minimizing risks.[707] This standard was updated in 2013 with ISO/IEC 27001:2013, entitled "Information Technology - Security Techniques - Information Security Management Systems – Requirements," which "specifies the requirements for establishing, implementing, maintaining and continually improving an information security management system within the context of the organization. It also includes requirements for the assessment and treatment of information security risks tailored to the needs of the organization. The requirements set out in ISO/IEC 27001:2013 are generic and are intended to be applicable to all organizations, regardless of type, size or nature."[708]

ISO 31000:2018, entitled "Risk Management – Guidelines," provides "guidelines on managing risk faced by organizations. The application of these guidelines can be customized to any organization and its context. ISO 31000:2018 provides a common approach to managing any type of risk and is not industry or sector specific. ISO 31000:2018 can be used throughout the life of the organization and can be applied to any activity, including decision-making at all levels."[709]

ISO/IEC 27005:2018, entitled "Information Technology - Security Techniques - Information Security Risk Management," provides information system security risk management guidelines, in support of ISO/IEC 27001 implementation. "This document is applicable to all types of organizations (e.g. commercial enterprises, government agencies, nonprofit organizations) which intend to manage risks that can compromise the organization's information security."[710]

ISO/IEC 27002:2013, entitled "Information technology – Security Techniques – Code of practice for information security controls," "gives guidelines for organizational information security standards and information security management practices including the selection, implementation and management of controls taking into consideration the organization's information security risk environment(s)."[711]

---

[707] Accessed 12/2/19 at https://www.iso.org/the-iso-story.html#16
[708] Accessed 12/2/19 at https://webstore.ansi.org/Standards/ISO/ISOIEC270012013
[709] Accessed 12/2/19 at https://webstore.ansi.org/Standards/ISO/ISO310002018
[710] Accessed 12/2/19 at https://webstore.ansi.org/Standards/ISO/ISOIEC270052018
[711] Accessed 12/11/19 at https://www.iso.org/standard/54533.html

Generally Accepted Privacy Principles (GAPP)

The AICPA and Canadian Institute of Chartered Accountants (CICA) first developed the Generally Accepted Privacy Principles (GAPP) in 2003, and updated them in 2006 and 2009.[712] They look like FIPs:

1. "Management. The entity defines, documents, communicates, and assigns accountability for its privacy policies and procedures.
2. Notice. The entity provides notice about its privacy policies and procedures and identifies the purposes for which personal information is collected, used, retained, and disclosed.
3. Choice and consent. The entity describes the choices available to the individual and obtains implicit or explicit consent with respect to the collection, use, and disclosure of personal information.
4. Collection. The entity collects personal information only for the purposes identified in the notice.
5. Use, retention, and disposal. The entity limits the use of personal information to the purposes identified in the notice and for which the individual has provided implicit or explicit consent. The entity retains personal information for only as long as necessary to fulfill the stated purposes or as required by law or regulations and thereafter appropriately disposes of such information.
6. Access. The entity provides individuals with access to their personal information for review and update.
7. Disclosure to third parties. The entity discloses personal information to third parties only for the purposes identified in the notice and with the implicit or explicit consent of the individual.
8. Security for privacy. The entity protects personal information against unauthorized access (both physical and logical).
9. Quality. The entity maintains accurate, complete, and relevant personal information for the purposes identified in the notice.

---

[712] See http://www.oecdprivacy.org/#gapp

10. Monitoring and enforcement. The entity monitors compliance with its privacy policies and procedures and has procedures to address privacy related complaints and disputes."[713]

The establishment and maintenance of an effective privacy program requires

1. "Strategizing. Performing privacy strategic and business planning.
2. Diagnosing. Performing privacy gap and risk analyses.
3. Implementing. Developing, documenting, introducing, and institutionalizing the program's action plan, including establishing controls over personal information.
4. Sustaining and managing. Monitoring activities of a privacy program.
5. Auditing. Internal or external auditors evaluating the organization's privacy program."[714]

GAPP is based on ISO 27002, and derives key concepts from the aforementioned OECD Guidelines.[715]

Enterprise Services Come to Government

With the 1996 Information Technology Management Reform Act (ITMRA), Congress required the Director of the Office of Management and Budget (OMB) to:

1. Improve acquisition, use and disposal of federal IT to improve federal program productivity, efficiency, and effectiveness, including through dissemination of public information and the reduction of information collection burdens on the public;
2. Develop a process to manage risk and results of IT investments;

---

[713] AICPA/CICA, "Generally Accepted Privacy Principles", August 2009. Accessed 12/28/19 at file:///Users/lesliegruis/Downloads/00250-Generally-Accepted-Privacy Principles.pdf

[714] "Generally Accepted Privacy Principles: CPA and CA Practitioner Version", August 2009, accessed 12/6/19 at https://iapp.org/media/presentations/11Summit/DeathofSASHO2.pdf

[715] See Julie Gable, CRM, CDIA, FAI, "Principles for Protecting Information Privacy", Information Management (magazine), September/October 2014. Accessed 12/6/19 at https://magazine.arma.org/wp-content/uploads/simple-file-list/2014_05_IM_principles_for_protecting_information_privacy.pdf

3. Encourage agency heads to use best practices in IT acquisition and resource management;
4. Oversee development and implementation of federal IT system standards and guidelines with NIST; and
5. Enforce accountability on agency heads for IT investment and resource management.[716]

For each agency, ITMRA designated a Chief Information Officer (CIO), responsible for "developing, maintaining, and facilitating the implementation of a sound and integrated information technology architecture," and "promoting the effective and efficient design and operation of all major information resources management processes." ITMRA defined ''information technology architecture'' as

> "an integrated framework for evolving or maintaining existing information technology and acquiring new information technology to achieve the agency's strategic goals and information resources management goals."

The 2002 E-Government Act[717] recognized the benefits of providing access to government information and services through the effective use of the internet and computer technologies, while still respecting laws and individual rights like privacy. It required the Office of Management and Budget (OMB) to make maximum use of commercial standards, and oversee the development of enterprise architectures; the implementation information system security programs, and the adoption of the privacy impact assessment (PIA)[718] process.

---

[716] Accessed 12/12/19 at https://www.govinfo.gov/content/pkg/PLAW-104publ106/pdf/PLAW-104publ106.pdf

[717] Accessed 12/12/19 at https://www.govinfo.gov/content/pkg/STATUTE-116/ pdf/ STATUTE-116-Pg2899.pdf

[718] OMB defined a PIA as: "an analysis of how information is handled that ensures handling conforms to applicable legal, regulatory, and policy requirements regarding privacy; determines the risks and effects of collecting, maintaining and disseminating information in identifiable form in an electronic information system; and examines and evaluates protections and alternative processes for handling information to mitigate potential privacy risks."

OMB released its Federal Enterprise Architecture (FEA) Consolidated Reference Model Document Version 2.3 in October 2007.[719] [720] FEA established a "common language and framework to describe and analyze IT [information technology] investments, enhance collaboration and ultimately transform the Federal government." Its designers assumed that it was most useful when guided by and aligned with the strategic goals (business objectives) of each agency. It relied on proactive collaboration from across the federal government to ensure its development, evolution and adoption. It also assumed that improvements in government efficiency and effectiveness would be realized through application of "businessapproved architecture" to all IT investments.

A tantalizing description of the "Platform for Privacy Preferences (P3P)" appears in the FEA version 2.3:

> A specification allowing users' web browsers to automatically understand web sites' privacy practices. Privacy policies will be embedded in the code of a web site. Browsers will read the policy, and then, automatically provide certain information to specific sites based on the preferences set by the users. For instance, if the site is an e-commerce site, the browser will automatically provide shipping info. If the site is requesting demographic info, then the browser will know to provide it anonymously. The P3P specification was developed by the W3C P3P Syntax, Harmonization, and Protocol Working Groups, including W3C Member organizations and experts in the field of web privacy. P3P is based on W3C specifications that have already been established, including HTTP, XML and Resource Description Framework (RDF). Privacy is policy that deals with the degree to which an individual can determine which personal information is to be shared with whom and for what purpose.

We'll look more deeply into this idea in our final chapter.

---

[719] Office of Management and Budget, "FEA Consolidated Reference Model Docum ent, Version 2.3", October 2007. Accessed 12/11/19 at https://www.reginfo .gov/public/jsp/Utilities/FEA_CRM_v23_Final_Oct_2007_Revised.pdf

[720] OMB had released its original Federal Enterprise Architecture Framework (FEAF Version 1.1) in 1999. FEAF was renamed FEA by OMB in 2002.

OMB updated the 2007 framework with "The Common Approach to Federal Enterprise Architecture" on May 2, 2012.[721] Now the framework was presented as a COSO-like cube, as shown in the figure below.

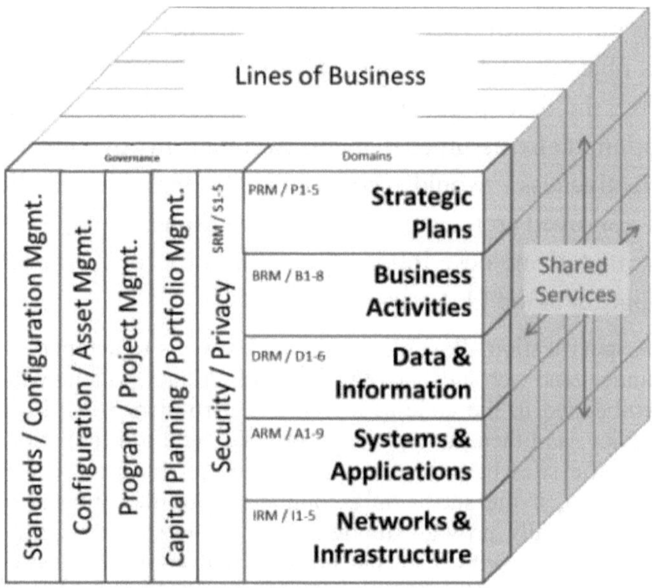

Figure: Federal Enterprise Architectural Framework v2 (FEAF-II)[722]

EO 13800[723] of May 2017 held agency heads accountable for "implementing risk management measures commensurate with the risk and magnitude of the harm that would result from unauthorized access, use, disclosure, disruption, modification, or destruction of IT and data." It required each agency to use the NIST Cybersecurity Framework for Critical Infrastructures to manage cybersecurity risk.

[721] Office of Management and Budget (OMB), "The Common Approach to Federal Enterprise Architecture" on May 2, 2012. Accessed 12/7/19 at https://obama whitehouse.archives.gov/sites/default/files/omb/assets/egov_docs/common_approah _to_federal_ea.pdf

[722] FEA 2012, 22.

[723] EO 13800, Strengthening the Cybersecurity of Federal Networks and Critical Infrastructure, 11 May 2017, accessed 12/12/19 at https://www.whitehouse.gov/ presidential-actions/presidential-executive-order-strengthening-cybersecurity-federal -networks-critical-infrastructure/

Risk Management and a Federal Framework

Title III of the E-Government Act, known as the Federal Information Security Management Act of 2002 (FISMA, 2002), established the requirement for an overall framework for information security controls throughout the federal government. This included ensuing information security risk management and oversight. Information security was defined as:

> "protecting information and information systems from unauthorized access, use, disclosure, disruption, modification, or destruction in order to provide -
>
> 1. Integrity, which means guarding against improper information modification or destruction, and includes ensuring information nonrepudiation and authenticity;
> 2. Confidentiality, which means preserving authorized restrictions on access and disclosure, including means for protecting personal privacy and proprietary information; and
> 3. Availability, which means ensuring timely and reliable access to and use of information."

It held the head of each agency responsible for "providing information security protections commensurate with the risk and magnitude of the harm resulting from unauthorized access, use, disclosure, disruption, modification, or destruction of … information collected or maintained by or on behalf of an agency…."

Section 208 of the act specified privacy provisions. It required each agency to conduct a PIA before acquiring or developing any information technology that "collects, maintains, or disseminates information that is in an identifiable form" or initiates any new collection of information that will be "collected, maintained, or disseminated using information technology." A PIA should include:

1. "what information is to be collected;
2. why the information is being collected;
3. the intended use of the agency of the information;
4. with whom the information will be shared;
5. what notice or opportunities for consent would be provided to individuals regarding what information is collected and how that information is shared;

6. how the information will be secured; and
7. whether a system of records[724] is being created."

The FISMA Amendment of 2014 defined an (information security) incident as "an occurrence that

1. actually or imminently jeopardizes, without lawful authority, the integrity, confidentiality, or availability of information or an information system; or
2. constitutes a violation or imminent threat of violation of law, security policies, security procedures, or acceptable use policies."[725]

It empowered the Department of Homeland Security to operate a federal information security incident center to:

1. provide technical assistance to the government;
2. "compile and analyze information about incidents that threaten information security;"
3. provide information across the government about "current and potential information security threats;" and
4. "provide … intelligence and other information about cyber threats, vulnerabilities, and incidents to agencies to assist in risk assessments."

Each government agency was responsible for its own information security program, to include periodic assessment, policies and procedures to reduce risk to an acceptable and cost-effective level, ensure compliance, provide security awareness training for all personnel and contractors, perform periodic testing of information system controls, and "procedures for detecting, reporting, and responding to security incidents."

The amended law also required each agency to perform an annual independent evaluation "of the information security program and practices

---

[724] The Privacy Act defined a system of records as "a group of any records under the control of any agency from which information is retrieved by the name of the individual or by some identifying number, symbol, or other identifying particular assigned to the individual." It also required each agency "to publish in the Federal Register at least annually a notice of the existence and character of the system of records…." These came to be known as System of Record Notices, or SORNs.

[725] Accessed 12/4/19 at https://www.govinfo.gov/content/pkg/PLAW-113publ283/pdf/PLAW-113publ283.pdf

of that agency to determine the effectiveness of such program and practices." The traditional idea of the financial audit was now an information security program audit in the government.

The US National Institute of Standards and Technology (NIST) (formerly the National Bureau of Standards or NBS) had originally been authorized by Congress to develop computer standards with the Computer Security Act of 1987.[726] The E-Government Act of 2002 made NIST responsible for information technology standards and guidelines to support e-government implementation. NIST's ongoing responsibility to provide such standards and guidance would lead to NIST's Federal Information Processing Standards (yet another kind of FIPS) Publications 800 series, which are designed to address security and privacy needs of USG information and information systems. We turn to these next.

NIST Standards

SP 800-122 Guide to Protecting the Confidentiality of Personally Identifiable Information

NIST SP 800-122 notes the sensitivity of PII. Security breaches pose risks to both individuals (identity theft, embarrassment, blackmail) and organizations (loss of public trust, legal liability, costs associated with remediation). It is reminiscent of the HEW study we explored in chapter seven.

SP 800-122 defines PII as "any information about an individual maintained by an agency, including:

1. Any information that can be used to distinguish or trace an individual's identity, such as name, social security number, date and place of birth, mother's maiden name, or biometric records; and
2. Any other information that is linked or linkable to an individual, such as medical, educational, financial, and employment information."[727]

---

[726] Accessed 12/12/19 at https://www.govinfo.gov/content/pkg/STATUTE-101/pdf /STATUTE-101-Pg1724.pdf

[727] Erika McCallister, Tim Grance, Karen Scarfone, "Guide to Protecting the Confidentiality of Personally Identifiable Information (PII)", NIST 800-122, April 2010, p. ES-1. Accessed 12/6/19 at https://nvlpubs.nist.gov/nistpubs /Legacy/SP/ nistspecialpublication800-122.pdf

It urges organizations to "minimize the use, collection, and retention of PII to what is strictly necessary to accomplish their business purpose and mission."[728]

Confidentiality safeguards for PII can include operational safeguards, like policies and procedures, and workforce education. They can also include privacy-specific safeguards, like: minimizing use, collection, and retention of PII; conducting PIAs;[729] de-identifying[730] PII; and anonymizing[731] information. They can also include security controls, like access control and enforcement, auditable events, audit review/analysis/reporting, protection of information as rest and in transit, appropriate media access/marking/storage/sanitization, and information system monitoring for unusual or suspicious events.[732] Incident response to PII breaches requires preparation; detection and analysis; containment, eradication, and recovery; and post-incident activity.[733]

Citing Fair Information Practices (FIPs) as the foundation of most privacy laws, NIST 800-122 notes that the OECD privacy guidelines as "the most widely-accepted privacy principles [which] were endorsed by the Department of Commerce in 1981."[734] As we've already seen, the OECD FIPs include collection limitation, data quality, purpose specification, use limitation, security safeguards, openness, individual participation, and accountability.

SP 800-39 Managing Information Security Risk

SP 800-39 opens by talking about the variety of threats to information and information systems. These include human and machine error, purposeful attacks, and environmental effects. Such threats have the

---

[728] NIST 800-122, ES-2.

[729] NIST cites OMB's definition of a PIA. See NIST 800-122, E-1 to E-2.

[730] Records can de-identified by removing or obscuring enough PII "such that the remaining information does not identify an individual and there is no reasonable basis to believe that the information can be used to identify an individual." See NIST 800-122, E-1

[731] Anonymized information is "previously identifiable information that has been de-identified and for which a code or other association for re-identification no longer exists." See NIST 800-122, E-1.

[732] NIST 800-122, 4-1 to 4-8.

[733] NIST SP 800-122, 5-1 to 5-4.

[734] NIST SP 800-122, 2-3.

potential to "result in great harm to the national and economic security interests of the United States."[735]

SP 800-39 advocates for senior leaders to be held responsible and accountable for information system (IS) risk management. These leaders must also communicate the organization's risk tolerance threshold.[736]

SP 800-39 in intended to

> provide guidance for an integrated, organization-wide program for managing information security risk to organizational operations (i.e., mission, functions, image, and reputation), organizational assets, individuals, other organizations, and the Nation resulting from the operation and use of federal information systems... The risk management guidance described herein is complementary to and should be used as part of a more comprehensive Enterprise Risk Management (ERM) program. (3)

Components of risk management process include

1. Framing a risk management strategy to include risk assumptions, constraints, tolerance, and trade-offs;
2. Assessing the threats, vulnerabilities, potential consequences, impact, and harm likelihood;
3. Designing consistent responses to risk, which can include acceptance, avoidance, mitigation, sharing, or transferring risk; and
4. Continuous monitoring of the risk response readiness and effectiveness, and for new risks brought by new information systems.[737]

Relationships with entities outside the organization - to include, suppliers, customers, partners, and service providers - also pose risks which must be considered. Some organizations face advanced persistent threats (APTs)[738], and sharing of risk-related information originating from

---

[735] NIST SP 800-39, "Managing Information Security Risk: Organization, Mission, and Information System View", March 2011, p 1. Accessed 12/8/19 at https://csrc.nist.gov/publications/detail/sp/800-39/final [735]SP 800-39, 2.

[736] SP 800-39, 2.

[737] SP 800-39, 6-7.

[738] An APT is defined as "a long-term pattern of targeted, sophisticated attacks". See SP 800-39, 8.

the organization or others (like Computer Emergency Response Teams or CERTs) can pay dividends for all.

SP 800-53 Security and Privacy Controls for Federal Information Systems and Organizations

The security controls of NIST SP 800-53 were designed to be technology and policy neutral, focusing on safeguards and countermeasures to protect information at rest, during processing, and during transmission. NIST 800-53 recommended that the risk management process be conducted at the organizational, mission/business process, and information system levels "with the overall objective of continuous improvement in the organization's risk-related activities and effective inter-tier and intra-tier communication among all stakeholders having a shared interest in the mission/business success of the organization."[739] Security controls must be aligned with privacy controls. Many useful definitions of terms appear in appendix 11B.

Government has a fundamental responsibility to protect the privacy of individuals. PII lives at the core of the privacy issue. Its many definitions add to the confusion.[740] Similar concerns about privacy exist in the private sector, "where healthcare, financial, and other services continue to be delivered via the web with increasingly higher levels of personalization."[741]

Privacy controls in SP 800-53 are "based on the Fair Information Practice Principles (FIPPs)[742] embodied in the Privacy Act of 1974,

---

[739] NIST SP 800-53 Revision 4, "Security and Privacy Controls for Federal Information Systems and Organizations" April 2013, p. 7. Accessed 12/2/19 at https://nvlpubs.nist.gov/nistpubs/SpecialPublications/NIST.SP.800-53r4.pdf

[740] We have already seen one in a previous chapter. Alternatively, OMB defined it as "information which can be used to distinguish or trace an individual's identity, such as their name, social security number, biometric records, etc. alone, or when combined with other personal or identifying information which is linked or linkable to a specific individual, such as date and place of birth, mother's maiden name, etc." See Office of Management and Budget Memorandum 07-16, accessed 12/5/19 at https://www.whitehouse.gov/sites/whitehouse.gov/files/omb/memoranda/2007/m07-16.pdf

[741] SP 800-53, J-1.

[742] "The FIPPs are widely accepted in the United States and internationally as a general framework for privacy and are reflected in other federal and international laws and

Section 208 of the E-Government Act of 2002, and Office of Management and Budget (OMB) policies. The FIPPs are designed to build public trust in the privacy practices of organizations and to help organizations avoid tangible costs and intangible damages from privacy incidents." There are "eight privacy control families, each aligning with one of the FIPPs."[743] These include:

1. Authority and Purpose;
2. Accountability, Audit, and Risk Management;
3. Data Quality and Integrity;
4. Data Minimization and Retention;
5. Individual Participation and Redress;
6. Security;
7. Transparency; and
8. Use Limitation.

See appendix 11C for additional details.

The NIST Cybersecurity Framework

NIST was instructed to reduce cybersecurity risks to critical infrastructure by Executive Order 13636 in 2013.[744] The PATRIOT Act had defined critical infrastructure way back in 2001 as "systems and assets, whether physical or virtual, so vital to the United States that the incapacity or destruction of such systems and assets would have a debilitating impact on security, national economic security, national public health or safety, or any combination of those matters."[745] EO 13636 specified that NIST's Cybersecurity Framework should contain "standards, methodologies, procedures, and processes that align policy, business, and technological approaches to address cyber risks." It should incorporate best practices from industry and voluntary standards "to the

---

policies. In a number of organizations, FIPPs serve as the basis for analyzing privacy risks and determining appropriate mitigation strategies. The Federal Enterprise Architecture Security and Privacy Profile (FEA-SPP) also provided information and materials in development of the privacy controls." NIST SP 800-53, J-2.

[743] SP 800-53, J-2.

[744] See EO 13636, "Improving Critical Infrastructure Cybersecurity", February 2013. Accessed 12/6/19 at https://obamawhitehouse.archives.gov/the-press-office/2013/02/12/executive-order-improving-critical-infrastructure-cybersecurity

[745] See US PATRIOT Act of 2001, accessed 12/6/19 at https://www.govinfo. gov/content/pkg/PLAW-107publ56/pdf/PLAW-107publ56.pdf

fullest extent possible," and "be consistent with voluntary international standards when such international standards will advance the objectives of this order...." The framework should use a "flexible, repeatable, performance-based, and cost-effective approach" and be technology agnostic. The Secretary of the Department of Homeland Security was required to establish a voluntary critical infrastructure cybersecurity program to encourage usage of the framework among critical infrastructure owners and operators (public and private), and other interested parties. Congress formalized this instruction with the Cybersecurity Enhancement Act (CEA) of 2014[746], and NIST responded by issuing a revised cybersecurity framework for critical infrastructure in 2018.[747] The framework is intended to improve cybersecurity risk management but does not replace an overall risk management process for an organization. It is, however, generic enough that it can be applied to other sectors besides the critical infrastructure.

The Framework Core performs five continuous and concurrent functions:

Identify: "Develop an organizational understanding to manage cybersecurity risk to system, people, assets, data, and capabilities."[748]

Protect: "Develop and implement appropriate safeguards to ensure delivery of critical services."[749]

Detect: "Develop and implement appropriate activities to identify the occurrence of a cybersecurity event."[750]

Respond: "Develop and implement appropriate activities to take action regarding a detected cybersecurity incident."[751]

---

[746] See Cybersecurity Enhancement Act (CEA) of 2014, accessed 12/6/19 at https://www.congress.gov/bill/113th-congress/senate-bill/1353/text

[747]NIST, "Framework for Improving Critical Infrastructure Cybersecurity", version 1.1, April 16, 2018. Accessed 12/2/19 at https://nvlpubs.nist.gov/nistpubs/CSWP/NIST.CSWP.04162018.pdf

[748] NIST Framework 1.1, 7.

[749] Ibid.

[750] Ibid.

[751] NIST Framework 1.1, 8.

Recover: "Develop and implement appropriate activities to maintain plans for resilience and to restore any capabilities or services that were impaired due to a cybersecurity incident."[752]

In this document, NIST defines risk management as "the ongoing process of identifying, assessing, and responding to risk." By understanding the probabilities of risks and their associated impacts, organization can make cybersecurity investments which align with their risk appetite. The NIST framework "gives organizations the ability to dynamically select and direct improvement in cybersecurity risk management."[753]

The NIST Cybersecurity Framework is explicitly aligned with other standards and frameworks, including CIS CSC[754], COBIT 5, ISA 62443-2-1: 2009 and ISA 62443-3-3: 2013[755], ISO/IEC 27001: 2013, and NIST SP 800-53 Rev. 4. The framework urges the incorporation of privacy principles into cybersecurity programs, like:

1. "Data minimization in the collection, disclosure, and retention of personal information material related to the cybersecurity incident;
2. Use limitations outside of cybersecurity activities on any information collected specifically for cybersecurity activities; 3. Transparency for certain cybersecurity activities;
4. Individual consent and redress for adverse impacts arising from use of personal information in cybersecurity activities;
5. Data quality, integrity, and security; and
6. Accountability and auditing."[756]

---

752 Ibid.

753 NIST Framework 1.1, 4.

754 Center for Internet Security (CIS) is a group of international IT security experts designing cyber benchmarks and controls to protect against cyber threats. CIS Control 17 Implement a Security Awareness and Training Program, 18 Application Software Security.

755 International Society for Automation (ISA) created the ISA 62443 standard describing security for industrial automation and control systems. ISA was created in 1945 to create a better world through automation.

756 NIST Framework 1.1, 19.

The NIST Privacy Framework

The latest discussion draft of the NIST Privacy Framework is dated September 6, 2019.[757] It is intended to build customer trust, fulfill compliance obligations, and facilitate communication about privacy practices among "customers, assessors, and regulators."[758] It is designed to be used by any size organization and it "agnostic to any particular technology, sector, law, or jurisdiction."[759] Accountability is a key privacy principle.

The Privacy Framework follows the structure Cybersecurity Framework to facilitate their use together. The Privacy Framework Core performs five functions concurrently and continuously:

1. Identify: "Develop the organizational understanding to manage privacy risk for individuals arising from data processing."[760]
2. Govern: "Develop and implement the organizational governance structure to enable an ongoing understanding of the organization's risk management priorities that are informed by privacy."[761]
3. Control: "Develop and implement appropriate activities to enable organizations or individuals to manage data with sufficient granularity to manage privacy risks."[762]
4. Communicate: "Develop and implement appropriate activities to enable organizations and individuals to have a reliable understanding about how data are processed and associated privacy risks."[763]
5. Protect: "Develop and implement appropriate data processing standards."[764]

---

757 "Discussion Draft: NIST Privacy Framework: An Enterprise Risk Management Tool", September 6, 2019. Accessed 12/6/19 at https://www.nist.gov/system/files/documents/2019/09/09/nist_privacy_framework_preliminary_draft.pdf

758 NIST Privacy Framework, 3

759 NIST Privacy Framework, 4.

760 NIST Privacy Framework, 10.

761 Ibid.

762 Ibid.

763 Ibid.

764 Ibid.

The alignment between cybersecurity and privacy risks is shown in the below NIST graphic:

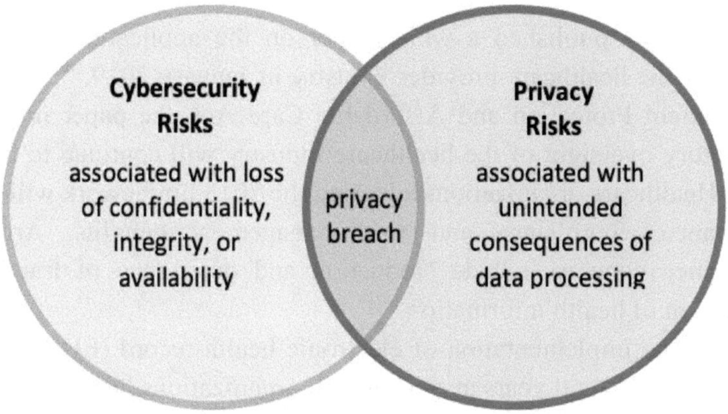

Figure: Cybersecurity and Privacy Risk Relationship[765]

Conclusion

Democratic nations are responsible for protecting their citizens' privacy. Terms like "PII" are used to generically describe the information about citizens that needs to be protected. US FIPs spawned international fair information practices which eventually led to GDPR.

GRC practices evolved quickly in the late twentieth century. Financial improprieties prompted passage of laws like SOX, bringing new regulation and potentially burdensome oversight. Companies adopted the COSO framework after the SEC recommended it, and ERM to manage corporate uncertainties. COSO's popularity probably gave its 2015 framework for information system security risk traction among for-profit institutions.

Congress mandated increased government usage of computers and networks while also preserving individual rights like privacy. New law emphasized ERM for information system security risks. This led eventually to NIST's Cybersecurity and Privacy frameworks.

All this knowledge about frameworks, especially as they are applied to the privacy of information held in cyberspace, could be used to inform a new federal privacy law. Let's consider that now.

---

[765] Ibid.

Appendix 11A

COSO and Patient Privacy

COSO published a white paper on the application of internal control to the healthcare provider industry in January 2019.[766] Citing the 2010 Patient Protection and Affordable Care Act, the paper noted that "regulatory oversight of the healthcare industry will continue to be very high." Healthcare organizations adopting the 2013 Framework will derive governance, compliance and risk management benefits. Areas of compliance concern include "reduction and deterrence of fraud" and "protection of health information."[767]

"The implementation of electronic health record (EHR) systems over the past several years at most health organizations has added further to the pressure on clinicians, support staff, and management to show improvement in care and efficiency and provide evidence of proper implementation to the government in order to maximize appropriate reimbursement."[768]

The 2013 Framework "Explicitly considers IT controls and identifies the need for fraud risk consideration not limited to financial statements but also within compliance and operations."[769]

"Consideration also needs to be given to the various IT systems (EHR, billing, etc.) that are used throughout the process. If these processes are not designed and implemented effectively, the healthcare organization may not achieve its operational, compliance, and reporting objectives within the revenue cycle."[770]

"There are several areas of risk... including operational performance, quality of care, patient and employee safety, regulatory

---

[766] Annette Schandl & Philip L.Foster, "COSO Internal Control –Integrated Framework: An Implementation Guide for the Healthcare Provider Industry" January 2019), accessed 11/19/19 at https://www.coso.org/Documents/COSO-CROWE-COSO-Internal-Control-Integrated-Framework.pdf

[767] Schandl, 4.

[768] Schandl, 3.

[769] Schandl, 5.

[770] Schandl, 7.

compliance, IT capacity, and infrastructure, cybersecurity, and leadership capabilities and capacity."[771]

Implementation of the 2013 Framework require commitment to planning and scoping; assessment and documentation; remediation planning and implementation; design, testing and reporting of controls; optimization of effectiveness and internal control.[772]

"Cybersecurity risk ... has increased dramatically over the past several years, especially with the widespread use of EHR in healthcare. It is a reality today for all organizations that the question is ono longer if a breach will occur but when. Identifying key controls and control gaps is imperative to reducing the volatility in potential breaches."[773]

Types of controls: preventative vs. detective, manual vs. automated. Need for continuous monitoring, determining the root cause of control failures.[774]

Key observations include:

1. "The accomplishment of significant goals and objectives is affected by prioritizing and bringing attention to managing operational, financial, compliance, and IT processes.
2. Senior management and members of the board of directors – in particular members of the audit committee – generally should understand the 2013 Framework and implementation benefits, costs, and approaches. Messaging and strong tone from the top will increase the likelihood of full cooperation through the in-scope departments.
3. Strong internal control functions can help mitigate many of the risks associated with current and future complex legislative, regulatory, and market pressures."[775]

---

[771] Schandl, 9
[772] Schandl, 23.
[773] Schandl, 9.
[774] Schandl, 21-22.
[775] Schandl, 23.

Appendix 11B

Useful Definitions from NIST SP 800-53

Advanced Persistent Threat: "An adversary that possesses sophisticated levels of expertise and significant resources which allow it to create opportunities to achieve its objectives by using multiple attack vectors (e.g., cyber, physical, and deception). These objectives typically include establishing and extending footholds within the information technology infrastructure of the targeted organizations for purposes of exfiltrating information, undermining or impeding critical aspects of a mission, program, or organization; or positioning itself to carry out these objectives in the future. The advanced persistent threat: (i) pursues its objectives repeatedly over an extended period of time; (ii) adapts to defenders' efforts to resist it; and (iii) is determined to maintain the level of interaction needed to execute its objectives."[776]

Availability: "Ensuring timely and reliable access to and use of information."[777]

Confidentiality: "Preserving authorized restrictions on information access and disclosure, including means for protecting personal privacy and proprietary information."[778]

Cyber Attack: "An attack, via cyberspace, targeting an enterprise's use of cyberspace for the purpose of disrupting, disabling, destroying, or maliciously controlling a computing environment/ infrastructure; or destroying the integrity of the data or stealing controlled information."[779]

Cyber Security: "The ability to protect or defend the use of cyberspace from cyber attacks."[780]

Cyberspace: "A global domain within the information environment consisting of the interdependent network of information systems infrastructures including the internet, telecommunications

[776] NIST SP 800-53, B-1.
[777] NIST SP 800-53, B-2.
[778] NIST SP 800-53, B-5.
[779] NIST SP 800-53, B-6.
[780] Ibid

networks, computer systems, and embedded processors and controllers."[781]

Enterprise: "An organization with a defined mission/goal and a defined boundary, using information systems to execute that mission, and with responsibility for managing its own risks and performance. An enterprise may consist of all or some of the following business aspects: acquisition, program management, financial management (e.g., budgets), human resources, security, and information systems, information and mission management."[782]

Enterprise Architecture: "A strategic information asset base, which defines the mission; the information necessary to perform the mission; the technologies necessary to perform the mission; and the transitional processes for implementing new technologies in response to changing mission needs; and includes a baseline architecture; a target architecture; and a sequencing plan."[783]

Information: "Any communication or representation of knowledge such as facts, data, or opinions in any medium or form, including textual, numerical, graphic, cartographic, narrative, or audiovisual. An instance of an information type."[784]

Information Security: "The protection of information and information systems from unauthorized access, use, disclosure, disruption, modification, or destruction in order to provide confidentiality, integrity, and availability."[785]

Information Security Risk: "The risk to organizational operations (including mission, functions, image, reputation), organizational assets, individuals, other organizations, and the Nation due to the potential for unauthorized access, use, disclosure, disruption, modification, or destruction of information and/or information systems."[786]

---

[781] Ibid.
[782] NIST SP 800-53, B-7.
[783] Ibid.
[784] NIST SP 800-53, B-9.
[785] NIST SP 800-53, B-10.
[786] Ibid.

Integrity: "Guarding against improper information modification or destruction, and includes ensuring information non-repudiation and authenticity."[787]

Metadata: "Information describing the characteristics of data including, for example, structural metadata describing data structures (e.g., data format, syntax, and semantics) and descriptive metadata describing data contents (e.g., information security labels)."[788]

Non-repudiation: "Protection against an individual falsely denying having performed a particular action. Provides the capability to determine whether a given individual took a particular action such as creating information, sending a message, approving information, and receiving a message."[789]

Personally Identifiable Information: "Information which can be used to distinguish or trace the identity of an individual (e.g., name, social security number, biometric records, etc.) alone, or when combined with other personal or identifying information which is linked or linkable to a specific individual (e.g., date and place of birth, mother's maiden name, etc.)."[790]

Privacy Act Statement: "A disclosure statement required by Section (e)(3) of the Privacy Act of 1974, as amended, to appear on documents used by organizations to collect personally identifiable information from individuals to be maintained in a Privacy Act System of Records (SORN)."[791]

Privacy Impact Assessment: "An analysis of how information is handled: (i) to ensure handling conforms to applicable legal, regulatory, and policy requirements regarding privacy; (ii) to determine the risks and effects of collecting, maintaining, and disseminating information in identifiable form in an electronic information system; and (iii) to examine and evaluate protections and alternative processes for handling information to mitigate potential privacy risks."[792]

---

[787] NIST SP 800-53, B-12.
[788] NIST SP 800-53, B-14.
[789] NIST SP 800-53, B-15.
[790] NIST SP 800-53, B-16.
[791] NIST SP 800-53, B-17.
[792] Ibid.

Risk Management: "The program and supporting processes to manage information security risk to organizational operations (including mission, functions, image, reputation), organizational assets, individuals, other organizations, and the Nation, and includes: (i) establishing the context for risk-related activities; (ii) assessing risk; (iii) responding to risk once determined; and (iv) monitoring risk over time."[793]

Service-Oriented Architecture: "A set of principles and methodologies for designing and developing software in the form of interoperable services. These services are well-defined business functions that are built as software components (i.e., discrete pieces of code and/or data structures) that can be reused for different purposes."[794]

Appendix 11C

Privacy Control Definitions from NIST SP 800-53

Authority and Purpose: "This family ensures that organizations: (i) identify the legal bases that authorize a particular personally identifiable information (PII) collection or activity that impacts privacy; and (ii) specify in their notices the purpose(s) for which PII is collected."[795]

Accountability, Audit, and Risk Management: "This family enhances public confidence through effective controls for governance, monitoring, risk management, and assessment to demonstrate that organizations are complying with applicable privacy protection requirements and minimizing overall privacy risk."[796]

Data Quality and Integrity: "This family enhances public confidence that any personally identifiable information (PII) collected and maintained by organizations is accurate, relevant, timely, and complete for the purpose for which it is to be used, as specified in public notices."[797]

Data Minimization and Retention: "This family helps organizations implement the data minimization and retention requirements to collect, use, and retain only personally identifiable information (PII)

---

[793] NIST SP 800-53, B-19.
[794] NIST SP 800-53, B-23.
[795] NIST SP 800-53, J-6.
[796] NIST SP 800-53, J-7.
[797] NIST SP 800-53, J-12.

that is relevant and necessary for the purpose for which it was originally collected. Organizations retain PII for only as long as necessary to fulfill the purpose(s) specified in public notices and in accordance with a National Archives and Records Administration (NARA)-approved record retention schedule."[798]

Individual Participation and Redress: "This family addresses the need to make individuals active participants in the decision-making process regarding the collection and use of their personally identifiable information (PII). By providing individuals with access to PII and the ability to have their PII corrected or amended, as appropriate, the controls in this family enhance public confidence in organizational decisions made based on the PII."[799]

Security: "This family supplements the security controls … to ensure that technical, physical, and administrative safeguards are in place to protect personally identifiable information (PII) collected or maintained by organizations against loss, unauthorized access, or disclosure, and to ensure that planning and responses to privacy incidents comply with OMB policies and guidance. The controls in this family are implemented in coordination with information security personnel and in accordance with the existing NIST Risk Management Framework."[800]

Transparency: "This family ensures that organizations provide public notice of their information practices and the privacy impact of their programs and activities."[801]

Use Limitation: "This family ensures that organizations only use personally identifiable information (PII) either as specified in their public notices, in a manner compatible with those specified purposes, or as otherwise permitted by law. Implementation of the controls in this family will ensure that the scope of PII use is limited accordingly."[802]

---

[798] NIST SP 800-53, J-14.
[799] NIST SP 800-53, J-17.
[800] NIST SP 800-53, J-20.
[801] NIST SP 800-53, J-22.
[802] NIST SP 800-53, J-24.

PART III
The Future of Privacy

Chapter 12
Future: Now What?

T.S. Eliot famously said that at the end of all our journeys, we shall arrive at the place from which we started and know it for the first time. This book has taken us on a journey of discovery from the origins of privacy to the modern era, only to return to the place from which we began. Privacy affects us all, profoundly and on a daily basis, from the writer, to the reader, to Alice, the thirteen-year-old girl we met in the first chapter. In the end, it will be Alice's world, and the decisions we make today will affect her and her children long after they cease to matter to us.

Let's review what we've learned, redefine privacy, describe the current course of privacy, and finally, outline the actions needed to preserve it. Here we go.

What History Teaches Us

a. Modern Privacy Hails from Historical Roots

American privacy was born out of a long European tradition the colonists brought with them to the New World. In Part I, we traced its origins and growing pains in English constitutionalism. We followed it to the New World, where the colonists chafed under British rule. As we know, the colonists finally decided enough was enough, declared their independence, and fought the Revolutionary War. The U.S. Constitution emerged from the rights they had asserted - life, liberty, and the pursuit of happiness.

b. The U.S. Constitution Implicitly Protects Privacy

The word "privacy" does not appear in the U.S. Constitution, but it is implicitly there. It is there in the First Amendment, in its five freedoms of religion, speech, press, assembly, and petition for redress. It also shows up in the Third Amendment about quartering soldiers in people's homes.

Likewise, it appears in the Fourth Amendment, according people the right to be secure in their persons, houses, papers, and effects; and protecting them against unreasonable search and seizure. It's there in the Fifth Amendment, giving the individual the right not to bear witness against herself, and the right to due process. And it's there in the Ninth Amendment, which reminds us all that the enumeration of rights does not deny or disparage any other rights which might have gone unmentioned.

c. "Privacy" Entered into the US Legal Vernacular in 1890

The word "privacy" finally entered the US legal vernacular in 1890 when Warren and Brandeis published their law review article. We charted its evolution in common law and constitutional law. The bottom line is that privacy has a basis in both tort and constitutional law.

d. Government Has Legitimate Needs for Information about its Citizens

Governments have always needed information about their citizens. In England, William the Conqueror conducted a survey of all the king's estates and their tenants. Historians debate the true purpose of the resulting Domesday Book. Some suggest William undertook it to assert his authority, others argue it was intended to assess taxes.

In the United States, Article I of the Constitution specified the need to conduct a census every ten years to assess taxes and representation. The Great Depression gave rise to Roosevelt's social welfare programs, requiring yet more information about its citizenry. Perceived threats against the nation's security caused still more private information to be collected for internal security purposes. By the time computers made the idea of an automated federal data conceivable, Congress had stepped in to curtail the erosion of privacy.

e. Constitutionalism both Empowers and Constrains

The Magna Carta was England's first written concession of rights. The people of the kingdom still agreed to live under the monarch's rule for protection, but certain classes were protected by affirmed rights. The Magna Carta described these rights, and created a council of barons to hold the sovereign accountable to respecting those rights. By the time of the

American Revolution, Great Britain had had considerable debate about representative government, equality, freedom of speech, freedom of assembly, freedom of the press, free elections, private property rights, due process, and had also fought its own civil war over the balance of power.

Participatory government was extended to the colonies from the time of the first charter to the Virginia Company of London in 1618. The Mayflower Compact spelled out a social contract where the people empowered the government in exchange for safety and abiding by the law. The Massachusetts Body of Liberties of 1641 asserted the rights of due process, freedom of speech, trial by jury, the right to bail, the right to written notice of court proceedings, and freedom from cruel and unusual punishment. Both Maryland and Rhode Island were early proponents of religious freedom. The Declaration of Independence describes these things as inalienable rights. The colonists took all the English and colonial lessons learned and incorporated them into a government framework they called the U.S. Constitution.

The Federalist Papers give us insight into the issues considered during the writing of the Constitution. The nation, because of its potential geographic size, became a republic, not a democracy. People needed to retain their individual rights while granting authority to the government to act. The government was responsible for protecting the nation and its citizens, and a standing army was necessary to accomplish this. Checks and balances had to be established among the three branches of government because men – and women - were not angels. Taxes, always a hot button issue, were necessary to produce a source of revenue for the fledgling government. Congress was given the power of the purse.

f. Privacy and Democracy are Symbiotic

Individual rights, like privacy, are rights accorded to the individual. Such rights cannot, however, be preserved without government acknowledging and enforcing them. Government inherently acknowledges this by operating under the Constitution, which was designed to restrain government action in order to preserve individual rights and collective civil liberties. Government protects its citizens' rights by guaranteeing equal protection (and social opportunities) under the law.

These civil rights are intended to ensure that all people can participate equally in the democracy.

In this way, privacy and democracy are symbiotic. Lawrence Lessig argued that "government is necessary to help establish [and support] the conditions necessary for [collective values like] liberty to exist. This is because there are collective values that, active as individuals, we will not realize.... The freedom to contract, to own property, to travel, to vote – all these rights require massive governmental support."[803]

g. New Law is Shaped by Legal Tradition, Social Values, and Technology

Roman law and Christian values provided a complex heritage for English language regulation.

Even Cicero saw that slanderous verses about state officials undermined the individual's reputation, and posed seditious threats to the community. It's not a leap to see how Elizabeth could consider any of the rumors spread about her seditious, even treasonous. Defamation cases were heard in ecclesiastical courts, civil courts, and the notorious Star Chamber.

While England had estranged itself from Catholicism, it retained its Christian values. These values shaped the way they thought about slander and libel. Heresy had been linked to the First Commandment's prohibition against worshipping any god but the one true Christian god. Now, seditious libel and treason were the serious crimes of English courts. They were crimes which undermined the one true monarch, who also happened to be the head of the Anglican church. The prohibition against blasphemy of the Second Commandment became the monarch's prohibition against oral and written communications which could disturb the sovereign's peace. The Eighth Commandment prohibited defamation, which of course included slander and libel. Underlying all this are essentially Christian values, like loving one's neighbor, honor, dignity, charity, and forgiveness.

---

[803] Lawrence Lessig, Code and Other Laws of Cyberspace. New York: Basic Books, 1999, p. 209.

The printing press also shaped free speech law in England. The printing press gave the population access to dangerous ideas, like the thought crimes of heresy and treason, in a vernacular tongue. By 1530, Henry VIII began regulating books, to include the language used and the printing presses on which they were produced. He realized that the printing press made material available to the citizenry which might give it thoughts, blasphemous and seditious, that undermined the king's peace. Prosecution for heresy in England declined after 1558, when Elizabeth I narrowed its definition to include only the denial of Christian fundamentals. Instead, dangerous ideas were prosecuted as libel, seditious libel, and treason.

The point is essential. Elizabeth did not seek to have a window into men's souls when it came to their religious beliefs. But she, and her father before her, absolutely could not tolerate the spread of Vatican propaganda – oral or written - in the kingdom.

h. National Security Threats Trump Individual Values

In the sixteenth century, the political threat posed by Spain, France, and other Catholic powers induced Henry VIII and Elizabeth I to assert protective powers which eroded individual rights. Anyone uttering or writing any words against Henry VIII, his family, and Elizabeth I were considered guilty of high treason.

In the United States in the twentieth century, anarchists, socialists, communists, fascists, and terrorists threated the internal security of the homeland. This mood was further fueled by US participation in wars among international powers which perturbed world order. The gradual rise of domestic surveillance was a natural government response.

i. Individual Rights Can Violently Reassert Themselves Once the Perceived Threat Passes

In seventeenth century England, the heavy-handed rule of the previous century brought unrest and civil war. The biggest problem faced by all the remaining Stuart monarchs was money. Parliament accused both James I and Charles I of imposing taxes without prior Parliamentary debate on the subject. Both kings dissolved the sitting Parliament, effectively cutting off their noses to spite their faces. Without Parliament, no appropriation could be made to the king to conduct the business of his realm. From that time onwards, Parliament held the kingdom's purse strings, tightly.

1649 was a turbulent year in England. The people reasserted their rights and beheaded their former king. Parliament enacted the Agreement of the People "for a secure and present peace upon grounds of common right, freedom, and safety." It accorded all people equality under the law, regardless of "tenure, grant, charter, patent, degree, or birth." It also called for people to elect their own Parliamentary representatives every two years. The goal was for the representatives to be apportioned according to population. The colonists embraced these lessons learned in the New World.

Individual rights reasserted themselves in the United States during the Civil Rights movement.

Fed up with government infringements on their rights, the people took the law into their own hands with acts of civil disobedience. Congress finally responded, with things like the Civil Rights Act in 1964, the 1968 Wiretap Act. The judiciary responded, with decisions like Katz v. U.S.

Then the 1970s, came along. People had been opposed to the Vietnam War in the previous decade, but the Pentagon Papers confirmed that the government had been misleading the public about how successful the war effort had been. In 1973, the Watergate scandal confirmed that the government was corrupt all the way up to the President. Nixon resigned, pursued by Congressional impeachers, and the Privacy Act was passed. But constitutional crisis was upon us, and things were about to get a lot worse. The Church and Pike committees revealed that the government had been taking liberties with people's freedom for most of the twentieth century. One could argue that the government's actions were at least partially justified by the national security threats faced since the new century dawned. But technology had given the government many tools that empowered it to infringe on civil rights in ways previously unimagined. The committees revealed information about government surveillance programs that shocked and awed. They paralyzed the public with righteous indignation. And then we got mad and insisted that Congress must act. And that's why we have FISA.

j. Democracy Must Balance National Security Concerns Against Citizen's Rights

The US Constitution created a framework for national government. Government was empowered to protect its own national security and the safety of its constituents. Its power was limited through checks and balances. The incorporated Bill of Rights enumerated the rights of the people which the government was foresworn to preserve.

Perturbations to surveillance laws continue. Government surveillance powers are more restricted in times of government scandal, especially when such events capture international media attention. Edward Snowden's 2013 sensationalized leaks reinvigorated public indignation about government surveillance powers. But of course, the reason surveillance laws had become more powerful was because of palpable threats to national security, like 9/11. Cyber threats began posing serious risk to the nation's critical infrastructure, and FISA was extended to cyber actors in 2017. And so, the tide of surveillance legislation goes in and out, ebbing and flowing as community needs for freedom and protection pull in opposite directions.

k. Technology Can Unleash Unprecedented Powers

The printing press upended the world, catalyzing the Renaissance, the Reformation, and the Scientific Revolution. It made books readily available to populations in vernacular language. Language standardized, and more and more people became literate. People no longer turned to the Catholic Church as their only source of guidance. Learning from books became a part of everyday life. Parents, not priests, were responsible for the spiritualization of the household. Literacy empowered people – individually and collectively – to act against the tyranny of Rome, fueling political consciousness, activism, and nationalism. Norms changed.

Scientific thought began to challenge the beliefs of the Catholic Church. The Vatican was not amused. Galileo lived out his days under house arrest for his Copernican-leaning world view. Yet because of the printing press, his works would be republished in Protestant lands and made widely available. The Scientific Revolution was launched, and the scientific method began helping humankind sort out the differences between facts, beliefs, and myths.

Four hundred years later, a new revolutionary technology came along: the telegraph. The telegraph made the geographic world smaller. It started with small companies operating locally, congealing slowly into fewer companies operating across larger expanses. Eventually, telegraphic services operated coast to coast, and then across the Atlantic.

The telegraph also made the world run faster. In business, stock tickers began transmitting fluctuating stock prices to investors. In news, information about national and international events became accessible to populations through wire services that fed the newspapers. In wars, the telegraph allowed the politicians at home to interfere in the affairs of military commanders in the field.

And then the telephone arrived, eventually ousting the telegraph. Bell and its telephone system leveraged and improved upon the precedents of telegraphy, causing time and space to shrink further.

Technological innovation from AT&T was a hallmark of the telephone company even before Bell Labs came officially into existence in 1925. The 1912 invention of a workable repeater made transcontinental telephone service possible by 1915. Telephone technology and the AT&T workforce played a tremendous role during World War I. The Lab's research in radio technology allowed AT&T to establish trans-Atlantic telephone service by radio by 1927. The FCC was created in 1934, introducing a government regulator dedicated to the telephone industry. Bell Labs devoted its resources to the war effort during U.S. involvement in World War II.

Mobile radio telephone service became available shortly after the end of the war. Bell Labs invented the transistor in 1947, and its undersea repeater would finally make trans-Atlantic telephone communications possible by cable in 1956.

The technological advances of World War II and the Cold War spurred U.S. investment in innovative technologies like computers, ARPANET, and data storage. Now a few decades later, our technology is generations beyond that. The commercial world has brought us mobile phones, allowing us to communicate 24/7 nearly anywhere with nearly anyone on the planet. Such devices allow us to access the internet, a worldwide network containing a vast repository of digital information.

Technology continues to proliferate and mature as long as markets for it continue to emerge and exist.

Looking forward, cyberspace "promised a kind of society that real space could never allow – freedom without anarchy, control without government, consensus without power."[804] One of the pundits of the emerging virtual world claimed: "We reject: kings, presidents and voting. We believe in: rough consensus and running code."[805] Today, this same mentality fuels a desire for continued lawlessness on the cyberspace frontier.

l. New Technology Enables Entities to Circumvent the Spirit of the Law

Since the time of our first post offices, U.S. law has protected the right to private communications. The privacy concepts associated with letters were challenged by the advent of the telegraph. During the Civil War, both Union and Confederate soldiers tapped telegraph lines as a valuable source of information about the enemy. After the war, some unemployed soldiers, looking to reassimilate back into the civilian world, put their wiretapping skills to use, sometimes in ways that circumvented the spirit of the law. Telephone tapping and eavesdropping came next. Then radio technology came along to confound the issues.

The telegraph and telephone gave individuals new ways to circumvent the spirit of the law. Madison was right, men were not angels, and people creatively devised new ways of using modern communications systems to infringe on individual rights and take advantage of others. Many of these activities were not unlawful per se, because the old laws did not anticipate nor prohibit the innovative abuses made possible by technology.

As a commercial venture, Ma Bell developed the technology needed to provide 99.999% reliability and bill its customers on a per call basis. This infrastructure also made it possible for the federal government to get information about customers – who they called, what they said, etc. Increased public awareness about government oversteps into the private

---

[804] Lessig, 4.
[805] Ibid.

lives of individuals during the 1970s, would lead to passage of new laws like FISA.

m. The Pace of Technological Innovation Laps Government Response

The capabilities of the technologies, and the companies that supported, them were remarkable. The telegraph and telephone companies had always needed to understand their own technology in order to provide reliable service to their customers. Legitimate "taps" into systems helped communications companies monitor the health and status of their systems. It helped them pinpoint failures to expedite repairs, and to minimize interruptions to service. The real problem arose when third parties wanted to implement their own tapping technology, or to accomplish the same thing with the complicity of the common carriers.

In 1934, Congress finally created the Federal Communications Commission, authorized to regulate all communications by wire and radio. Section 605 of the 1934 Communications Act tried to make such interceptions illegal, but ambiguities over its real meaning and intent left the barn door open to federal, state, and local government surveillance practices. Nor did Congress or the Supreme Court come down with clear guidance, especially during the threatening times of anarchism, fascism, communism, and the Cold War. It would take the restoring force of the Civil Rights Movement to steer the ship away from the national security state to the individual rights state. Two 1967 Supreme Court decisions and the 1968 Wiretap Act codified the reversal judicially and legislatively.

The Privacy Act came about after twenty years of Congressional haggling. Historical events shaped the debate. Technological innovations had matured into commercial products which allowed the government, and others, to eavesdrop with impunity. The spread of mainframe computers to other parts of government raised concerns about the computerized information the government had about its citizens. The Cold War, McCarthyism, and sensationalized spy case spread fears that the Soviet enemies were living among us, and had infiltrated our government. The Civil Rights movement exploded in response to the overreach of government. The Bay of Pigs, the Vietnam War, the Pentagon Papers, and the Watergate scandal fueled public disillusionment in government. FOIA had been a forward step, but insufficient. The Privacy Act finally moved to restore the balance between individual rights and overbearing national security behaviors. It leveraged the five FIPS of the Department of Health, Education, and Welfare (HEW) report on "Records, Computers, and the Rights of Citizens" into what the Privacy Protection Study Commission (PPSC) report would describe as eight FIPS.

In 1995, the President of Intel, Andy Grove, was quoted as having said: "High tech runs three-times faster than normal businesses. And the government runs three-times slower than normal businesses. So we have a nine-times gap."[806] It took decades and the specter of the Cold War to successfully drive government investment in the technological capability that would emerge as the internet.

n. Technology Can Support or Thwart Government and Leaders' Objectives

The printing press emerged as the champion of the Reformation. Both Martin Luther and Henry VIII capitalized on the printing press as a propaganda machine against the ecclesiastical and temporal power of the papacy. No matter how hard the Vatican tried to put the genie back in the bottle, the viral success of anti-Catholicism spread from multiple safe harbors in Europe. Vatican book-banning backfired, generating explosive demand for forbidden texts.

Bell Telephone aspired to grow into a national service, and to make money. It grew up as a utility instance of the big business monopolies of the Robber Baron era. Such monopolies began to be reined in by the Sherman and Clayton antitrust acts. U.S. appetite for trustbusting brought hostility towards AT&T's monopoly status. To settle an ICC investigation, AT&T agreed in 1913 to dispose of its Western Union stock, to stop buying up independent telephone companies, and to allow interconnection between local telephone systems and the AT&T long distance service.

---

[806] Lillian Cunningham, "Google's Eric Schmidt expounds on his Senate testimony," Wash Post, 1 October, 2011. Accessed 12/17/19 at https://www.washingtonpost.com/national/on-leadership/googles-eric-schmidt-expounds-on-his-senate-testimony/2011/09/30/gIQAPyVgCL_story.html

Terrorism against U.S. interests, at home and abroad, fueled government funding to companies with big data and associated analytics. The attacks of 9/11 were the turning point. The government had clearly failed to protect the nation and once again, the pendulum swung towards national security priorities and away from individual rights. FISA authorities were strengthen by Congress, but government surveillance authorities remained more constrained than they had been before passage of the Wiretap Act and the original FISA. Government was further constrained by its lack of technological prowess. This was something better left to the entrepreneurs, and the synergy of government funding and innovative technology would give wing to the success of companies like Google.

o. Technology Shapes Social Norms

The Privacy Protection Study Commission (PPSC) report highlighted the social dimension of the information age. With computers, individuals no longer had a personal relationship with another individual, shaped by common values, beliefs, or human agreement. Personal information could now ooze to other locations. Existing laws did not prohibit it, so the Privacy Act was a good step towards protecting the private information held by the government about its citizens.

The PPSC usefully pointed out that there was a balance to be struck for effective privacy protection policy. Firstly, the information requested by any organization to provide individuals with goods and services should be minimally intrusive. Secondly, record keeping operations should maximize the fairness of decisions made about the individual. Thirdly, there should be agreed-upon expectations for confidentiality, to include rules about and legal rights over disclosure of personal information by the organization. This would be accomplished by incentives for compliance, use of existing regulatory and enforcement mechanisms, and minimizing the cost burden on organizations. These principles were equally applicable across the public and private sectors. The crucial conclusion was that at that point in time, 1977, the PPSC did not believe that a one-size-fits all privacy law could accomplish its intent for the U.S. commercial world.

p. The Commercial World Prioritizes Privacy Only When Required

The Privacy Act did nothing to deter commercial erosion of personal privacy. In some sectors, the USG has chosen to enact laws to protect the privacy of individuals and their information in the private business world. The 1950s, rise of consumerism finally made consumer protection an important enough issue to address with congressional action. The Fair Credit Reporting Act (FCRA) was the first U.S. law to address the information privacy issue across a single industry, four years before the 1974 Privacy Act. It required Credit Reporting Agencies (CRAs) to perform their credit reporting function with fairness, impartiality, and a respect for the consumer's privacy. This was important because such information could affect an individual's ability to get employment, credit, or insurance. A key player in this became the Federal Trade Commission (FTC), which was named the FCRA administrative enforcement authority. By 1999, the Gramm-Leach-Bliley Act (GLBA) affirmed that financial institutions had an obligation to protect the security, confidentiality, and integrity of Non-Public Information (NPI) in consumer records.

The Health Insurance Portability and Accountability Act (HIPAA) was not passed until 1996. It had the benefit of everything that had been debated and learned with FCRA, the HEW report, the Privacy Act, and the PPSC report. HHS leveraged this knowledge to compactly describe the HIPAA Privacy Rule for protecting the privacy of IIHI. The Security Rule described the security protections required for e-PHI. The HITECH Act of 2009 was passed to promote a nationwide health information technology infrastructure. It was intended to improve health care, reduce its costs, and still secure and protect patients' health information. HITECH specifically prohibited the sale of electronic health records and protected health information.

In commercial sectors unconstrained by privacy law, the FTC has tried to step in and exercise privacy protection as a failure to exercise fair consumer protection practices.

q. GRC Evolved to Protect Both Big Business and Consumers

Governance, risk management, and compliance techniques evolved to protect big business and the interests of consumers. The Depression brought massive financial reforms imposed by the government. The SEC was created in 1934, and authorized to collect annual reports from regulated entities to protect investors and ensure fair dealing. The SEC worked with the accountants, and over time, the GAAP emerged as accepted fair practices in accounting.

Financial crises from the 1980s, into the new century prompted passage of new laws intended to hold governance controllers more accountable for their publicly held businesses and financial institutions. SOX held senior executives directly accountable for the activities of their organizations. It required usage of internal controls, auditing, and the usage of GAPP and transparency in their financial reporting.

Enterprise Risk Management (ERM) became popularly favored by businesses and government alike. It involved access and analysis of complete information, an understanding of the risk appetite of an organization, an assessment of risks across the organization and their alignment with the risk appetite, the use of computer models to stress test the risk management strategy under ordinary and extraordinary events, and an appreciation for the behavioral economics of the situation. Suddenly, ERM became the term of the times.

In corporations, a tradition of compliance has evolved. Many laws and frameworks require senior leadership to "set the tone at the top," i.e. to establish and model the values to which it expects every employee to subscribe. Collectively this becomes the organizational culture, which should align with applicable laws and regulations. Their purpose is to minimize the organization's risk with respect to civil and criminal liability to maximize its profits. Compliance is about enforcing organizational norm.

r. The Commercial World and the Government Need One Another

Nobody wants to be told what to do, especially by the government. But we are assembled together as a nation which subscribes to a framework of government. The agreement is that the government will keep us safe, yet leave us alone.

Companies don't want the government to tell them what to do, but they do want to know the minimally required actions they must take to comply with the law, regulations, and policies which apply to them. No single compliance program fits every business like a glove; this is how we got to frameworks like COSO. Nor does the government have the resources to prosecute every infringement of its rules. Prosecutors pursue the most egregious violators, taking a far more sympathetic view towards businesses that act without malicious intent, make honest efforts to comply, and are open to compromise. The question remains as to whether a new U.S. privacy law could strengthen the informational privacy of individuals.

Government is not going to let anyone else tell it what to do, but it does value best business practices from for-profit entities. Adoption of such practices allows government to leverage the painful and expensive lessons learned in the competitive world to increase government efficiency and act in the public good. Congress pushed government to manage IT resources and move towards e-Government. The executive branch responded with enterprise architecture and risk management principles pinched from commerce. As a traditionally sensitive subject, provisions for the protection of integrity, confidentiality, and availability of information - and the information systems on which they were housed – was emphasized. By 2014, each agency was responsible for its own information security program, as well as independent assessment - think audit - of its information security program.

So, government and commerce participate in this elaborate dance. Each thinks it is stopping the other from leading, but in fact they are playing shadow tag with one another.

s. The Concept of FIPs Emerged in the U.S. and Overseas

Technology drove public concern about what the government was doing with citizens' private information. The 1973 HEW report described these concerns. It also framed the fair information practices (FIPs) which were incorporated into the Privacy Act. The OECD created a European version of the FIPs. All future privacy principles regarding personal data were underpinned by democratic mindsets committed to individual rights. These principles rippled worldwide in laws, regulations, policies, and standards.

Technology was also affecting the corporate world. Because of SOX, COSO enjoyed great popularity in the commercial world. The framework was updated in 2013 to reflect the emerging challenges associated with cyberspace. Risk analysis and anti-fraud measures were central to its continuous improvement strategy. Its 2015 paper addressed application of the COSO framework to information system security risk. Its keys to effective control of risk in the cyber era include a clear tone from the top, an ongoing evaluation program to assess design and effectiveness of control for cyber risk, the help of cyber experts, monitoring of cyber risks and controls related to outsourced service providers, timely recognition of and communication about cyber deficiencies, and holding owners accountable.

t. Security and Privacy Frameworks Emerged for the Cyber Age

The National Institute of Standards and Technology (NIST) published number reports on security and privacy in USG information and information systems. NIST specifically addressed the protecting the confidentiality of personally identifiable information (PII), and managing information system risk. SP 800-53 addresses security and privacy controls for federal information systems and organizations. It is based on the fair information practices embodied in the Privacy Act, and other later laws and policies. With this build-up, NIST was finally able to propose its relatively mature Cybersecurity Framework, and showed its alignment with ISO standards, and the COSO and COBIT frameworks. Now NIST is refining its draft Privacy Framework, which explicitly shows the relationship between privacy concerns and security concerns.

Defining Privacy

We have spent a whole book talking about privacy. Hopefully, we agree it is not a thing to be glibly dismissed. We have traced the who, what, where, when, why, and how of it being a part of our democracy and freetrade capitalism. But what is privacy, really? Is it "a claim, a right, an interest, a value, a preference, or merely a state of existence?"[807] Is it like a property right, which suggests a contract has been entered into which acknowledges the transfer of property from one individual to another? Or is it a tort claim, which never involved a contract but resulted in reputational injury? The fuzziness of its definition is aptly captured by legal discussions about "privacy penumbra," a metaphor used to describe the implied privacy rights of the constitution.

Privacy encompasses all of these dimensions. In chapter six, we looked at its legal dimensions: physical, informational, decisional, proprietary, associational, and intellectual. The ones we really focused on in the second part of the book were physical privacy, intellectual privacy, and informational privacy.

Physical privacy contains a sense of solitude and seclusion. It is partly summed up in Coke's idea that "a man's home is his castle." It can include the privacy of one's physical, bodily, territorial, or spatial domain.[808] Warren and Brandeis would not have disagreed. Zuboff goes so far as to suggest that privacy guarantees the individual the right to an unplunderable sanctuary.[809]

Mixed up in this, however, is the fact that privacy is about more than a right to the unfettered and uninfringed-upon use of one's property and effects. It is also the privacy of one's non-material space, the right to be enjoy one's thoughts in private without being judged. This is

---

[807] Helen Nissenbaum, Privacy in Context: Technology, Policy and the Integrity of Social Life. Stanford: Stanford Law Books, 2010, p. 2.

[808] Anita L. Allen and Marc Rotenberg, Privacy Law and Society. St. Paul, MN: West Academic Publishing, 2016, 3rd edition, p. 5.

[809] Zuboff, 478.

intellectual privacy.[810] Warren and Brandeis described this when they said: "The common law secures to each individual the right of determining, ordinarily, to what extent his thoughts, sentiments, and emotions shall be communicated to others."[811] In his dissent in *Warden v. Hayden*, Supreme Court Justice Douglas stated that "Privacy involves the choice of the individual to disclose or to reveal what he believes, what he thinks, what he possesses."[812]

Informational privacy is about the protection of individuals' information. Technological advances throughout the twentieth century made electronic surveillance easier. Congress began talking about information privacy in 1965 after the government proposed creating a National Data Center.[813] The HEW study stated that the use of automated data systems posed serious concerns for privacy and due process.[814] The FIPs tried to address this.[815] Concerns about the storage of private individual information in government repositories would bring us FOIA, the Privacy Act, and eventually FISA. In 1998, the legal scholar Jerry Kang described privacy as "the control of the flow of personal information in all stages of processing – acquisition, disclosure, and use."[816]

As the cyber age progressed from a science fiction fantasy to reality, the many versions of FIPs and FIPPs emerged to describe a set of norms for the handling of information given to others. These can take on

---

[810] This is, of course, distinct from intellectual property, a different legal subject outside the scope of this book.

[811] Warren and Brandeis cited Judge Yates in the 1769 English copyright case of Millar v. Taylor: "It is certain every man has a right to keep his own sentiments, if he pleases. He has certainly a right to judge whether he will make them public, or commit them only to the sight of his friends." Yates, J., in Millar v. Taylor, 4 Burr. 2303, 2379 (1769), accessed 12/24/19 at https://www.jstor.org/stable/pdf/1321160.pdf?refreqid=excelsior%3A31514a85881b279ad7c387a04616adcb

[812] Warden v. Hayden, 387 U.S. 294 (1967), accessed 12/16/19 at https://supreme.justia.com/cases/federal/us/387/294/

[813] Priscilla Regan, Legislating Privacy: Technology, Social Values, and Public Policy. Chapel Hill, NC: University of North Carolina Press, 1995, p. 7-8.

[814] HEW, viii.

[815] Regan, 75-80.

[816] Jerry Kang, "Information Privacy in Cyberspace Transactions". Stanford Law Review 50(4): 1193-1294. Accessed 12/24/19 at https://papers.ssrn.com/sol3/papers.cfm?abstract_id=631723

a greater authority if we describe them as the fiduciary responsibilities of the data custodians. Concerns about data safety and overall protection in cyberspace lead to basic information system security principles - confidentiality, data integrity, and availability – and privacy frameworks.

Psychological descriptions of privacy capture a similar diversity of meaning and intent. Psychologist Darhl Pedersen[817] describes privacy as a "boundary control process in which the individual regulates with whom contact will occur and how much and what type of interaction it will be." He enumerates six kinds of privacy: "solitude, isolation, anonymity, reserve, intimacy with friends, and intimacy with family." Pedersen found that the privacy functions of "contemplation, autonomy, rejuvenation, confiding, freedom, creativity, disapproved consumptions, recovery, catharsis, and concealment" fulfilled privacy needs vital to the human. Privacy provides "freedom from censure and ridicule" and promotes mental health.[818]

But privacy is still more. It is a collective right of society which underpins our democracy.

Legal scholar Ruth Gavison tells us that privacy is "essential to democratic government because it fosters and encourages the moral autonomy of the citizen, a central requirement of a democracy. Part of the justification for majority rule and the right to vote is the assumption that individuals should participate in political decisions by forming judgements and expressing preferences. Thus, to the extent that privacy is important for autonomy, it is important for democracy as well."[819]

At the opening of his book on privacy, law professor Raymond Wacks observes:

> The modern distinction between public and private realms arose out of a twin movement in modern political and legal thought. On the one hand, the emergence of the nation-state and theories of sovereignty in the sixteenth and seventeenth centuries

---

[817] Darhl Pedersen, "Psychological Functions of Privacy", Journal of Environmental Psychology (1997) 17, 147-156. Accessed 12/24/19 at https://www.deepdyve.com/lp/elsevier/psychological-functions-of-privacy-KzTnLfz1rl

[818] Ruth Gavison, "Privacy and the Limits of Law". The Yale Law Journal 89(3), 1980, p. 448. Accessed 12/24/19 at https://digitalcommons.law.yale.edu/cgi/view content .cgi?article=6581&context=ylj

[819] Gavison, 455.

> produced the idea of a distinctly public realm. On the other hand, a delineation of a private sphere free from the encroachment of the state emerged as a response to the claims of monarch and, subsequently, parliaments, to an untrammeled power to make law.[820]

Nissenbaum claims that "a right to privacy is neither a right to secrecy nor a right to control but a right to appropriate flow of personal information."[821] She argues that the privacy of information needs to be associated with the context in which it is shared. She proposes a framework of contextual integrity which includes social and informational contexts. It is intended to establish the norms by which the players (the owner, the sender, the recipient) agree to share, transmit, and protect information. Any violation of privacy is considered a violation of contextual norms, which should aspire to become legal norms over time.

There is a subtle but essential difference between the U.S. and European perspectives on privacy. The U.S. Bill of Rights enumerates the individual rights related to privacy which Americans retain. The government is not only prohibited from violating them, but constitutionally bound to preserve them. The Europeans consider privacy to be an inherent right.[822] While government violation of them is not even conceivable, the Europeans expect the EU and their governments to enforce these rights.

We've already seen many different versions of fair information practices and classes of private data. There are many versions of FIPs. There are many flavors of PII, which is different from non-public information (NPI) and individually identifiable health information (IIHI). These are distinct, of course, from public record information (PRI), which is only sometimes eligible to be held as confidential. Yes, it is confusing. But all the definitions of private information attempted to circumscribe a zone of privacy around the most sensitive information about an individual.

---

[820] Raymond Wacks, Personal Information: Privacy and the Law. Oxford: Clarendon Press, 1993, pp. 7-8.
[821] Nissenbaum, 126.
[822] This is a very Hamiltonian point of view. As you recall, Alexander Hamilton argued against a bill of rights being incorporated in the Constitution because it specified exceptions to a power never formally granted to government.

All the fair information practices aim to describe what is considered a fair use of the private information provided to someone else.

What is privacy? In this book, we conclude that privacy is the right for each individual to enjoy her physical and spiritual spaces, realized only when affirmed as a collective value of a democratic society. It guarantees sanctuary in one's home. It allows one to be alone with one's thoughts, both written and unwritten. It grants each individual the right to share those thoughts, or hold them in reserve. And it should extend to personal information about oneself in cyberspace.

The Future Arc of Privacy

a. Google and the Other Privacy Pirates as Digital Totalitarians

Companies like Google and Facebook are doing amazing things with your private information. Google actually pioneered what Shoshana Zuboff called "surveillance capitalism" by being the first to link and actuate your online behavioral data for targeted advertising.[823] She calls these companies "digital totalitarians." I will call them *Privacy Pirates*.

Google's capabilities seem like magic to the new user, matching advertisements with user's interests. But access to such powerful magic does not come without a cost. The user actually gets access to Google capabilities by undetectably paying with his or her behavioral data, and being force-fed targeted advertising. Google has always been deliberately silent and secretive about the ways they use users' information to target the advertising, as Zuboff says, because "they took things from users

---

[823] Zuboff defines surveillance capitalism as, among other things: 1. "A new economic order that claims human experience as free raw material for hidden commercial practices of extraction, prediction and sales"; 2. A mutated capitalism which concentrates unprecedented amounts of knowledge, wealth and power in the hands of the few to enable a surveillance economy; 3. A market-driven threat to human nature which could be used to control human behavior, eliminating the uncertainties associated with exercising free will; and 4. "An overthrow of the people's sovereignty." See Shoshana Zuboff, The Age of Surveillance Capitalism: The Fight for a Human Future at the New Frontier of Power. New York: Public Affairs, 2019, opening pages.

without asking and employed those unilaterally-claimed resources to work in the service of others' purposes."[824]

Privacy Pirates have both public and private personas.[825] They cultivate benign public personas, demonstrating their commitment to helping humankind, connecting families and friends, making your work easier, anticipating your every need, etc. But their true intentions and activities are squirreled away in secrecy. If I try to understand what they are going to do with my private information, I'm confronted with the complex and obtuse language of a privacy agreement. I have to agree to the Pirates' terms before I can use their services.

Like regular pirates, Privacy Pirates want to secure wealth. The way they make money is by having the most data and the best algorithms. The plundering of privacy on their way to recovering treasure is at best collateral damage in their minds. At worst, they see privacy as an impediment to their success which needs continued undermining on their way to its eradication. They wrap themselves in the Constitution to assert their free right to use our data however they see fit, privacy be damned.

Zuboff suggests that the Privacy Pirates are hell bent on digital dispossession of individual behavioral information to "impose a new kind of control on individuals, populations, and whole societies."[826][827] Digital totalitarianism does not use the violent methods of traditional totalitarianism, but rather "it grows through declaration, selfauthorization, rhetorical misdirection, euphemism, and the quiet, audacious backstage moves specifically crafted to elude awareness as it replaces individual freedom with others' knowledge and replaces society with certainty."[828] Google dispossesses you of your information through incursion into your digital devices, habituation legitimizes its actions as norms, adaptation

---

[824] Zuboff, 89.

[825] Truth be told, we all do. Law professor Richard Posner talks about privacy as the "right to misrepresent one's character." See Richard Posner, "The Right to Privacy". Georgia Law Review 12(3), 393-422. Accessed 12/24/19 at http://chicagounbound.uchicago.edu/cgi/viewcontent.cgi?article=2803&context=journal_articles

[826] Zuboff, 192.

[827] Zuboff describes totalitarianism's goal as "the reconstruction of the human species through the dual mechanisms of genocide and the 'engineering of the soul.'" See Zuboff, 353

[828] Zuboff, 381.

designed to placate government and public opinion, and redirection in order to appear compliant.[829]

Europeans associate totalitarianism with the atrocities of World War II, which helped drive passage of the Universal Declaration of Human Rights in 1948. We see this ethos shaping European privacy concepts today. GDPR presumes that human rights are never eligible to be given away or sold to anyone. That includes to any government, to any commercial entity, or to anyone else. GDPR is very specific about the kinds of privacy protections it wants for its EC citizens, including the aspirational right to be forgotten. GDPR and the Privacy Pirates are on a collision course. Already the EU is levy large fines against the Pirates for GDPR violations.

Perhaps the Privacy Pirates see themselves as modern utopians who believe they can use their code and our behavioral data to solve all the world's problems, including "questions of individual authority, moral reasoning, social norms and values, privacy, decision rights, politics and law."[830] Sociologists since the time of B.F. Skinner have argued that rewards of a behaviorally driven society are far greater than the potential losses. Harvard data scientist Alexander Pentland argues that in such a perfect world, there would be no war, no famines, and no need for government or individual rights.[831]

The Privacy Pirates need us to believe that the decline of privacy is inevitable. Way back in 2010, Mark Zuckerberg claimed that "privacy was no longer a 'social norm.'"[832] Such claims allow the Pirates freedom to harvest more and more behavioral data. Perhaps the failures of Facebook and Cambridge Analytica to protect the private of information of individuals were not anomalies, but the visible tip of this dytopian iceberg.

---

[829] Zuboff, 139-140, 292.

[830] Zuboff, 223.

[831] "See Alex Pentland, Social Physics: How Good Ideas Spread – The Lessons from a New Science. NewYork: Penguin, 2014."

[832] This was in line with "recent controversial changes to Facebook's privacy settings, which not only reduced the control users have over their personal data and pushed more personal information public, but [also] sparked a federal complaint." See Huffington Post, 3/18/2010, updated 12/7/16. Accessed 12/22/19 at https://www.huffpost.com/entry/facebooks-zuckerberg-the_n_417969

In 1999, Lessig described the harvesting of web-based information in terms of Oscar Gandy's "panoptic sort," "a vast structure for collecting data and discriminating on the basis of that data." While the intent is to make the market operate more smoothly, it reeks of manipulation, profiling, and discrimination.[833] It also undermines our individual and collective right to privacy.

Privacy craves autonomy. One should be free define and present oneself in different roles in life. One should have freedom from scrutiny in thought and action, as long as it does not hurt other people or otherwise violate laws or fundamental social norms.[834] Privacy abhors the idea of the cyber panopticon, a prison in which all thoughts, words, and deeds can be seen and behaviors can be controlled.

b. The Power of Digital Totalitarianism is Visible

The overwhelming power of digital totalitarianism has become most visible in one place: China. China today controls its population's access to dangerous ideas on the internet with the Great Firewall, the "largest system of censorship in the world."[835] It began in 2000 as part of the Golden Shield Project, an automated surveillance system designed to accumulate and make available records about each citizen. Government monitoring capabilities are complemented by compelled cooperation from telecommunications and technology companies.

Foreign companies are attracted to doing business in China. Labor and manufacturing costs are low, and its population represents a huge potential consumer market. But foreign companies find themselves greatly restricted by China's rules. China blocks internet sites and applications regularly. It compels foreign companies to cooperate with its surveillance objectives. After being blocked for the first time in 2002, Google released a censored version of its site, Google.cn.[836] Google.cn was removed from China in 2010 after the company was hacked, and amidst furor over online

---

[833] Lessig, 153-154.

[834] See Nissenbaum, 81-82.

[835] Bloomberg News, "The Great Firewall", November 5, 2018, accessed 12/26/19 at https://www.bloomberg.com/quicktake/great-firewall-of-china

[836] Elizabeth C. Economy, "The great firewall of China: Xi Jinping's internet shutdown", The Guardian, 6/29/18. Accessed 12/26/19 at https://www.theguardian .com/news/2018/jun/29/the-great-firewall-of-china-xi-jinpings-internet-shutdown

search censorship. Then Google embarked upon its ill-fated Dragonfly project to a build search engine which adhered to Chinese censorship rules. Public uproar and a request from Vice President Mike Pence later induced Google to cancel the project.[837] Google subsequently refused to support Pentagon projects in artificial intelligence "because its employees object to having their work used for military ends."[838]

Now we are hearing about China's social credit scores, derived from dossiers of information about an individual. This of it as a traditional credit rating expanded to include all dimensions of one's life. At this point, participation in government run and private credit scoring is voluntary, but incentivized. In the future, participation in the state sponsored program will be mandatory. Bad behavior causes deductions in one's social credit score. These include things like financial delinquencies, traffic violations, jaywalking, time spent playing video games, and stealing electricity. Good behavior, like donating to charities or being a parent, rewards the individual with an increased social credit score. Social credit scores are today being normalized in Chinese society, for example, by inclusion on dating websites. In the hands of the state, the credit scores can be used to blacklist individuals.[839]

c. Code is Law

In 1999, Lessig broadly declared "code is law," suggesting that West Coast (computer) code was threatening the authority of East Coast (legal) code. He saw that cyberspace code was challenging traditional laws and norms about privacy, intellectual property, free speech, and sovereignty. Lessig then stated that we are free to "build, or architect, or code cyberspace to protect values that we believe are fundamental, or we can build, or architect, or code cyberspace to allow those values to disappear."[840] What values do we want?

---

[837] Matt Sheehan, "How Google took on China – and lost", MIT Technology Review, 12/19/18. Accessed 12/26/19 at https://www.technologyreview.com/s/612601/how-google-took-on-china-and-lost/

[838] Ibid.

[839] Nichole Kobie, "The complicated truth about China's social credit system", Wired magazine, 6/7/19. Accessed 12/26/19 at https://www.wired.co.uk/article/china-social-credit-system-explained

[840] Lessig, 6,8.

The measure of the Privacy Pirates' power is not just in their ability to invade our lives. It includes their ability to influence East Coast code with West Coast code. Even before 9/11, the government was trying to make investments in innovative technologies to address the terrorist challenge on the horizon. Zuboff does an admirable job detailing the funding and cooperation that occurred between government and the nascent behavioral capitalists. 9/11 allowed "surveillance exceptionalism" to prevail. It helped Google et al gestate, thrive and mature. The Privacy Pirates emerged from their chrysalises capable of meeting the government's need to "rapidly bypass legal and bureaucratic restrictions."[841] As legal scholar Jack Balkan said in 2008, government came to "rely on private enterprise to collect and generate information for it."[842] As a result of this affinity, the "fledgling practices of surveillance capitalism were allowed to root and grow with little regulatory or legislative challenge."[843] Sentiment analysis became a useful tool for predicting future behaviors of our unseen enemies.

Zuboff asks and answers three important questions. Who knows? The Privacy Pirates know. Who decides? The market decides. Who decides who decides? Competition among the Privacy Pirates decides who decides. Do we really want the Privacy Pirates knowing everything, deciding on the rules of engagement, and deciding on deciding who makes the rules?

The Roman poet Juvenal asked *Quis custodiet Ipsos custodes?* Who watches the watchers? We should be watching the Privacy Pirates.

Since the time of Adam Smith and his *The Wealth of Nations* (1776), the "invisible hand" has been guiding society's evolution towards "perfect liberty" through competition among individuals. His perfect liberty would over time come to be called laissez-faire capitalism. In *On Liberty*, Mill

---

[841] Zuboff, 115.

[842] Jack Balkin, "The Constitution of the National Surveillance State" (2008), Faculty Scholarship Series. 225. Accessed 12/17/19 at http://digitalcommons.law.yale.edu/cgi/viewcontent.cgi?article=1224&context=fss_papers

[843] Zuboff, 120.

claims that the only source of human progress is liberty; government, even democratic government, breeds mediocrity.[844]

What then is the role of government in a free society? Milton Friedman argues it is "to provide a means whereby we can modify the rules, to mediate differences among us on the meaning of the rules, and to enforce compliance with the rules on the part of those few who would otherwise not play the game." [845] It regulates behavior between individuals, ensuring that one person's freedom is checked when it violates another's. Friedman tells us that one Supreme Court Justice succinctly put this as: "My freedom to move my fist must be limited by the proximity of your chin."[846] Government also performs a function which "the market cannot do for itself, namely to determine, arbitrate, and enforce the rules of the game" in the commercial world.[847]

Zuboff argues that the rules of capitalism have changed with surveillance capitalism. Capitalists have traditionally argued that the market was unknowable, and therefore they needed every freedom from government intervention. Through surveillance capitalism, the market is today more knowable. Zuboff claims they now "know too much to qualify for freedom."[848]

We have left the Privacy Pirates largely in control of the invisible hand in cyberspace. Without constitutional agreements in this new domain, Lessig argues, "cyberspace will become a perfect tool of control."[849]

d. Code Is Replacing the Social Contract with an Anti-Contract

Since the seventeenth century, political theorists have talked about the social contract. The social contract is negotiated agreement between the governed and the government. It enumerates the rights and

---

[844] John Stuart Mill, On Liberty. London: Longmans, Green, Reader, and Dyer, 1880, pp. 39 and 41.
[845] Milton Friedman, Capitalism and Freedom. Chicago: The University of Chicago Press, 2002, p. 25.
[846] Friedman, 26.
[847] Friedman, 27.
[848] Zuboff, 495, 498-499.
[849] Lessig, 5-6.

responsibilities of each. Our social contract is the Constitution. Our government has acted to fulfill its contractual responsibilities to protect the rights of its citizens by passing new privacy laws.

The first glaring instance of the anti-contract was the noncontractual relationship people had with CRAs when they emerged. CRAs collected lots of information about consumers and shared it with others. The consumer had (and still has) no contractual relationship with the CRA. Her actions as an individual consumer were no match for the national interests of CRAs. Eventually, Congress started stepping in with legal restrictions and regulatory authorities.

And so, we set down the path of uncontract dystopia. Personal relationships and formal contracts gave way to databased consumer profiles and automated judgements. Social trust has already been replaced by a financial credit score. The Chinese are already going for a social credit score.

e. Cyberspace has given rise to a non-territorial domain which requires translation of national and international privacy laws and norms

The internet released unprecedented powers like an atomic blast. It tantalizingly offered early adopters a virtual world imbued with "freedom without anarchy, control without government, consensus without power."[850] In this, it failed.

Because of cyberspace and its internetwork, information now permeates every corner of the earth more quickly than ever before. internet technology and code allow the commercial world to access, collect, search, sort, analyze, synthesize, aggregate, correlate, manipulate, lease, share, and sell information about consumers in unprecedented ways. In order to remain competitive in today's market, businesses have learned to morph adeptly in virtual space and cyber time. This also allows them to color around existing laws and regulations intended to protect the individual rights of the consumer and the collective good. Democratic government can only respond slowly, trying to enforce shifting norms with consent orders, judicial proceedings, and legislation. Such instruments of

---

[850] Lessig, *Code*, 4.

government are quickly obsolesced by new technology and commercial creativity. Collective norms and the individual right of privacy begin vanishing in the dust of cyber-charged commercial profit motives.

This is complicated by the emergence of international cyberspace, that place where individuals from different countries meet to exchange ideas, goods, and services. How much should local, state, national, and international laws apply in cyberspace? Many laws, rules, and norms of real space are unenforced and/or unenforceable in cyberspace. The world's nations, from totalitarian to democratic, have responded in different ways. The Chinese built the Great Firewall of China to regulate the internet, limiting their citizens' access to foreign websites and content. The Europeans passed the General Data Privacy Regulation (GDPR) to protect the "fundamental rights and freedoms of natural persons and in particular their right to the protection of personal data."[851] Rooted in the American values of its birthplace, the internet is being modified overseas to cohere with other nations' concepts of individual rights and the collective good.

Cyber technology challenges our sovereignty today in ways that the printing press challenged the sovereigns of its era. Cyber actors, both foreign and domestic, can attack our critical infrastructure, causing havoc with hacking, advanced persistent threats, ransomware, and social engineering and phishing attacks. Government, businesses, and individuals are not always prepared to repel these invasions into our way of life. We embrace new devices and services which promise efficiencies, without necessarily thinking about our increased vulnerability in cyberspace. Too little, sometimes too late, we realize we should have proactively managed the risks to our individual rights and collective values with better network and information security.

Because of the internet, ubiquitous networks transcend the territorial boundaries so carefully constructed after World War II. They provide opportunities for many actors, not just nation states, to exercise state-like powers in cyberspace. Now sovereign states find their territorial integrity violated by not just by peers, but non-nation states, terrorists, and

[851] General Data Privacy Regulation, Art. 1., https://gdpr-info.eu/art-1-gdpr/, accessed November 1, 2019.

others. The foundation on which the internet was built-a utopian ideal of openness-has left our cyber borders porous to malevolent actors.

Actions We Can Take

ACTION I: Understand the capabilities and intentions of the Privacy Pirates.

John Milton argued that God gave man reason so he could understand the difference between good and evil. Milton saw any licensing of books as a "tyranny over learning" which abridged man's liberty. Are the Privacy Pirates good or evil?

We see the modern conveniences of a cyberized world as good. The Privacy Pirates aim to fill our lives with magic, anticipating our needs and fulfilling them before we ask. We rely on them because their capabilities are tempting, the convenience addictive, and the goods and services rewarding. But what wasn't so obvious when you signed up is that they are monetizing your private information as a surplus commodity they use for their own ends. Knowing that now, would you still make the same choices? Do you remember agreeing to give away your privacy? Are we really too blind, too self-absorbed, too stupid, too apathetic or too whatever to see how this is undermining our democracy?

Are the Privacy Pirates evil? Their digital totalitarianism delivers the power craved by the twentieth century's dictators, and most feared by its dystopians. The inattention of government to the Privacy Pirates agenda is alarming.

Throughout the twentieth century, the United States and its citizens opposed totalitarian regimes, like Hitler's Third Reich, Stalin's Russia, and Mao's China. In *Privacy and Freedom*, Alan Westin said the "modern totalitarian state relies on secrecy for the regime, but high surveillance and disclosure for all other groups. With their demand for a complete commitment of loyalties to the regime, the literature of both fascism and communism traditionally attacks the idea of privacy as 'immoral,' 'antisocial,' and 'part of the cult of individualism.'"[852]

The Privacy Pirates are not inherently evil, they just don't care about you, or your privacy. In fact, they'd prefer your privacy to go away

---

[852] Alan Westin, Privacy and Freedom. New York: Atheneum, 1967, 23.

because it interferes with their agenda. They have a boundless appetite for human information, aggregating it into insights about human behavior that are far greater than the sum of its parts. These powers equip Privacy Pirates to control our behavior. The question is, are you okay with that?

ACTION II: Acknowledge that our freedom depends on a foundation of individual rights like privacy, and a democratic form of government to preserve them.

To say that the preservation of privacy is a lost cause is to abandon democracy and freedom. As Lessig tells us: "Liberty in cyberspace will not come from the absence of a state. Liberty will come from a state of a certain kind. We build a world where freedom can flourish not by removing from society any self-conscious control; we build a world where freedom can flourish by setting it in a place where a particular kind of selfconscious control survives. We build liberty, that is, as our founders did, by setting society upon a certain ... architecture."[853] This is an architecture of "not just a legal text but a way of life", incorporating the fundamental values we hold dear above and beyond politics.[854]

Right now, computer code is masquerading as law. Its architecture or framework could have been built to protect our fundamental values.[855] At present, the code is undermining these values, making compromises about our privacy because the Privacy Pirates want to monetize our behavioral data.

ACTION III: Insist on ethical and civic behavior in cyberspace.

In 1992, the Computer Ethics Institute the Ten Commandments of Computer Ethics: [856]

1. Thou Shalt Not Use A Computer to Harm Other People.

---

[853] Lessig, 5.

[854] Ibid.

[855] Lessig, b.

[856] The *Ten Commandments of Computer Ethics* were first presented in Dr. Ramon C. Barquin's paper, *"In Pursuit of a 'Ten Commandments' for Computer Ethics."* Accessed 12/26/19 at http://computerethicsinstitute.org/publications/ten commandments.html

2. Thou Shalt Not Interfere with Other People's Computer Work.
3. Thou Shalt Not Snoop Around in Other People's Computer Files.
4. Thou Shalt Not Use A Computer to Steal.
5. Thou Shalt Not Use A Computer to Bear False Witness.
6. Thou Shalt Not Copy or Use Proprietary Software for Which You have Not Paid.
7. Thou Shalt Not Use Other People's Computer Resources Without Authorization or Proper Compensation.
8. Thou Shalt Not Appropriate Other People's Intellectual Output.
9. Thou Shalt Think About the Social Consequences of The Program You Are Writing or The System You Are Designing.
10. Thou Shalt Always Use A Computer in Ways That Insure Consideration and Respect for Your Fellow Humans.

Think back again to our earlier discussions about how Christianity shaped the law. This 1992 view of ethical behavior in what would become cyberspace was framed in the context of fundamental Christian values, shared beliefs that appear in law, social norms, and human behaviors. Unfortunately, it is the norm today to ignore such ethical values.

Now let's compare that with the Google Declarations, written down by Shoshana Zuboff as her interpretation of what Google informally declared it was conquering by declaration:[857]

1. We claim all human experience as raw material free for the taking. On the basis of this claim, we can ignore considerations of individuals' rights, interests, awareness, or comprehension.
2. On the basis of our claim, we assert the right to take an individual's experience for translation into behavioral data.
3. Our right to take, based on our claim of free raw material, confers the right to own the behavioral data derived from human experience.
4. Our rights to take and to own confer the right to know what the data disclose.
5. Our rights, to take, to own, and to know confer the right to decide how we use our knowledge.

[857] While not attributable to Google, they are instructive to all.

6. Our rights to take, to own, to know, and to decide confer our rights to the conditions that preserve our rights to take, to own, to know, and to decide.[858]

You should be laughing and crying. Is it opposite day? How did we come to this?

The Privacy Pirates have gotten away with misbehaving in cyberspace because we let them. We've let them exercise their algorithms without bound, make decisions about our lives, and abridge our free will. That should make you angry. And if enough of us feel like Alice in chapter one, then it's time to push back.

Can we not find ways to extend genuine protections to this new virtual space? Could we talk about netiquette? Can we build on the rules that emerge from polite behavior? Can we establish new social norms of our own choosing? Can't they be aligned with the preservation of privacy and democratic values?

We need to teach such values to our children as part of a civics and ethics curriculum. As Supreme Court Justice Thurgood Marshall reminded us: "Education is not the teaching of the three R's. Education is the teaching of the overall citizenship, to learn to live together with fellow citizens, and above all we learn to obey the law."[859]

ACTION IV: Take a stand on privacy.

Law is designed to lag behind in a democracy. Milton Friedman believed that "legislative and judicial action invariably reflect the public opinion of twenty to thirty years earlier."[860] Another way of saying this is that Congress is waiting for its constituents to make up their minds. It took a long time to get to the Privacy Act. It took a long time to get to FISA. Now we need something like the Wiretap Act and/or FISA to rein in the Privacy Pirates and their surveillance capitalism.

As a republic, the United States Government is responsible for representing its citizenry and acting in the public interest. Congressmen and congresswomen must be seen to respond to their constituents. These

---

[858] Zuboff, 179.

[859] Lessig, 93.

[860] Zuboff, 520.

constituents can be individuals, corporations, or special interest groups, anyone in fact that has sway over the next congressional election. Congress cannot muster sufficient support for new laws until disparate popular views about new technologies have annealed into norms. The views of individuals in a representative's district may be vastly different than those of a corporate entity lobbying a senator. Along the way, judicial decisions may generate case law precedents worth noting. It usually takes years of public debate about an issue before Congress feels it can take on new legislative bills which have any hope of congressional passage and presidential signature. A stable national view on any subject empowers Congress to respond with meaningful legislation.

The Privacy Pirates have been very successful lobbyists in Washington. Section 230 of the 1996 Communications Decency Act codified the liability exemption for any provider or user of an interactive computer service who made available *or* restricted access to any material posted by a third party. Under this amendment, Facebook quite legally restricts some content, to include what they see as disinformation, propaganda, and offensive posts. Is that right? Is that wrong? Meanwhile, the commercial world is starting to argue that its First Amendment rights are being violated when the government prohibits companies from sharing/selling information about private citizens to others.

Whether they meant to or not, the Privacy Pirates have catapulted the public debate about privacy to the forefront. Take a stand.

ACTION V: Demand that Privacy Pirate code respects your privacy.

The time has come for a new federal privacy law. The Privacy Pirates are commoditizing our private information and compromising our privacy. We should each chose how we want our data to be used. Lessig talks about a "data butler," a machine to machine protocol which negotiates privacy protections.[861] The Federal Enterprise Architecture suggested a similar idea, the Platform for Privacy Preferences. Such ideas have been with us for a long time, and are ripe for adoption.

---

[861] Lessig, 160.

A modern understanding of privacy is nuanced. It has all sorts of dimensions. Sometimes it appears to be a property right. Property law gives you the right to negotiate before entering into a contract to transfer ownership. Sometimes it appears to be a liability right. When an entity invades someone's privacy without permission, the aggrieved party can sue for liability and be compensated for her suffering. This occurs after the privacy has already been transferred.[862]

We hail from a tradition of constitutionalism and democracy. Our country's founders created a new nation based on inalienable rights. Among those rights, implicitly, was privacy.

Our government continues to oscillate between less and more heavy-handedness. National security crises allow government to exercise more powers, further abridging individual rights. This balance is restored after the crisis when the people reassert their rights.

It is time to reassert our right to privacy. The Privacy Pirates have filled the vacuum left by the absence of East Coast code with their own West Coast regulation. Lessig aptly observed: "To push the antigovernment button is not to teleport us to Eden."[863] We don't want the Privacy Pirates left free to create their own sovereignty over our rights in cyberspace.

Conclusion

We should not blithely sell our democratic souls to the cyber tyrant. Privacy is a core tenet of democracy worth preserving. As an individual right, it has been defined as "the right to be left alone" and "the right to control information about oneself." But such a right can only be enjoyed if government is empowered to protect it as a collective democratic value.

America's great strength has always been the freedom to choose. But with that comes to obligation to choose wisely. We now need to choose privacy, because we want our government to preserve our freedom.

The Privacy Pirates don't win until we give up. Stop being stunned and disbelieving. Stop assuming it's a lost cause. It's time to get mad.

It's time to act.

---

[862] Ibid.
[863] Lessig, 220.

Bibliography

Adams, John. John Adams Diary, 1770. Accessed 5/28/18 at https://www.masshist.org/digitaladams/archive/doc?id=D15&bc=%2Fdigitaladams%2Farchive% 2Fbrowse%2Fdiaries_by_date. php

AICPA. AICPA Code of Professional Conduct. Accessed 3/14/20 at https://www.aicpa.org/research/standards/codeofconduct.html

AICPA/CICA. "Generally Accepted Privacy Principles: CPA and CA Practitioner Version," August 2009. Accessed 12/6/19 at https://iapp.org/media/presentations/11Summit/ DeathofSASHO2.pdf

Allen, Anita L. and Marc Rotenberg. Privacy Law and Society. St. Paul, MN: West Academic Publishing, 2016, 3rd edition.

Ames, William. The Conscience with the Power and Cases Thereof. 1639. Accessed 3/15/18 at https://archive.org/stream/conscpo00ames#page/146/mode/2up/search/good+repute.

Aquinas, Thomas. Summa Theologica, SS Treatise on the Theological Virtues, Q[33] Of Fraternal Correction, trans. The Fathers of the English Dominican Province, 1947. Accessed 3/16/18 at http://www.sacred-texts.com/chr/aquinas/summa/sum288.htm

Bacon, Francis. A Collection of Some Principal Rules and Maximes of the Common Lawes of England. London: Affignes of J. More, 1636. Accessed 3/16/18 at https://archive.org/stream/elementsofcommon00baco#page/n123/mode/2up.

Bacon, Francis. Novum Organum, 29, originally published in England in 1620. Accessed 1/6/18 at http://www.gutenberg.org/files/45988/45988-h/45988-h.htm

Balkin, Jack. "The Constitution of the National Surveillance State." Faculty Scholarship Series, 225, 2008. Accessed 12/17/19 at http://digitalcommons.law.yale.edu/cgi/viewcontent.cgi?article=1224&context=fss_papers

Barquin, Ramon. "The Ten Commandments of Computer Ethics." Accessed 12/26/19 at http://www.computerethicsinstitute.org/publications/tencommandments.html

Baskir, Lawrence M. "Reflections on the Senate Investigation of Army Surveillance," Indiana Law Journal, v 49 is 4, Summer 1974.

Accessed 5/22/19 at https://www.repository.law.indiana.edu/cgi/viewcontent.cgi?referer=&httpsredir=1&article=3019&context=ilj

Baudouin, Francois. Ad Legis de Famosis Libellis et de Calumniatoribus, Commentarius. PARISIIS: Apud Andream Wechelum, 1562. Accessed 3/18/18 at https://ia800504.us.archive.org/6/items/bub_gb_1KfLKIXMhoEC/bub_gb_1KfLKI XMhoEC.pdf

BBC. "William Caxton (c. 1422-1492)." Accessed 3/14/20 at http://www.bbc.co.uk/history/historic_figures/caxton_william.shtml

Blake, Aaron. "Neil Gorsuch, Antonio Scalia and originalism explained," Washington Post, 2/1/17. Accessed 6/17/18 at https://www.washingtonpost. com/ news/the-fix /wp/2017/02/01/neil-gorsuch-antonin-scalia-and-originalism-explained/?utm_term=.dcc8f03d077e

Bloomberg News. "The Great Firewall," 11/5/18. Accessed 12/26/19 at https://www.bloomberg.com/quicktake/great-firewall-of-china

British Association of Paper Historians. "History of Papermaking in the United States." Accessed 3/14/20 at http://baph.org.uk/uk paper history.html

Brooks, John. Telephone: The First Hundred Years. New York: Harper & Row, 1976.

Center for Cryptologic History (CCH), National Security Agency (NSA). "The Friedman Legacy: A Tribute to William and Elizebeth Friedman,"1992, second printing.

Chrimes, S.B. English Constitutional History. London: Oxford University Press, 1958, Second Edition.

Church Committee. "Intelligence Activities and the Rights of Americans: 1976 US Senate Report on Illegal Wiretaps and Domestic Spying by the FBI, CIA and NSA." St. Petersburg, FL: Red and Black Publishers, 2008.

Cicero, M. Tullius. The Oration of Marcus Tullius Cicero, literally translated by C. D. Yonge. London: George Bell and Sons, 1891. Accessed 3/12/20 at http://www.perseus.tufts.edu/hopper/text?doc=Perseus%3Atext%3A199.02.0020%3Atext%3DDom.%3Achapter%3D41%3Asection%3D109

Coke, Edward. The Reports of Sire Edward Coke, Kt. in in English, in Thirteen Parte Compleat. Pt. V, 1738. Accessed 3/14/18 at http://lawlibrary.wm.edu/wythepedia/library/ReportsOfSirEdwardCoke1738Pt5. pdf

Committee of Sponsoring Organizations of the Treadway Commission (COSO). "Enterprise Risk Management – Integrated Framework: Executive Summary," September 2004. Accessed 12/11/19 at https://www.coso.org / Documents/COSO – ERM – Executive - Summary.pdf

Committee of Sponsoring Organizations of the Treadway Commission (COSO). "Enterprise Risk Management: Integrating with Strategy and Performance Executive Summary," June 2017. Accessed 11 /19/19 at https://www.coso.org/Documents/2017-COSO-ER M - Integrating-with-Strategy-and-Performance-Executive-Summary .pdf

Cooley, Thomas M. "Inviolability of Telegraphic Correspondence," University of Pennsylvania Law Review, v. 27, 1882. Accessed 7/26/19 at https://scholarship.law.upenn.edu/penn_law_review/ vol27/iss2/1/

Cooley, Thomas M. Treatise on the Law of Torts or the Wrongs Which Arise Independent of Contract. Chicago: Callaghan and Co, 1879. Accessed 6/2/18 at https://repository. law.umich.edu/books/11/

Court of Justice of the European Union (CJEU), case C-362-14 3/13/14. Accessed 3/2/20 at http://curia.europa.eu/juris/document/docum ent.jsf?text=&docid=169195&pageIndex=0&doclang=EN&mod e=lst&dir=&occ=first&part=1&cid=2156760

Cunningham, Lillian. "Google's Eric Schmidt expounds on his Senate testimony," Washington Post, 10/1/11. Accessed 12/17/19 at https://www.washingtonpost.com/national/on-leadership/google s-eric-schmidt-expounds-on-his-senate-testimony/2011 /09/30/gIQAPyVgCL_story.html

Department of Commerce, Safe Harbor Privacy Principles, 2000. Accessed 3/13/20 at https://2016.export.gov/safeharbor/eu/eg_ main_018475.asp

Department of Defense. Pentagon Papers. Accessed 6/23/19 at https: //www.archives.gov/ research/pentagon-papers

Department of Health and Human Services. "Summary of the HIPAA Privacy Rule," May 2003. Retrieved 5/7/19 at https://www.hhs. gov/sites/default/files/privacysummary.pdf

Department of Health and Human Services. "Summary of the HIPAA Security Rule." Accessed 5/6/19 at https://www.hhs.gov/hipaa / for-professionals/security/ laws- regulations/index.html? languag e=es

Economy, Elizabeth C. "The great firewall of China: Xi Jinping's internet shutdown," The Guardian, 6/29/18. Accessed 12/26/19 at https://

www.theguardian .com/news/2018/jun/29/the-great-firewall-of-china-xi-jinpings-internet-shutdown

Eisenstein, Elizabeth L. The Printing Press as an Agent of Change: Communications and Cultural Transformations in Early-Modern Europe. Cambridge, UK: Cambridge University Press, 2009, 14th printing.

European Parliament and Council. "Directive 95/46/EC of the European Parliament and of the Council of 24 October 1995 on the protection of individuals with regard to the processing of personal data and on the free movement of such data," 1995. Accessed 12/6/19 at https://eur- lex.europa.eu/legal-content/EN/TXT/HTML/?uri=CELEX:31995L0046

European Union."Charter of Fundamental Rights of the European Union," 2012/C 326/02, 2012. Accessed 12/6/19 at https://eur-lex.europa.eu/legal-content/EN/TXT/PDF/?uri= CELEX:12012P/TXT&from=EN

European Union. "Regulation (EU) 2016/679 of the European Parliament and of the Council of 27 April 2016 on the protection of natural persons with regard to the processing of personal data and on the free movement of such data, and repealing Directive 95/46/EC (General Data Protection Regulation)," 2016. Accessed 12/6/19 at https://eur-lex.europa.eu/legal-content/EN/TXT/PDF/?uri=CELEX:32016R0679

Everson, Miles E.A. et al. "Internal Control – Integrated Framework: Executive Summary," Committee of Sponsoring Organizations of the Treadway Commission (COSO), May 2013. Accessed 11/26/19 at https://www.coso.org/Documents/ 990025P-Executive-Summary-final-may20.pdf

Federal Bureau of Investigation. "Custodial Detention Part 2 of 3." Accessed 6/11/19 at https://vault.fbi.gov/Custodial%20Detention/Custodial%20Detention%20Part%202%20of%203/view

Federal Trade Commission. "Protecting Consumer Privacy in an Era of Rapid Change: Recommendations for Businesses and Policy makers," FTC Report, March 2012. Accessed 3/14/20 at https://www. ftc . gov / reports / protecting-consumer - privacy - era-rapid-change-recommendations-businesses-policymakers

Federal Trade Commission. "Privacy Online: Fair Information Practices in the Electronic Marketplace," May 2000. Accessed 3/14/20 at https://www.ftc.gov/reports/privacy-online-fair-information-practices-electronic-marketplace-federal-trade-commission

Federal Trade Commission. "Privacy Online: A Report to Congress," 1998. Accessed 3/14/20 at https://www.ftc.gov/sites/default/files/documents/reports/privacy-online-report-congress/priv-23a.pdf

Friedman, Milton. Capitalism and Freedom. Chicago: The University of Chicago Press, 2002.

Gable, Julie. "Principles for Protecting Information Privacy," Information Management (magazine), September/October 2014. Accessed 12/6/19 at https://magazine.arma.org/wp-content/uploads/simple-file-list/2014_05_IM_principles_for_protecting_information_ privacy.pdf

Galligan, Mary and Kelly Rau. "COSO in the Cyber Age," Committee of Sponsoring Organizations of the Treadway Commission (COSO), January 2015. Accessed 11/19/19 at https://www.coso.org/documents/COSO%20in%20the%20Cyber%20 Age_FULL_r11.pdf

Gavison, Ruth. "Privacy and the Limits of Law." The Yale Law Journal 89(3), 1980. Accessed 12/24/19 at https://digitalcommons.law.yale.edu/cgi/viewcontent .cgi?article=6581&context=ylj

Gellman, Robert. "Fair Information Practices: A Basic History." Accessed 12/27/19 at https://bobgellman.com/rg-docs/rg-FIPshistory.pdf

George Washington University, The National Security Archive. FOIA Legislative History. Accessed 3/14/20 at https://nsarchive2.gwu.edu//nsa/foialeghistory/legistfoia.htm

Godkin, E.L. "The Rights of the Citizen. IV. To His Own Reputation." Scribner's Magazine, New York, 1890, v. 8, pp. 58-67. Accessed 5/15/18 at https://babel.hathitrust.org/cgi/pt?id=coo.31924097287480;view=1up;seq=66

Gorman, Siobhan and Jennifer Valentino-DeVries. "New Details Show Broader NSA Surveillance Reach." Wall Street Journal, 8/20/13. Accessed 6/22/19 at https://www.wsj.com/articles/new-details-show-broader-nsa- surveillance-reach-1377044261?tesla=y

Hamilton, Alexander, James Madison and John Jay. The Federalist. Cambridge, MA: The Belknap Press of Harvard University Press, 1974, 4th printing, ed. Benjamin Fletcher Wright.

Hamlin, Hannibal and Norman W. Jones, ed. The King James Bible after 400 Years: Literary, Linguistic, and Cultural Influences. Cambridge, UK: Cambridge University Press, 2010.

Hairiri, Oren. "Quotations from Chairman Powell: A Leadership Primer," 1996. Accessed 12/29/19 at https://govleaders.org/powell.htm

Health, Education and Welfare (HEW) Secretary's Advisory Committee on Automated Personal Data Systems. "Records, Computers and the Rights of Citizens." Washington: U.S. Government Printing Office, 1973. Accessed 10/12/18 at https://www.justice.gov/opcl/docs/rec-com-rights.pdf

Hochman, Brian. "Eavesdropping in the Age of 'The Eavesdroppers; or, The Bug in the Martini," Post 45, 2/3/16. Accessed 12/27/19 at http://post45. research. yale.edu/ 2016/ 02 /eavesdropping-in-the-age-of-the-eavesdroppers-or-the-bug-in-the-martini-olive/#identifier_71_6796

Hoofnagle, Chris Jay. Federal Trade Commission Privacy Law and Policy. New York: Cambridge University Press, 2016.

International Association of Independent Private Sector Inspectors General. Accessed 3/14/20 at http://www.iaipsig.org/

ISACA website. Accessed 11/29/19 at http://www.isaca.org/COBIT/PublishingImages/20th/ COBIT-Timeline-lg.jpg

ISO website. Accessed 12/2/19 at https://www.iso.org/the-iso-story.html #16

Johnson, Ben. Queen Elizabeth I. Accessed 3/14/18 at http://www.historic-uk.com/HistoryUK/HistoryofEngland/Queen-Elizabeth-I/

Johnson, Lyndon Baines. "State of the Union Address," January 10, 1967. Accessed 7/21/19 at https://millercenter.org/the-presidency/ presidential-speeches/january-10-1967-state-union-address

Kang, Jerry. "Information Privacy in Cyberspace Transactions," Stanford Law Review 50(4): 1193-1294. Accessed 12/24/19 at https://papers.ssrn.com/sol3/papers. cfm?abstract_id=631723

Kobie, Nichole. "The complicated truth about China's social credit system," Wired magazine, 6/7/19. Accessed 12/26/19 at https://www.wired.co.uk/article/china-social-credit-system-explained

Lawfare Blog. "FISA: 215 Collection." Accessed 6/22/19 at https://www.lawfareblog.com/topic/fisa-215- collection

Leavitt, Mike. Speech by HHS Secretary Mike Leavitt, 12/5/08. Accessed 12/28/19 at https:// www.govtech.com / dc / articles / HHSs-Leavitt-Announces-New-Privacy-Principle s.html

Lessig, Lawrence. Code and Other Laws of Cyberspace. New York: Basic Books, 1999.

Maitland, Frederic William. The Constitutional History of England: A Course of Lectures Delivered. Cambridge: Cambridge University Press, 1908. Reprinted by The Lawbook Exchange, Clark, NJ, 2013.

Man, John. The Gutenberg Revolution: How Printing Changed the Course of History. London: Bantam Books, 2009.

Mandel, Lewis. The Credit Card Industry: A History. Boston: Twyne Publishers, 1990.

McCarthy, Joseph. "Enemies Within" Speech, delivered in Wheeling, West Virginia (1950). Accessed 10/12/18 at https://liberalarts.utexas.edu/coretexts/_files/resources/ texts/1950%20McCarthy%20Enemies.pdf

McNally, Stephen J. "The 2013 COSO Framework & SOX Compliance," Strategic Finance magazine, June 2013. Accessed 11/26/19 at https://www.coso.org/documents /COSO

Mill, John Stuart. On Liberty. London: Longmans, Green, Reader and Dyer, 1880.

Miller, Geoffrey Parsons. The Law of Governance, Risk Management, and Compliance. New York: Wolters Kluwer Law & Business, 2014.

Milton, John. Aeropagitica. New York: Doubleday, Page and Co., 1901.

Monk, Linda. The Words We Live By: Your Annotated Guide to the Constitution. New York: Stonesong Press, 2015.

Morris, Richard B. Basic Documents of American History. New York: D. Van Nostrand Company, 1965.

National Commission on Terrorist Attacks. "The 9/11 Commission Report: Final Report of the National Commission on Terrorist Attacks Upon the United States (Authorized Edition)." New York: W.W. Norton & Company, 2004.

National Institute of Standards and Technology (NIST). "Discussion Draft: NIST Privacy Framework: An Enterprise Risk Management Tool," September 6, 2019. Accessed 12/6/19 at https://www.nist.gov/system/files/

National Institute of Standards and Technology (NIST). "Framework for Improving Critical Infrastructure Cybersecurity," version 1.1, April 16, 2018. Accessed 12/2/19 at https://nvlpubs.nist.gov /nistpubs/CSWP/ NIST .CSWP .04162018.pdf

National Institute of Standards and Technology (NIST). "NIST SP 800-122: Guide to Protecting the Confidentiality of Personally Identifiable Information (PII)," April 2010. Accessed 12/6/19 at https://nvlpubs.nist.gov/nistpubs/Legacy/ SP/ nistspecialpublication800-122.pdf

National Institute of Standards and Technology (NIST). "NIST SP 800-39: Managing Information Security Risk: Organization, Mission, and Information System View," March 2011. Accessed 12/8/19 at https://csrc.nist.gov/publications/detail/sp/800-39/final

National Institute of Standards and Technology (NIST). "NIST SP 800-53 Revision 4: Security and Privacy Controls for Federal Information

Systems and Organizations," April 2013. Accessed 12/2/19 at https://nvlpubs.nist.gov/nistpubs/SpecialPublications/NIST.SP.800-53r4.pdf

National Research Council. "Bulk Collection of Signals Intelligence: Technical Options." Washington, DC: National Academies Press, 2015.Accessed 7/21/19 at https://www.nap.edu/read/19414/chapter/1

Nissenbaum, Helen. Privacy in Context: Technology, Policy, and the Integrity of Social Life. Stanford: CA: Stanford University Press, 2010.

Organisation for Economic Co-operation and Development (OECD). "Generally Accepted Privacy Principles." Accessed 3/14/20 at http://www.oecdprivacy.org/#gapp

Organisation for Economic Co-operation and Development (OECD). "OECD Guidelines on Protection of Privacy and Transborder Flows of Personal Data," 1980. Accessed 12/6/19 at http:// www.oecd.org /sti / ieconomy / oecdguidelinesontheprotectionof prvacyandtransborderflowsofpersonaldata.htm

Organisation for Economic Co-operation and Development (OECD). "OECD Privacy Framework," 2013. Accessed 12/6/19 at http://www.oecd.org/sti/ieconomy/oecd_privacy_framework.pdf

Office of Management and Budget (OMB). "The Common Approach to Federal Enterprise Architecture," May 2, 2012. Accessed 12/7/19 at https://obamawhitehouse.archives.gov/sites/default/files/omb /assets/egov_docs/common_approac h_to_federal_ea.pdf

Office of Management and Budget (OMB)."FEA Consolidated Reference Model Document, Version 2.3," October 2007. Accessed 12/11/19 at https://www.reginfo.gov/public/jsp/Utilities/FEA_CRM_v23_Final_Oct_2007_Revised.pdf

Office of Management and Budget. "Safeguarding Against and Responding to the Breach of Personally Identifiable Information," OMB Memorandum 07-16, May 22, 2007. Accessed 12/5/19 at https://www.whitehouse.gov/sites/whitehouse.gov/files/omb/memoranda/2007/m07-16.pdf

Office of the National Coordinator for Health Information Technology, Department of Health and Human Services. "Nationwide Privacy and Security Framework for Electronic Exchange of Individually Identifiable Health Information," 15 December 2008. Accessed 12/28/19 at https://www.healthit.gov /sites/default/files/ nationwide-ps-framework-5.pdf

Pedersen, Darhl, "Psychological Functions of Privacy," Journal of Environmental Psychology (1997) 17, 147-156. Accessed 12/24/19 at https://www.deepdyve.com/lp/elsevier/psychological-functions-of-privacy-KzTnLfz1rl

Pentland, Alex. Social Physics: How Good Ideas Spread – The Lessons from a New Science. New York: Penguin, 2014.

Pettegree, Andrew. Brand Luther. New York: Penguin Press, 2015.

Pickering, Lewis. Poem. Accessed 3/14/18 at http://www.earlystuartlibels.net/htdocs/early_jacobean_section/B11.html

Pike Committee. "The Unexpurgated Pike Report: Report of the House Select Committee on Intelligence, 1976." New York: McGraw Hill, 1992. Accessed 7/31/19 at https://archive.org /details/PikeCommitteeReportFull

Posner, Richard. "The Right to Privacy," Georgia Law Review 12(3), 393-422. Accessed 12/24/19 at http://chicagounbound. uchicago.edu/cgi/viewcontent.cgi?article=2803&context=journal_articles

Privacilla. "How U.S. State Law Quietly Leads the Way in Privacy Protection," Special Report, July 2002. Accessed 5/31/18 at http://www.privacilla.org /releases /Torts_Report.pdf

The Privacy and Civil Liberties Oversight Board website. Accessed 11/3/18 at https://www.pclob.gov/about/

The Privacy Protection Commission. "Personal Privacy in an Information Society: The Report of the Privacy Protection Commission." Washington: U.S. Government Printing Office, 1977.

Prosser, William L. "Privacy," 48 Cal. L. Rev. 383 (1960). Accessed 5/29/18 at https: //scholarship.law.berkeley.edu/cgi/viewcontent.cgi?article=3157&context=california lawreview

Raithby John, ed. The Statues At Large of England and Great-Britain from Magna Carta to the Union of the Kingdoms of Great Britain and Ireland. London, 1811, v. 4. Accessed 3/13/18 at https://archive.org/stream/statutesatlarge02raitgoog#page/n727/mode/2up/search/ to+restrain+abuses

Regan, Priscilla. Legislating Privacy: Technology, Social Values, and Public Policy. Chapel Hill, NC: University of North Carolina Press, 1995.

Risen, James and Eric Lichtblau, "Bush Lets U.S. Spy on Callers Without Courts." New York Times, December 16, 2005.

The Royal Society. "History of the Royal Society." Accessed 3/14/20 at https://royalsociety.org/about-us/history/

Schandl, Annette and Philip L. Foster. "COSO Internal Control – Integrated Framework: An Implementation Guide for the

Healthcare Provider Industry." Committee of Sponsoring Organizations of the Treadway Commission (COSO), January 2019. Accessed 11/19/19 at https://www.coso.org/Documents/COSO-CROWE- COSO-Internal-Control-Integrated-Framework.pdf

Securities and Exchange Commission. "Final Rule: Compliance Programs of Investment Companies and Investment Advisers." Accessed 11/19/19 at https://www.sec.gov/rules/final/ia-2204.htm

Securities and Exchange Commission. "Final Rule: Management's Report on Internal Control Over Financial Reporting and Certification of Disclosure in Exchange Act Periodic Reports," SEC Release No. 34-55929. Accessed 12/28/19 at https://www.sec.gov/rules/final/33-8238.htm#iia

Securities and Exchange Commission and US Department of Justice. "A Resource Guide to the U.S. Foreign Corrupt Practices Act," November 14, 2012. Accessed 11/19/19 at https://www.sec.gov/spotlight/fcpa/fcpa-resource-guide.pdf

Segrave, Kerry. Wiretapping and Electronic Surveillance in America, 1862-1920. Jefferson, NC: McFarland and Company, Inc., 2014.

Sheehan, Matt. "How Google took on China – and lost," MIT Technology Review, 12/19/18. Accessed 12/26/19 at https://www.technologyreview.com/s/612601/how- google-took-on-china-and-lost/

Shuger, Debora. Censorship and Cultural Sensibility: The Regulation of Language in Tudor-Stuart England. Philadelphia: University of Pennsylvania Press, 2006.

Standage, Tom. The Victorian Internet: The Remarkable Story of the Telegraph and the Nineteenth Century's On-line Pioneers. New York: Walker and Company, 1998.

Steinberg, S. F. Five Hundred Years of Printing. Mineola, NY: Dover Publications, 2017.

Stephenson, Carl and Frederick George Marcham, ed. Sources of English Constitutional History: A Selection of Documents from A.D. 600 to the Present. New York: Harper and Row, 1937.

Storey, Read K. & Sylvia Storey, "FASB Special Report: The Framework of Financial Accounting Concepts and Standards," No. 181-C, January 1998. Accessed 11/21/19 at https://www.fasb.org/jsp/FASB/Document_C/DocumentPage?cid=1176171746896&acceptedDisclaimer=true

Turner, Frederick Jackson. "The Significance of the Frontier in American History 1893." Accessed 5/31/18 at http://nationalhumanitiescenter.org/pds/gilded/empire/ text1/turner.pdf

Wacks, Raymond. Personal Information: Privacy and the Law. Oxford: Clarendon Press, 1993.

Warren, Samuel D. and Louis Brandeis, "The Right to Privacy," Harvard Business Review, 1890. Accessed 6/2/18 at http://www.jstor .org/stable/pdf/1321160.pdf?refreqid=excelsior%3A0df8ef50658 f2e2204b9fb82667f3e28

Westin, Alan. Privacy and Freedom. New York: Atheneum, 1967.

The White House. "National Strategy for Trusted Identities in Cyberspace: Enhancing Online Choice, Efficiency, Security, and Privacy," April 2011. Accessed 12/28/19 at https://obamawhitehouse. archives.gov/sites/default/files/ rss_viewer/ NSTICstrategy_0415 11.pdf

The White House. "Consumer Data Privacy in a Networked World: A Framework for Protecting Privacy and Promoting Innovation in the Global Digital Economy," February 2012. Accessed 12/28/19 at https://obamawhitehouse.archives.gov/sites/default/ files/ priv acy-final.pdf

United Nations. "Universal Declaration of Human Rights," 1948. Accessed 12/6/19 at https://www. un.org/en/universal-declarat ion-human-rights/index.html

US Congress. Freedom of Information Act and Amendments of 1974. Washington: Government Printing Office, 1975. Accessed 10/31/ 18 at http:// www.loc.gov/rr/frd/Military_Law/pdf / FOIA-1974 .pdf

US Congress. Legislative History of the Privacy Act of 1974: Source Book on Privacy. Government Printing Office, September 1976. Accessed 10/31/18 at http://www.loc.gov/rr/frd/Military_Law/ pdf/LH_privacy_act-1974.pdf

USC Annenberg School for Communication and Journalism. "Top Secret: The Battle for the Pentagon Papers." Accessed 6/23/19 at http://topsecretplay.org/the-courts/

US Sentencing Commission. 2018 Guidelines Manual. Accessed 11/19/19 at https://www.ussc.gov/guidelines/2016-guidelines-manual /201 6 -chapter-8

Wilson, Woodrow. "Proclamation Nationalizes All Telephone and Telegraph Networks," July 22, 1918. Accessed June 10, 2019 at https: //cybertelecom.blogspot.com/2016/08/aug-1-1918-pres-wo odrow-wilson.html

Zuboff, Shoshana. The Age of Surveillance Capitalism: The Fight for a Human Future at the New Frontier of Power. New York: Public Affairs, 2019.

---. Edward Snowden Embracing the American Flag, Wired Magazine, September 2014. Accessed 6/22/19 at https://time.com/3107153/edward-snowden-embraces-american-flag-on-wired-cover/

---. "Joint Statement: NSA and the Office of the Director of National Intelligence." Accessed 3/14/20 at https://www.intelligence.gov/index.php/ic-on-the-record-database/results/33-joint -statement-nsa-and-office-of-the-director-of-national-intelligence

---. Transcript: NSA Deputy Director John Inglis on NPR, January 10, 2014. Accessed 11/3/18 at https://www.npr.org/ 2014 /01/10/261282601/transcript-nsa-deputy-director-john-inglis

--. "Union Men Demand Wire Tapping List." The New York Sun, June 13, 1916. Accessed 6/10/19 at http://nyshistoricnewspapers.org/lccn/sn83030272/%201916-06-13/ed-1/seq-6/

Index

C

D

E

F

Printed by Libri Plureos GmbH in Hamburg,
Germany

9 781680 531268